MW01706053

TO KILL A NAKED BIRD

Some Names Have Been Changed to Protect the Privacy of the Individuals Involved

The story you are about to read is true….

I can't believe what I'm seeing! This all seems so unreal. I'm in this strange new world surrounded by all these sexy, beautiful, scantily clad, young, and not so young, women – or "girls" as they're usually known in places like this. I keep thinking, "*What on earth am I doing here…?*" And yet, inwardly, I'm also smiling and congratulating myself. After all, many have tried and failed, and yet I've made it into *this* place – the famous "Sundowner Gentlemen's Club" – on my first go! I feel excited, even privileged to be starting work in the *hottest* hotspot in all Canada. To be completely honest though … I'm also nervous and just a little frightened.

I'm sitting in front of a wall covered by a mirror that reaches up from a long counter to the ceiling. Behind me are rows and rows of lockers. Facing the mirror and a countertop loaded with beauty supplies are several gorgeous women seated on stools and high chairs. I glance into the mirror, my makeup clustered before me on the counter – but my eyes aren't on me so much as "the competition."

It's like a buffet of female delicacies! Black girls, white girls, Asian girls, blondes, brunettes, redheads – and even a few "skunks," you know: those girls with the black hair on top and blonde on the bottom. Some are getting dressed or undressed while others are just standing around openly in the nude. The atmosphere is loud – not as bad as the bar area downstairs with its blaring music – but still noisy as hell from the chatter of girls who seem to be shouting as much as talking.

I glance at the girls' bodies. Big breasts, small breasts and some fucked-up, lop-sided, uneven breasts; big asses, small asses, flat and curvy asses; thin girls, athletic girls, voluptuous girls. Not one of them over a hundred and forty pounds. Despite their variety, they all seem to have emerged out of a similar mold, a master cookie cutter.

No one seems to notice me. I'm like a fly on the wall....

Candy walks into the room with two shot glasses filled with vodka, and the girls greet her with smiles. She introduces me, and their response is warm and friendly. Candy then pushes over beside me, depositing the shots on the counter. She leans into me, whispering that she'd been waiting for me downstairs, and then gives me a big hug.

Candy is a beautiful, olive-complexioned woman with long black hair that almost touches the curvature of her lower back. She owns a smile that can melt your heart, a small mouth with delicate lips, a straight nose, and round eyes framed in a longish face – a stunning woman, who prides herself on her figure and the hard workouts in the gym that maintain it. Long-legged and lean, she stands about 5-8 in her bare feet.

She hands me a shot glass and makes a toast to a successful night. We knock it back. The feeling of straight vodka hitting my empty stomach induces a warm, cozy feeling. She hurries me to get started with my makeup, which I do, and gives me an update about her son. He's decided he no longer wants her to walk him to school because he's "a big boy" now – at the age of six! Although she jokes about it, her laugh is bittersweet, and I can tell she's a bit hurt. She loves her son dearly; she lives for that boy.

I notice her pussy area is smooth shaven, like many of the other girls. I curl my finger, inviting her to lean toward me. "I'm not shaved down there," I whisper as her ear comes close to my lips.

"Who cares babe?" she replies. "Different strokes, you know…? Lots of guys love some bush."

I pull out my outfit and show it to her. She asks where I got it. I tell her Wal-Mart. She takes it from my hand, holds it up for everyone to see and bursts out laughing. The rest of the girls join in as one says, "My little girl has that same outfit!"

Candy asks to see my shoes, and I raise them up for everyone to see. I swear – I've become the comedy relief, as the laughter grows louder. Even I join in. The girls are asking about my sizes, from bra to shoes. They spread outfits before me on the counter and shoes at my feet. Candy hands me a fancy looking bra. I try it on and it swallows up my ample tits like the Grand Canyon. The laughter rises to a crescendo.

Another girl hands me three strings that resemble a slingshot. I'm confused until she helps me with it. *This shit barely covers my nipples!* Then she hands me two more strings to cover my bottom. I tell her I don't wear other peoples' undergarments, but she assures me it's clean and insists I need it. *Okay, if you say so!* I put it on and it *just* covers my bush. I stand back and stare at myself – my brown chocolate skin in bold contrast to this white and gold outfit. *I look fantastic*. I thank the girls excitedly. I try on four different pairs of shoes and luckily find a pair that fit. They're more like glass slippers really, with hard clear plastic on top and platform heels. *I'd never find these at Wal-Mart!*

Candy sits me down and attaches false eyelashes to my eyelids and then applies gold sparkling eye shadow. She teases my hair and adds some fake extensions that make my hair look fuller. *I'm looking so, so hot! I should really be on the cover of Victoria's Secret catalogue!* I gaze at myself for a while until Candy snaps me back to reality and orders me to put my stuff away in her locker. I gather my clothing from the chair and hand it to her.

As I'm about to sit down, a girl grabs my arm and I recoil quickly as if there's a fire on the chair. She warns me to *never* sit on the chairs with my bare buns and hands me a white towel with flowers printed on it. I inspect the towel as Candy tells me to cover the chair.

I sit waiting for Candy to finish her makeup. She sprays herself and then me.
I'm thinking, *her smile could make stars blink.*

I place my hand between my thighs. *I'm wet.* I stand up and see blood on my fingers and towel. *Shit, no! If this isn't a sign for me to leave, I don't know what is!*
"Where's the washroom?" I ask urgently.

"Down the hall," Candy answers. I ask her for a tampon, and tell her I've got to go home because my period is starting. She accompanies me to the washroom. I do a quick rinse and position the nozzle so I can wash my thighs. I then insert the tampon.

The tampon string is dangling from my pussy as I again insist, "I've got to leave!" Candy asks me why, and I point to the string. She tells me to stick it up inside me. That's the oldest trick in the book, but how am I supposed to know? I wash my G-string and return to the change room. Candy hands me an active blow dryer, and

I aim the hot air directly at my G-string. Then I put it on and lotion my skin.

I'm done – and I'm ready for business.

Phew, that was a close call! No one will know a damn thing. Crazy! Without Candy's help I'd be on my way home. I feel calm now, and reassured knowing I have a friend who can help me through a minor crisis like that.

I follow Candy down the stairs, feeling just a little apprehensive as she pushes the door open into the bar area. We make our grand entrance, like two queens entering a royal gala.

The music is loud and the bar is packed with dozens of men sitting, talking, standing, clapping, and moving about. The ambience is a cross between a party and a marketplace. Young men, old men, businessmen and working stiffs, students and professionals, able-bodied and disabled men – the male of the species in all its great diversity seems gathered here, *united in one singular, unwholesome purpose.*

The music is so loud that, as I call out to my friend walking just ahead, she isn't able to hear me. We make our way through the crowd and eventually find seats at the bar. After drinking half a dozen shots I'm feeling increasingly at ease. This unfamiliar new environment is looking more and more like a fun house.

I start to move to the beat of the music, smiling as I notice a guy across the bar ogling me. Instinctively, I look away. I'm thinking, *this is going to be so easy*. I had thought that the girls upstairs would be my competition, but no, there are at least sixty more girls down here on the floor.

My eyes fix on a blonde girl performing on the main stage who's slowly removing her top. The men are clapping wildly, enjoying the tease and urging her to reveal more. She jumps on a brass pole and rotates quickly around it. As her legs swing freely in several directions, they spread wide.

Now the real tease is beginning, and some of the guys are shouting something about a "naked bird." While spinning round the pole the dancer deftly removes her G-string. Men are throwing money onto the stage. *Money may not grow on trees, but in this place it falls like rain!*

Candy snaps me back to attention, grabbing my hand and leading me to the far side of the club. We step up onto a slightly higher level and enter a "VIP" area. It's partitioned into several small den-like rooms or booths. Each of these semi-private spaces has a large wall mirror, a couch and a small table, with a lamp providing dim illumination. The music from the public area is muted here – you can actually carry on a conversation. We look for an empty booth but they're all occupied. As a song ends, we notice a guy about to leave and a girl getting dressed to return to the floor, a.k.a. "the zoo." So we wait at the entrance of this soon-to-be-available booth. The man gives the girl some money and they make a quick exit.

We enter the cozy space and Candy pushes me down on the couch, a crazy smile on her face. I try to get up, but she instructs me to stay put and I submit. She tells me that when I get a guy into a cubbyhole like this, I shouldn't waste any time. Once a new song starts I need to start dancing. Candy glides her body erotically over mine. She then turns her back to me and plants her lovely butt on my lap. My poor legs, supported by those damn high-heeled shoes, feel like they're about to snap from her forceful grinding. *How can guys actually like this?* I remind myself and giggle: *Oh yeah, they have a cock between their legs!* Candy gets up and faces me, smothering my face with her breasts and slapping them side to side in rhythm with the music. I'm captivated by how wonderful she smells. She starts to nibble on my ears and, even though I'm not gay, a warm sensation spreads through my body.

I move my head away but she pursues my ear with her glossed lips. Slowly she slides her body down on me, kneeling on the floor as her hands massage my breasts and then move down to my waist. She rubs her upper torso around my crotch and inner thighs and then buries her face between my legs. She's nibbling on my inner thigh, and … *Oh my god, that's nice! Maybe I'm a little gay after all, 'cause this nibbling is definitely making me moist!*

Candy gets up abruptly as the music ends. She tells me that at the end of each song I must keep close and rub the guy's inner thigh and ask him if he wants another dance. What she really means is, I should rub close to his cock through his pants! She also instructs me to never remove my G-string during the first song. If I have a bunch of guys waiting, I should ask each guy how many songs (dances) he wants and line them up from high to low. The guys who intend to spend more get serviced first!

And that's it – my crash course in the exotic art of lap dancing!

We exit our booth, and I know this is the last I'll see of my friend Candy for a while. She wishes me good luck and hurries out to make her rounds among the customers.

I hesitate to re-enter the zoo. I'm standing at its threshold like a scared would-be tigress. Gazing at the spectacle before me, I'm reminded of my Sunday school lessons – Sodom and Gomorrah, and the revelry and idol worshiping and general sinfulness of Jehovah's Chosen People after Moses descends Mount Sinai after receiving the Ten Commandments – and I wonder, *what would Jesus think?*

I need another drink just to keep myself busy – and maybe to suppress such thoughts. So I push my way through the crowd to the bar. I stand next to this guy who looks about 45, balding but in good shape. He's wearing a really nice suit and what looks like a Rolex watch, although I honestly can't tell a fake Rolex from the real deal. Still, I'm somehow sure it's real. I sip on my drink and observe a blonde asking him if he wants a dance. He dismisses her with a wave of his hand. A brunette hits on him next and receives similar treatment. This one walks away slowly, extending her middle finger to him behind her back. Soon a really pretty Asian begins to chat him up, but she too disappears fast. I make eye contact with him but quickly look away.

The bartender hands me a shot compliments of another guy seated several stools down. I hold up the shot to thank him, and he gestures for me to come over. *Am I ready for this? No way, I'm not ready! Maybe I should just leave!* But I know I can't. I can't walk home, and I'm already passed the limit to drive legally. So I breathe deeply, summon my courage, and flap my way over to him.

"Hi there, thanks for the drink," I say by way of greeting.

Oddly, he says nothing. Feeling a little uncomfortable I ask him if he wants a dance. He nods his head yes and I give him my best smile. I start winding my way through the crowd as he follows behind me. We enter the VIP area.

It's now so full we're obliged to take our place in a line-up. The girls ahead of us are talking to their customers but I don't know what to say to mine. We stand there silently until a space finally becomes available. We enter the booth and my customer sits down on the well-worn couch.

I recall Candy's lesson and begin mimicking what she did to me. But this guy isn't me – he's not sitting there passively with his hands at his sides as I did. No, this is much more like Kung Fu – or fighting an octopus! I'm going for a hundred bucks from this dude but also trying to keep him from grabbing my breasts, ass and pussy. It's exhausting. *I need to sit.* I just want to leave, but I remember Candy's rule that I must try to get a hundred dollars or more out of each customer. So I swallow my pride and ask him if he wants another dance as the first song ends. He nods a yes and I start dancing for him again. *This fucking guy is totally ruining my buzz.* I'm fighting two hands that seem to be grabbing me everywhere at once. Over and over I ask him to *stop,* but he ignores me.

Finally, I explode: “That’s it! I can’t dance for you anymore!” He pulls me toward him on the couch.

“What’s your problem?” I ask angrily. He responds with a mumbling sound. I ask whether he just got out of jail, because he doesn’t seem to understand that he needs to keep his hands to himself when I tell him to. The fucker just keeps making the same meaningless mumbling noise, so I insist, like a mother scolding her four year old, that he must *use words*. He murmurs in a new and different way – a whiney sort of utterance. I ask him to just pay me the forty bucks he owes me, but he grunts in protest. I’m getting upset as this quest to get my money consumes most of another song, one that I may not be paid for – plus there’s a girl standing nearby with a customer, waiting to enter our booth.

I’m dressed now, standing in front of this fool with my hand out waiting for him to pay me. He grasps my arm and tugs me down once again as he pulls something out of his pocket. I think its money at first, so I thank him, but then he starts writing something on a blank piece of paper. I tell him he’s going to have to pay for this third song because all this bull is taking much too long. He hands me a note that reads: “WHAT’S YOUR NAME?” “Linda Lee,” I answer.

He grabs back the paper and writes: “THAT’S A NICE NAME.”

Bemused, I thank him and then ask why he can’t talk. I expect him to write that he has laryngitis or something. Instead, I’m shocked to read: “I HAVE NO TONGUE.” I’m thinking I must have read it wrong, so I ask him to confirm what he wrote.

"You have no tongue in your mouth, like right now?"

He quickly scribbles his answer: "I WAS BORN WITH NO TONGUE." Despite my frustration with his earlier behavior, I suddenly feel nothing but sympathy for him. *He was born that way, wow!* I tell him I'll continue to dance for him, but only if he behaves himself and keeps his hands on the couch. He nods his head in agreement.

I begin to dance to what is now our fourth song. He behaves for a few seconds but then the bullshit starts up again. I stop dancing and stare at him angrily for a moment before he yanks me down to the couch and scribbles another note. The scrawl is so bad I ask him to write the message again.

Slowly, he prints out five words: "CAN I EAT YOUR PUSSY?"

I'm out of patience, so I stand up defiantly to give him my unkind but fully appropriate answer: "How can you eat my pussy if you don't have a tongue?"

I demand my money, he hands over sixty dollars, and I leave him sitting there.

I had thought all this was going to be easy, but making those first sixty dollars was really hard work!

Guys keep asking me for dances all night. None is quite as troublesome as that first customer, but they all keep me busy, in a variety of ways. Most respect my dance rules, but quite a few try to take liberties and I have to tell them off. Some proposition me to go to a motel with them. I explain that I don't do any "extras" – I sell lap dances only. I'm so busy, I don't even get a chance to touch up my makeup.

I'm in a VIP booth dancing for a customer when the whole area is suddenly flooded with light and a bouncer tells me I need to collect my money and quit for the night. It's well past 2:00 a.m. The customer pays me and I run upstairs with my clothing in hand. Candy is sitting on the dirty floor, drunk and struggling to put on one of her shoes. A girl asks me if I can take care of her. I agree with a nod. *She's my friend and my neighbor. But how the hell do I get her up and out of here?*

Candy slurs, "Did you tip the DJ?" I go, "What?" Then another girl says, "Make sure you tip the DJ."

I explain that I paid an extra fifty dollars on top of my floor fee to avoid performing on stage. "The DJ's done nothing for me, so why should I tip him?"

With a grim look, the girl replies: "If you want to work here again, go tip the fucking DJ. This place has bullshit rules."

I run downstairs without even getting dressed and hand the DJ twenty bucks. He looks unimpressed. I rush back upstairs to help Candy. All the girls are now off the floor and crowded into the change room. There must be at least eighty women bumping into each other as they don their street clothes. The room is deafeningly noisy with many girls talking about meeting customers elsewhere; some are going to the casino and after-hour clubs.

All I know is I can't wait to get my ass home. I ask a girl named Shyanne to help me get Candy dressed, which she does. It's kind of funny because as we're struggling to get her dressed, Candy is reaching over and trying to make out with one of the other girls. I've never seen this side of her before…. *or maybe I have, like when she was giving me that lap-dance lesson?*

Shyanne and I finally walk Candy out to my car and then dump her into the front passenger seat. I have to swing her feet into the car and fasten her seatbelt since she's close to passing out, dead to the world. I place her purse on her lap.

I really shouldn't be driving. I'm not exactly drunk but I'm pretty sure I'll blow over the limit if I get stopped by the cops. I feel okay though. I get us home safely and it takes me a few minutes to wake up Candy. She tells me she doesn't want to go back to her own place – she wants to sleep at my house instead. I remember how she came on to that girl in the dressing room.

I don't like the idea of her sleeping over with me, but she explains almost deliriously that she doesn't want her son to see her like this. I suggest he's probably sleeping, but she insists that he often gets into bed with her when she comes home, and she doesn't want him smelling booze on her breath. I tell her she can spend the night. I help her into my house, and she soon falls asleep on my couch like a baby.

I enter my bedroom, dump the cash contents of my purse onto the bed, and then settle into the middle of the mattress. I feel like a five year old as I toss my accumulated earnings into the air. I lie back into the bed, surrounded by small piles of bills, and recall the events of the night. I can't help but giggle.

The room is spinning a little but I still manage to count up the money, more or less accurately. *No way! I made $860. I can't believe it!* A rush of adrenalin surges through me and keeps me awake for what seems a long time, but I eventually drift off to sleep.

Late in the morning a frantic Candy awakens me. Her voice is elevated and she's crying. I'm still groggy, dazed and confused. "What the fuck happened to the money?" she shrieks. I tell her I have all my money – that I made good money. "My money is missing," she retorts. I rush over to check her purse and then the pocket of her jacket. *No money!* I know for sure she should have a lot because her night was even busier than mine.

I try to help her relive the night, retracing her actions and movements, especially the time she spent in the dressing room at closing time. Over and over, out loud and in my head, I'm saying, "*I didn't take it.*" Candy says she believes me, but her eyes betray suspicion. My thoughts keep returning to those last minutes in the change room. I can't believe this is happening!
"What about the other girls in the change room?" I ask. Someone there must have taken her money when she was so out of it.

She cries out softly, "Anyone could have taken it." I feel guilty even though I know I'd done nothing wrong.

"Can't you go to management? Tell them someone took your money from the change room and get them to check the surveillance tapes!"

"Those cameras are all over that place," she replies, "but not in the bathrooms or the change room."

I feel like shit as I walk her to the door. I go back to bed but I can't sleep. I feel like I'm the thief because of the way Candy was looking at me. I just can't shake the feeling of guilt.

There was only one other time when I was suspected of stealing something, but on that occasion I really was guilty. When I was eight years old back in my native Jamaica I was on Miss Lyn's veranda with her kids and some other friends. There were seven of us playing marbles, hopscotch and a few other games.

Before leaving for work, Miss Lyn left a few mangos in a basket on the ledge of the veranda so the sun would ripen them faster. Well, when the other kids left to eat their lunch, I took one of those mangos and ate it. I swear – it was the best mango I ever tasted! I was so hungry, and the mango was juicy and deliciously sweet! I thought nothing of it and then all my friends returned and we played some more.

Well, Miss Lyn came home from work and we were still out playing, but a little later Miss Lyn called all us kids into the house. That's what she usually did when she finished her baking and was going to give us cookies. This time though she didn't take us to the kitchen. Instead she told us all to sit down in the living room.

"I want to know who took my blasted mango!" Everyone's reply, including mine, was "Not me!" She was so mad! She asked again: "Who took my mango off the veranda?" "Not meeees!" filled the room. Then she asked us to write down our names on a writing pad that she passed around. As soon as it got back to her, she left the room abruptly.

That's when I got scared. All I was thinking was, *the whip is coming out*. Back then, you see, the community

as a whole raised the children – and that whole community believed in the saying, "Spare the rod, spoil the child."
There were no child-care agencies, or social workers, or kids' help lines. Probably not a whole lot has changed since then either. Miss Lyn returned with a Bible, an old fashioned skeleton key and a long string that she placed in front of us.

"I'm going to ask again," she said angrily. "Who took the mango?" "Not me," came a couple of replies. "Yeah, yeah, yeah, NOT ME!" Miss Lyn thundered as if to complete the chorus of replies that she was expecting from the rest of the kids. "One of you is LYING!"

I watched her closely as she placed the key into the Bible and wrapped the string around the Bible till it made a cross. Then she read out one of the kids' names and said these words: "By St. Peter, by St. Paul … did William take the mango?" She held the key up in an awkward way, allowing the Bible to dangle in mid-air – but nothing much happened. She did the same thing for a few other kids with no results.

Then it was my turn.

"By St. Peter, by St. Paul … did *Thelma* take the mango?" The suspended Bible started to turn and then to spin ever faster! After a few moments, the inside pages of the Bible began to tear, as the string tightened around them.

In a low voice, Miss Lyn asked me directly: "You didn't take the mango?"
"No, Miss Lyn, it wasn't me."
"Get out of my house!" she said. "The Bible never lies!"

I knew she was right. What I witnessed was unreal. I never forgot it.

Around noon, I get up and call Candy. I ask her if we can get the names of all the girls working last night at the club. "That's easy," she replies, "Everyone has to sign in when we pay our floor fees." She'll talk to the manager and get back to me. Within an hour or so Candy is already back with the list. I get my Bible and a key. Then I remove a few laces from my running shoes and tie them together to make a string of sufficient length.

"I'm not sure if this is going to work, but I'm gonna try."

I place the key in the middle of the front cover of the Bible and then relate the mango story to Candy. I tie everything together just as Miss Lyn did and place the list of eighty-two names before me. I can't wait to start with the name Shyanne because that's the girl who helped me with Candy the most. She even helped me to get Candy out to my car in the club parking lot. I recite the spell: "By St. Peter, by St. Paul … did Shyanne take the money?" Nothing happens. I try again. Nothing!

I tell Candy I was sure it was Shyanne who did it, but nothing happens on the third try, so I move on.

I repeat the spell over and over again, making my way down the list and crossing out names as the Bible testifies to their innocence. I'm becoming discouraged as I reach Number 68 on the list.

"Did Aneed Aman take the money?" Suddenly the Bible begins to spin, as the shoelaces tighten around it.

Yes, we've found the thief! Candy is shocked. She had thought the whole thing was a joke, but now she doesn't know what to think.

To be absolutely sure, I repeat the procedure for the remaining fourteen names – uneventfully. Then I return to Number 68, Aneed Aman. "Did Aneed Aman take the money?" Once again, the Bible spins, this time even more furiously. Candy is looking on in amazement.

I've cleared myself and identified the real thief, and I'm pleased. But Candy is steaming mad and says she can't wait to get to work to knock this bitch out and demand her money back. I try to calm her down: "Like really Candy, is knocking her out going to bring back your money?"

"No, but I'll feel better!" she replies. "That bitch is taking food out of my kid's mouth, fucking stupid hoe! I can't wait to get my hands on her!" Candy continues her rant and prepares to leave.

But I have a better plan. "Let's just go over to her house and tell her we viewed the surveillance tape and saw her taking the money. Who cares if there's no video camera in the change room?"

"House, what house? Aneed Aman's got no house."

Candy points out that a lot of the girls don't have permanent homes, even after years of dancing, because they have pimp guys who take most of their money away from them. To add insult to injury, many have to bring home a quota of a thousand dollars, and if they can't make it by dancing, they'll leave with a customer they meet at the club or go walk a strip where all the street whores hang out. They don't own homes, and she suspects Aneed Aman is a girl who will steal to avoid a beating.

Candy knows exactly where to find Aneed Aman – at a seedy motel down the road from the club. We decide to pay her a visit. I'm scared she might call the cops but Candy assures me that if her man beats her on a regular basis, and she doesn't call the cops on him, then we have nothing to worry about. Her only concern is that "her fucking pimp" might be there.

Candy does the driving. She knocks on the door of the ground-level motel room and waits for it to crack open. When it does, Candy pushes her way into the dark room. Aneed Aman looks as if she just got up. Fortunately, she's alone.

Candy is at her threatening best. "Where's my money bitch? We have you on tape, so cough it up or I'm calling the cops!" Aneed Aman pulls open a nightstand drawer and hands an envelope to Candy. She insists she was going to give it back to her tonight – that the money had fallen out of Candy's purse and that she had merely kept it for safe keeping.

"Right bitch," Candy replies scornfully. "I totally believe you!"

We leave and Candy stops at the club to go talk to the manager. I wait in the bar area and observe men coming and going early in the afternoon. Many are enjoying a lunch buffet. Candy returns and tells me that Aneed Aman will never work there again.

She drives me home and I contemplate how the Bible had proven that I wasn't the thief. As joyful as I am, I'm also dead tired. I crawl back into bed just as soon as I get home.

A bit later, Candy wakes me up with a phone call and says she'll drive us to work tonight. She tells me I have to be ready for 8 p.m., which gives me a whole hour to eat, shower, fix my hair, and get dressed up like the sexy gal I am.

I remember a conversation I'd had with Candy when we were driving home earlier. She explained how she'd been able to make so much more than me – a "secret" that's a large part of her hustle. Candy told me to never wait for customers to approach me. Last night, I'd waited to make eye contact and then waited for them to invite me over to their table or come to me and ask for a dance. She suggested that as soon as I hit the floor I should start my hustle by walking around and asking every customer for a dance. If they say no, I shouldn't let it bother me but just move on to the next guy. By the end of the night, she insisted, this routine will definitely pay off, whether the club is busy or not.

I decide to get one step ahead of Candy tonight. I won't be driving, so I pour myself a glass of wine. By the time she picks me up I'll already have my liquid courage.

Time flies when you're drinking vino, listening to music and getting ready. Candy rings and I rush out to her car. As I get in, I notice a glass of wine in the cup holder. She asks me to remove it and hold it for her, since it doesn't fit securely in the cup holder. I can tell she's feeling tipsy. We drive by a truck that honks at us, and she flashes her breasts and giggles like a child. We blast the music and sing our heads off. We pull into the club parking lot like it's a pit stop on a racetrack.

We enter the bar back door and make our way through the crowded floor to the office where we pay our fee and then upstairs to the change room. It's filled with girls squeezed together trying to get a peek into the mirror as they awkwardly apply their makeup. We stand back from the crowd beside Candy's locker and get dressed.

Candy pulls out a bottle of wine and two glasses and pours us drinks, trying her best to conceal her actions from the others. "Outside" liquor isn't allowed in the change room. If the manager finds out we could be "fined" or even fired on the spot. As with most of the other rules in this place, this policy is all about maximizing profit. Candy is saving us the $7 we'd be charged for a glass of wine downstairs.

We toast each other and wish for another great night. Hurrying so we can hit the floor soon, we literally throw back our wine. Ready to go, Candy bids me adieu, while I rush to finish my make-up. I hit the floor ten minutes later.

I walk over to the bar and order two shots of vodka and down them like water. Determined to drown my sobriety as quickly as possible, I order two more. The second round of drinks burns their way down. I suck on a lime wedge to relieve the sensation.

The music is hitting me just right. I'm moving to the beat, but not yet making any money. No one is approaching me, and I can't seem to get up the nerve to ask anyone. *One more drink should bolster my courage!* Unfortunately, there's a lineup of dancers and customers at the bar, so I give up on the drink idea and decide to just go for it.

I walk over to a guy seated at a small table and slide onto his lap. He seems to welcome my boldness. I place my hand by his thigh and bring my mouth close to his ear.

"Hi how are you…?" I breathe into his ear. His arm pulls me closer and he replies in a low but clear voice: "I'm horny and looking for someone to fuck, so if you're here to ask me for a dance I'm not interested, but if you want to leave with me right now, I have five hundred burning a hole in my pocket with a naughty girl's name on it."

Without replying or even looking at him again, I rise from his lap and walk over to another table where there's a group of men talking. The fattest of the bunch reminds me of Jaba the Hut from one of the *Star Wars* films. "Can you come back in a bit?" Jaba says. "We're just finishing up our meeting." I walk back to the bar and try to find a spot to place an order. I can't squeeze in anywhere. So I stand by a post hoping someone will approach me for *something* – a waitress for an order, or a customer for a dance, *anything!* My head is beginning to spin and my sense of time and space seems warped. After a while I return to the counter of the bar, stopping in four different spots to get the bartender's attention. He's so busy he just ignores me.

Fuck this shit! As I start toward the door that leads to the upstairs, a waitress stops me and lets me know that a woman sitting at the bar wants a dance. *No way! How am I supposed to dance for a woman?*

Reluctantly, I approach the customer. She's not attractive at all and on the portly side – and she's dressed like she's stuck in the eighties. But money is money, so I introduce myself. She asks for a dance, so I tell her to follow behind me. I fight my way through the crowd and glance back for her once I reach the VIP entrance. *The stupid woman is still sitting on a stool at the bar! What the…?!?* I walk back to her thinking that maybe she missed my instruction. I tell her again to follow me, but as I start to walk away she grasps my top, tugging me back toward her. I pull away, but I hear her say something, so I relax and let her whisper in my ear.

"I'm blind, I need your help."

"Come again?"

"I said I'm blind, and I need your help."

"Oh, I'm sorry, I didn't realize…"

I try to lead her by the hand, but the bar is so packed that I end up holding her close as we make our way through the crowd. I feel like I'm giving her a dance lesson. With almost every step I have to shout instructions – "step down," "turn left," "step up" – until we reach the VIP area. There's a lineup, so I explain to her that we'll have to wait.

A booth becomes available and we enter. I guide her onto the couch and place her handbag on the side table. It's a little freaky because her eyes are wide open and seem to be looking right at me. I sit down beside her and wonder, *how am I going to do this?* I ask her how long she's been blind. "All my life," she replies. I ask her why she picked me and she says she loved my scent. A song starts and I get up and find myself standing motionless in front of her. Midway through the song I

start to dance as she "stares" at me, never blinking. She asks, "Are you dancing?"
"Yes," I reply.
"Oh...."

To prove I'm dancing I take her hand and slowly move it over my body so she can feel my movements. Then it dawns on me: her hands will need to be her eyes if she's to get anything out of this experience. So I guide one of her hands to trace the contours of my shoulder and then move it across my face, letting her fingers lightly touch my almond eyes, small nose and protruding full lips. I guide her other hand along my long neck and let her squeeze one of my C-size breasts.

As her hand moves to my waistline, I whisper, "I'm as dark as midnight." She pulls her hand away from me.
"You're black?" she asks. I say yes.
"No you're not!" she exclaims.
"Yes, I am – is there a problem?"
"You don't sound black," she mutters with an alarmed tone. I decide to lay it on thick and tell her that I'm so black even my tobacco-stained teeth look white.

I ask her if she wants me to continue and she says no. I call over a bouncer and ask him to help her. I don't ask for a dollar and she doesn't offer me any payment. I go upstairs and get dressed. I remember Candy saying that "you shouldn't let no john bother you" – but damn, to be treated so shabbily by a blind woman I'd treated so nicely and gone on out of my way for! *That* was upsetting! I've definitely had it for the night.

While riding home in a cab, I reconsider everything. *Maybe I'm just not cut out for this line of work.*

I take a few days off, staying home mostly and trying to decide what I should do. During that time my friends and family are calling, but I seldom answer the phone. I don't want the people closest to me to know about by new profession, but I'm so depressed I'm afraid I might unburden myself to them. I distance myself from everyone. Eventually, three days after the incident with the blind woman, my spirits are beginning to revive, and I make up my mind to recommit to my new life. Bottom line, I have to pay my bills, and I don't care what anybody thinks.

The very next day I go shopping for stripper shoes and outfits. I'm amazed I'd never noticed the specialty stores catering to strippers before – stores with names like "Miss Behaving Girls" and "Dancing Doll Diva." The prices they want for their stuff are crazy! You've got to be making big bucks, and probably making them as a stripper, to shop in these places. I spend $500, and I feel good knowing that I can now return the items I've been borrowing from the other girls.

I've decided the night shift might just be too busy for me, so the next morning I go into work for noon. The change room is practically empty compared to the night shift and there are so few girls around I'm thinking I'm going to make a killing. I hurry downstairs to the bar area. It feels empty, with only one customer in sight – and he's already sitting with a girl. The music is low and there are maybe 30 girls on the floor, some of them sitting on stools playing games on video machines. Half a dozen girls are clustered around a large table but I settle into a high stool right up at the bar. I feel weird about ordering a drink this early in the day, so I wave the bartender away. A guy walks in and just as soon as he sits down one of the girls from the cluster rushes over to him. *He hasn't even had time to order a drink.* This is nothing like the night shift, but a waitress tells me it'll get better soon. True, the club has just opened its doors, but after experiencing the night shift this kind of non-action seems pointless to me. I ask the manager if I can leave, but he refuses to let me go, explaining that once I'm on the floor I have to stay a minimum of five hours.

I can't understand this stupid rule. They don't pay me a cent, for god's sake. I'm a *freelancer* – a self-employed contractor selling a service to the club's customers. Actually, I have to pay the damn club for the privilege of working here and then they have the frigging nerve to boss me around! The manager's arrogance really pisses me off, but I have no choice but to deal with it. *I won't make this mistake again!*

A thin, frail-looking man who looks to be in his fifties enters the bar area and walks up to the table where most of the girls are gathered. Several rise to hug and kiss him. As he sits down with them, I'm thinking, *this guy must feel like some kind of rock star getting that kind of treatment.* A few minutes pass and the waitress who's just delivered a full tray of drinks to the busy table walks over to me and says, "That guy over there, his name is Paul, he's a regular here and he'd like to buy you a drink." I flash him a smile and ask the waitress for a rum and coke. I approach the table to thank him, and he invites me to sit down with them. As I'm waiting for my drink to arrive, Paul gets up and goes for a dance with one of the girls in the VIP area. They aren't gone long – maybe three or four songs. He then invites another girl "into the back" with him.

The girls aren't making me feel very welcome at their table, so I return to the bar counter. After getting back from a few more trips to the VIP area, Paul walks over and asks me for a dance. I go with him. I learn he has a "favorite spot" where he can hide and "do some dirt." I start to dance for him and he immediately commences to undo his pants.

Abruptly, I step back and say: "No, no, no – no way, you can't do that here!"
"Whuddya mean," he answers. "I don't want no blow job – I save that for when I'm ready to leave. What's the point gettin' a blow job now when I'm gonna hang out for a couple of hours? Just play with it, okay?"

I tell him straight: "Just leave your limp-ass dick in your pants!" Heaving an impatient sigh, he obeys my instruction and zips up.

"What the hells the matter with you man? I said I'd dance for you, not touch your penis!"

"Okay, okay," he says, "gimmee one dance. I can't be wasting my money on you."

It's all over in no time. I don't get close to him or even sit next to him because he's creeping me out – he reminds me of Skeletor from *Masters of the Universe*. He tosses me $20.

I walk out to a fuller club. A waitress informs me that two busloads of golfers have stopped by. We're finally in business! The golfers keep me busy for the rest of the afternoon. By 6:30, I'm hungry and tired, so I pack it in.

As soon as I get home, I count my money anxiously. *I've made more than I did during my most lucrative night shift.* On the down side, the guys I'd serviced were dirtier. The girls on the day shift can get away with anything because there's no bouncer. I personally didn't see any dirt, but I wasn't looking for any either. From the way they were talking, though, most of the customers seemed to want more "action" than I'd been willing to provide. All the same, I've done very well, almost a grand!

I call up Candy and tell her about my day. I explain that I prefer the day shift because I can treat it like a 9 to 5 job, and still enjoy my evenings. The night shift just kills me! After getting home about 4 in the morning, you can't wake up till real late in the day and you have just a few hours to spare before doing it all over again.

I can tell from her voice she'd love to be flexible enough to work day shift, but with a child to care for, she can't do it. Who would get her son to school, meet him later, make sure his homework is done, have supper with him, and read him stories before bed? Single moms have their work cut out for them! Sure, she has to pay for babysitting at night, but her son is asleep for most of the time she's away.

That evening, I go to the gym for a workout, make supper, and watch a movie before bed. Wouldn't you know it, it's that ridiculous movie with Demi Moore playing a stripper! The whole club scene is so wrong! Total bullshit – as far from reality as Julia Roberts' *Pretty Woman* glamour hoe! Speaking of which, I just bet if you were to talk to one of those high class hookers they'd tell you it's nothing like that with those rich johns.

I get a good night's sleep and start my second day shift promptly at noon.

I'm standing at the bar, dressed to the max, outfitted with jewelry and the sweetest scent. I look like a pro-stripper, but, damn, the only customer in the club is Paul. I can't stand him but I've already taken him for a few dances. He has a definite thing for me, even though I always take a hard line against his bullshit. As usual there are many girls doting on him, waiting to be picked for his next trip "to the back."

In walks this gorgeous guy dressed in a perfectly tailored Armani suite, his shoes glistening as he steps toward pervert row. After he takes a seat at a small table, I consider joining him – but I'm intimidated. He looks like a cross between Brad Pitt and Michael Jordan, except he has a full head of blond hair styled like a surfer dude. I sit there and watch as other girls approach him and then leave as they are each turned down in turn. As they walk past me they whisper things like "He's *so* cute!" One girl mentions that he has bright blue eyes and full lips. Every girl that walks by encourages me to go over and talk to him – not to get a dance but just to get a good look at him. I stay put – I'm just too shy and this guy isn't showing much interest in any of the girls.

I watch the guy as he sits there taking in the acts of a few girls on stage while continuing to refuse offers to go for dances. Finally I walk over, but instead of immediately sitting on his lap, I ask him if I can join him. "My pleasure," he replies. I'm overtaken by an intoxicating scent that conjures up an image of walking in a garden on a breezy night, a light, fresh aroma in the air. I lean close to him to indulge my sense of smell. I ask him where he's from. It's Los Angeles. Nice, so why is he so far north? He explains he's on business, being a corporate CEO and all. Although he came in to have a few drinks, he's still busy working, taking calls from time to time from employees all over North America on his Blackberry. I can't look at him; he's too beautiful! I stare at his glass, still amazed by his wonderful scent. He asks me if I want a drink, and I accept.

When I tell him he's a really attractive guy, he blushes like a big kid who's unaware of his good looks, and then asks me for a dance. I glance over at the other girls who are now looking in our direction in disbelief as we head off for dances. *Yes, girls, he's picked me, the only black girl in the club today, over all of you white chicks.* We find ourselves alone in the VIP area.

He's so sweet – he wants to know more about me. I tell him I don't want to dance forever. I want to start up a business, but first I want to pay off all my bills. He wants to know what kind of bills I could have to drive me to strip. I tell him I owe back taxes to Revenue Canada, and I have lots of other expenses. He nods sympathetically, and I ask him if he has a family. He speaks with pride about his two little girls, chuckling that at home he's ruled by women. He admits to spoiling his girls because his work takes him away from home more often than he'd like. Then he talks about his wife and shows me a picture of her that he's removed from his wallet. *Wow, she's so pretty!*

I excuse myself to go to the washroom. Something about this guy has me feeling uncomfortable and on edge. I need a refresher: a little perfume and makeup. Once inside the washroom, I find myself surrounded by several girls who want to know about him. All I say is, "He's nice." One girl says: "You must be making so much money." I say, "no, I haven't even started my dances yet."
Another girl asks if I've felt how big his cock is. *I haven't even started, and she's expecting a report on the dimensions of his dick!* I shake my head dismissively.

I rejoin my customer who kids me by saying that he'd almost given up on me and was just about to grab a blonde. I ask him why he'd do such a thing. "I was feeling lonely," he replies in a tone that reminds me of a little boy. He asks me if I like to be in control during lovemaking and I say yes. Then he asks if I like submissive men, and again I say yes. *But really, no. I'm just trying to be agreeable.*

I tell him I'm going to start dancing for him with the next song.

"Okay, but don't take off your outfit," he replies.
Now I'm truly shocked – I have a routine, and getting naked is always a part of it. I'm wondering, *what's this guy's game?*

The song starts up and I'm dancing for him face to face, running my fingers through his golden hair, and caressing his tan face, and touching his nicely built, buff body. I'm getting really hot and bothered. I start rubbing my breasts against his chest, looking him straight in the eye. I turn around and sit on his lap, grinding my butt cheeks into him. No hard-on yet! I grind harder but there's no response. *He must be into blondes – his beautiful wife is one.*

As I'm about to finish, he asks me to stay. He tells me he likes to be punished and humiliated for being in places like this. I take a moment to digest this information and then I order him to get down on his knees like a dog. He quickly complies. I climb onto his back and ride him like a horse around the near-empty VIP area from room to room. He keeps saying,

"Please mistress – stop, please stop!" And I say, "No, you must obey me, you bad boy!" As I'm laughing and thoroughly enjoying myself, I put my legs up on his head, and lose my balance.

My feet quickly hit the floor and he cries out: "Miss, my knees are really hurting!"
I command him: "Take us back to our booth," and he obeys. I dismount him and he's about to get up, but I order him to stay put. "Okay mistress," he responds sheepishly. I sit back on the couch and throw my legs over his back as if he's an ottoman. I pull a book out of my purse and start to read.

We remain like this for several songs as other girls and their customers pass us by, often glancing down at this immaculately dressed guy groveling beneath me.

"Miss, people are staring at us."

I just laugh and say: "So what? You deserve this humiliation. It was your decision to enter this den of iniquity and you're a very bad boy! So shut up and accept your punishment!"

I reach down and grab his dick. It's hard as a board and quite long, maybe 9 inches. I get him up, push him onto the couch and squeeze his nipples. He's groaning with ecstasy. I kneel on his hard dick and slap his face as he screams out: "Miss, please stop, please stop!" I say no. He changes his tone and says, "No, please – I've had enough." So I back off and ask him why he wants me to stop. He explains that he's on the verge of coming and has a meeting he must get to in an hour. He doesn't have time to change his suit and he can't show up with cum stains on his pants!

We're done, so he opens his wallet and asks: "How much miss?" I ask him how much he has in his wallet. He does a quick count and says "seven hundred and thirty five dollars." I say, "I want it all," and he nods his agreement. After he hands over the cash, I point toward my feet with a stern look, and he bends over to kiss them. Then he fixes his disheveled clothing and departs the club quickly.

As I exit the VIP area, Paul is waiting for me. *Shit!* He doesn't ask for a dance but he follows behind me till I reach the door leading to the upstairs change room – a doorway no customer is allowed to enter. As I look back at him to explain I'm going upstairs, he hands me a piece of paper with a phone number written on it. "Call me," he says. *Strange!* I rush through the door and up to the change room. Later one of the girls tells me Paul had been waiting for some time at the entrance to the VIP area while I'd been with Mr. CEO. I can't even begin to understand that, but I've been meeting the strangest people ever in this place, and Paul is definitely one of them.

I get dressed and pay my DJ fee, which is relatively low for the day shift. As I go to the office to sign out, the club owner and the manager are sitting there. The manager tells me I can't leave because I have yet to work a full five hours. I'm feeling cocky, maybe because of the role playing I'd been doing with Mr. CEO, so I reply that I'm a freelancer, which means I should be able to come and go as I please. The manager interrupts me and says that those are the rules and if I don't like them, I can go work somewhere else. If I need to leave early, I can pay $20 at the bar for a waiver.

"So I have to pay $20 for a get-out-of-jail free card?" I exclaim.

"Those are the rules," retorts the manager, knowing full well he has me over a barrel. I'm thinking, *this is the place to work, and I'm not going anywhere.*

Then the owner asks me how long I've been working at "the Downer"? I tell him it's been a few years. He asks me if I'm a cop. "No, of course not," I reply, surprised by his question. I pay the $20 and get the fuck out of there, but I'm a little rattled by the club owner's paranoia and his apparent suspicion toward me.

I go pay some bills, hit the gym, and I'm home in time to make myself a great, healthy supper. I'm in bed by ten. At around three in the morning I'm awakened by noises outside, seemingly on the roof or on the side of the house. They sound like footsteps. I'm too scared to look out the window, so I grab my cell-phone and call the police. The dispatcher sends out some cops who look around the property. After a few minutes, they come to the door and report to me that everything seems to be okay and safe. They suggest that I may have heard an animal, maybe raccoons because they're known to cause a big racket sometimes. I go back to bed but have trouble sleeping. I drift off to sleep around seven in the morning for a short time, but get up around nine to perform some chores before making it into work before noon.

As I'm putting on my makeup in the change room, I lose track of time. I'm listening to this stripper-hoe Diamond who's talking about how her life is shit and it's all her fault. She feels so very alone in this world because neither side of her family will talk to her. I'm so saddened by Diamond's story that I'm moved to go over and give her a hug.

Her father had started sexually molesting Diamond when she was just four years old. When she was ten her mother came home from work one day and caught this monster fucking the shit out of her. Her mother rushed him with her fists and then started hitting him with whatever she could grab, trying desperately to get the piece of shit off her daughter. As the fight between her parents continued, verbally and physically, Diamond called 9-1-1. By the time the cops arrived, Diamond's father had beaten her mother to death.

The fucker got a long prison term. Diamond's family on her mother's side won't talk to her because she looks like her dad and they now accuse her of "dressing like a slut." On her father's side of the family, they hate her because she told the truth about what happened, and they can't handle it. It's easier to accuse her of lying. Estranged from her relatives, Diamond spent most of her teenage years moving between foster homes and the streets.

Now she's a rough-edged but undeniably beautiful stripper with a pimp who beats her if she doesn't bring home her quota every night, either stripping in the club or selling her body on the streets.

Diamond's so caught up in the lifestyle that she's quick to start a fight with any and all of the other girls. Her pimp has three girls working for him, all working in the same bar, and believe it or not, they're all friends. Well, when Diamond sees one of her pimp mates and realizes that the other one hasn't show up for work, she asks her where the third girl is. She mutters something about her having the day off, and that's all it takes to get Diamond to "go gangster" and start yelling, "how can she get a fucking day off when I haven't had one in over a year."

I pull Diamond off her pimp-mate, a hundred-ten pound, teenage-looking girl. I'm guessing from her old make-up and the crack fragrance in her hair that, while she might look as young as twelve, she's likely been around for a while and is probably in her late teens. So she's probably "legal" – the minimum age for stripping, parading naked and grinding your ass into the laps of lecherous men in Niagara is eighteen.

I've had it with these two fools. I hurry my ass downstairs and run into Paul who's been waiting near the door to the upstairs change room since I first entered the bar. He asks me for a dance and I ask him why, since he's never satisfied with what I offer him. He says, "Let's start over." So I go with him. Within a minute or two of the first lap dance, he's reaching toward my breasts. I tell him to stop and demand my money. He tells me I suck at this, and he'll never get me again. I think, *I'm completely okay with that, because you're not at all appealing.*

Maybe, I think, I should try going on stage to advertise myself. So I talk to the DJ and ask him to let me do a stage show. He puts me on his list, and I quickly run upstairs to change my outfit. I'm supposed to be ready to perform following two other girls, but after the next song I hear the DJ calling my name over the P.A. system to come see him right away. So I run down stairs, only partially dressed, leaving my locker unlocked. The DJ wants to know what songs I'm using in my show. I pick three songs, which is the mandatory number: *Dirty Diana* by Michael Jackson, *She Works Hard for the Money*, and Mariah Carrey's *Hero*.

Soon, it's show time. The bar area only has about twenty scattered customers – a few seated at the edge of the stage but most at tables ten or more feet away. It's practically empty by club standards, but I have the jitters and, to make matters worse, I need to pee … but there's no turning back now. The music is starting and the DJ has just introduced me. I strut my stuff around the stage, dance my ass off, and take a few swings around the pole. By the end of the first song I have the attention of the whole room. The guys are going nuts, and all the girls are watching me. During my third song I even get tipped on stage. The men love me and I'm suddenly feeling a natural high. I make eye contact with a few customers knowing that as soon as I get off stage I'll have them lining up for dances.

As I exit the stage to wild applause, I'm stopped by Diamond backstage who's accusing me of "stealing" her song. I ask her when exactly she wrote it. She's carrying on like she wants to fight. I brush past her, eager to get dressed and back on the floor. She threatens to knock me on my ass if I ever cross her again. As I quickly dress, she continues yelling and acting like a hooligan. But I try my best to ignore her and then quickly make my way out to greet the customers who seem most interested in me. I walk over to a table and flop myself down in a chair beside this middle-aged fat guy who's dressed so well he could be a banker.

I introduce myself, and he replies by shaking my hand with a firm grip. "You can call me John," he says, and I'm thinking, *how appropriate!* It's probably a fake name – customers are at least as likely to use them as dancers. I'm still trying to catch my breath as he asks me for a dance. I get up and he leads the way. The fucker walks deep into the VIP area to the last booth. I suggest we go back to one of the other empty booths but he waves me down and we enter his preferred destination. He gives me a big hug, as if he's known me forever, and we sit. He tells me that he doesn't want me to dance and gives me two hundred up front. I slip it into my purse and place it on the floor under the side table. As I turn back toward him he's struggling to open a little plastic bag. He pours out some white powdery stuff on the table and makes two lines, He asks me to keep a look out, which I do, even though I'm thinking, *why? there's no bouncers on the day shift!* He proceeds to snort one of the lines. Then he hands me his rolled-up bill and tells me the other one is for me. I tell him I'm fine. He covers up the unused line on the table with his cigarette pack.

The fool is talking a mile a minute. He wants to know if I live on Fire-lane.

What the ...? More than a little shocked, I ask him why. He says he's seen me walking in that area a few times, so I answer, "yes, I live near there." Then he snorts the other line and gives me another two hundred bucks as if he's forgotten he's already paid me. Now I'm almost sure this guy was already fucked up even before he came to the club. His mouth just doesn't stop, but I'm being paid to listen to the fool, so I'm trying to be patient with him. Then he asks me if I live at No. 11 Fire-lane. *Shit no!* A chill runs through me.

I bolt up suddenly, and he tries to calm me down. "No, no, relax love. I know I've seen you there a few times, and you looked like a party girl to me, so a few different nights I took a chance and stopped by your house to invite you to a party."

Astonished, my reply is an almost breathless "Really?!?!" He pulls out his little baggie again and then reaches for his wallet and hands me more money.

He explains he only lives about twenty houses away from me. He says I must be a heavy sleeper because one night he knocked on my window and door and I didn't answer, so he just left. His words send a frightening shock through me again. *Oh my dear god, I have a nutcase on my hands. What do I do? That "animal" I heard at three in the morning ... could that have been him?*

He forms another big line of coke, and I get up. He asks what's wrong. I tell him I've got to call my friend. He asks me to wait a minute and watch out as he snorts his line. He holds my hand gently and says, "I'm sorry if I frightened you, but there's nothing to be frightened of." He tries to reassure me by saying that he had just recently separated from his wife and that he's a retired schoolteacher. He then explains that he's been watching me since before I started dancing and that he just loves the way I carry myself. I'm thinking, *what does he mean "how I carry myself," and how does he know when I started dancing*?

The guy won't shut up – he's totally wired. He tells me he's the head finance usher at his church, and really I shouldn't be worried. He's actually an extremely shy guy, partly because he has no siblings or friends, and that's why he likes cocaine: it gives him courage. Even when he stops talking, his mouth is still moving in a sideways grinding motion. He's sweating profusely. He keeps wiping his face with a handkerchief and his shirt is soaked. He stands up and says goodbye with a gentle handshake and a gallant kiss to the back of my hand.

I run upstairs and call Candy on the phone.

"Candy! Remember when I told you that I called the cops to my house because I heard noises outside? Well, I just found out that it was probably a customer."
"No way, what the fuck?"
"Yes, a retired school teacher …"

I tell her the whole story, how he did lines of coke but also treated me nicely.

"Do you feel threatened by him … like, do you think he might hurt you?" she asks.

"No, Candy, he's into church affairs. He told me I had nothing to fear from him."

"What does church have to do with anything? What the hell is he fucking doing at your house at that wee time in the morning?"

She's right of course, but I have no answer for her. *Did he really want to invite me to a "party" at that time in the morning? What sort of "party" could that possibly be?*

"So what should I do?"
"Does he creep you out?" she asks.
"Not really. For some reason, I feel kind of sad for him."
"I don't know," she replies. "That shit's crazy."
"What would I tell the cops, anyway? Plus Candy, I made over seven hundred dollars from the guy in under an hour."
"I don't know,… I guess you'll just have to see when and if he comes back."
"That's fine – I'll make money, and I'll tell him not to show up at my house again."

We say our good-byes and she jokes that I should introduce them so he can spot her a few lines.

I can't wait to hit the gym. I'm becoming addicted not so much to the energy I get from my workout as to the pleasing routine of my day. After the gym, I make fresh veggie juice – it makes my mouth water hearing the juicer extract the juices from all the carrots, beets and watercress. My day ends with a movie and a bag of Humpty Dumpty barbeque chips.

For some reason I wake up that night at 2:45 a.m. I keep the lights off but I stare out the window until I eventually drift off to sleep. Suddenly I wake up with a start. I'm relieved to reassure myself that I've had no unwanted visitors during the night. No raccoons…. and no retired, cokehead school teachers.

I'm not really in the mood for loud music or talking to customers, but once I'm dressed, I zap myself into work mode. *What character might I play today? Yes, a doctor! And I'm going to speak with a British accent.*

I hustle into the club and ask the girls in the change room if any of them want to work with me today. Diamond – yes *that* Diamond! – says she will. I'm surprised by her eagerness. *No hard feelings apparently. Besides, money takes precedence over everything, and she knows we can work well together.*

Two girls acting as a team can often make a killing because most customers during the dayshift show up as couples or in groups. Often, they're having drinks after a golf game or a business meeting. If one guy goes for a dance, the others usually follow.

Diamond and I approach this table where four guys are seated. Several of the girls have had their eyes on this table because the bar is pretty dead, and several have already sat with them briefly or been turned away. It's an unwritten rule that when customers are already occupied with girls, the other girls must stay away – unless a customer specifically invites a girl to his table. Sometimes a guy will point to a girl who's at another table and say, "she's the one I want." At that point it's appropriate to invite the girl over – but if you don't like her, you may try to sell the customer on one of your own friends. Most often it works.

Anyway, the coast is clear now, and it's our turn to take a crack at these guys.

So we're having drinks and getting engaged in their conversation about computers. I feel insecure because I really don't know anything about computers. Then Diamond walks off with one of the guys hand in hand, and I'm left sitting with the remaining three, one to my right, one to my left and the other directly across from me. I quickly establish that the one on my left likes one of the girls that has just walked by and the waitress is getting her. The other on my right is into blondes. I move my way around to the center of the table as two new girls join us. Before long all six of us are chatting up a storm. I ask "my guy" repeatedly if he's ready for a dance, but he keeps saying no. Soon all the others have gone off to the VIP and I'm sitting alone with this guy. He won't budge for nothing. When the others return, one of them asks if I've gone for a dance yet. I shake my head. So his friend pulls out a hundred dollar bill and tells me to take him for a dance.

So we go back to the VIP area and he immediately apologizes for not taking me earlier. He feels like a fool. I tell him not to worry. I start to dance for him but he asks me to stop. He tells me to keep the money and we can just sit and talk.

"I'm sorry," he says, "but you don't do anything for me."
Startled by his honesty, I ask: "I don't turn you on?"
"It has nothing to do with you, I love black people."

I'm confused, but he's quick to explain himself. "I'm gay," he says softly. "My boyfriend is black, okay? I just don't want you to feel offended."

"That's fine," I reply. "We'll just sit here for five songs, no problem. And I won't say a thing to your friends." He said he was cool with that.

I ask him why he was shy to tell me he's gay; we didn't have to come back here.

"I own the company," he explains. "We had a meeting here in town over a golf game, and then one of my workers suggested this place. So here we are. The reason I came with you is that my workers don't know I'm gay. You see, I'm actually married with kids." "Really!" I answered.

"In case you haven't noticed, I've been around a long time and I know how judgmental people can be."

"But if you have kids, you must be bisexual, not gay."

"No, I'm gay. I married a woman with kids from another man. She's my best friend, so when her asshole husband who used to beat the crap out of her got put in jail she got up the courage to get a divorce. My wife knows I'm gay. She wants nothing to do with men sexually. We do family things. I love my kids, and I love my wife. She knows everything about me." "Really!" I exclaimed.

"Yes I tell her everything. Well I spare her the details of my gay escapades." "So where do you meet your men?"

"Sometimes on the Internet," he answers, but he explains he doesn't have time for too many dates, so he mostly goes to bathhouses.

"Holy shit, what's with bathhouses?" I ask. He explains in detail. I know he's not making it up.

As he's talking about it I can see he's getting excited. I notice Diamond walking by with one of the other guys, and I know that the other three aren't digging me, so I've got to find a way to keep this guy after the five songs end. So I ask him what his favorite type of guy is. He says it's his boyfriend – this big, tall, black man named Neville. One of the reasons he likes Neville is he doesn't look gay. They go on dates and call it business meetings; they travel and he pays Neville's expenses. Neville is like a man-mistress. All he does is work out and shop, and …

I execute my plan. I get up and start dancing for him. He tries to stop me but I keep going and tell him how much I want to stick my finger up his ass and my hard cock down his throat. He starts rubbing his dick which soon turns into a raging hard-on.

Twenty-five songs and five hundred bucks later he's still moaning and groaning.

Finally he says he wants to rejoin his group. He admits he really enjoyed his time with me. He can't believe I kept him hard for so long.

When we return, his buddies rib him for having resisted going with me at first and then staying in the VIP the longest. I smile, but say nothing. One of his friends calls over another girl for him but he quickly rejects the suggestion. "Sorry guys, I'm going to stick with her," he says, as I slip onto his lap. He sticks another hundred in my purse. We drink and talk as the others make many more trips to the VIP room. Every now and then he deposits more money in my purse.

The group is just leaving as I hear my name being called to go see the DJ. The DJ tells me Paul has called a few times asking to talk to me, and he finally left his number for me to call him. I take the number and toss it into the garbage.

I pay the DJ and I'm about ready to leave when the manager asks me to stay because "we're short on girls." I'm tired and have had too much to drink but I say okay. The dinner and early evening hours are really slow, so I feel like I'm wasting my time. Finally Candy appears; the night shift is beginning.

I freshen myself upstairs, re-enter the floor and order a drink at the bar. As I'm being served, a man standing behind me pays the bartender. I look around … and it's John. He asks me to join him and we walk into the VIP area. After we settle in his favorite spot, he gives me four hundred dollars and asks if I can join him at his house. I tell him I'm not a whore. He says, "no sex, just for a drink." "I don't know," I respond hesitantly, as Candy sits down beside me. Candy, feeling her liquor, asks "what's crack a lacking?" I say my friend here would like me to join him at his house later. Candy goes "me too?" I say "No Candy," and John quickly adds "only Linda Lee." Candy says "you're not going with some strange guy without me." Candy takes over and tells him its three hundred an hour. He agrees to two hours with both of us after the club closes. John gives me his address and leaves without even taking a sip of his drink.
The night moves on, slowly. Tired and knowing I have more money coming to me later, I just sit and read for the next four hours.

When we arrive at John's house around 3:00 a.m., Candy is drunk and I'm exhausted. We knock on John's door and he answers with a brandy in his hand. He leads us into what he calls his red room. The carpet is red, the wallpaper is red and white, and all the furnishings are antique. What grabs my attention most is an old piano sitting under a floor lamp with a red frilly lampshade and silver and yellow stain Plexiglas buttons. One wall is completely covered by bookcases lined with old books. I sit down in this antique chair that has a curvaceous back but no arms. The feet of the chair are chiseled to a beautiful breathtaking design. John explains he was born in this house and that after his parents passed away he inherited it and he decided to live here. Most of the furnishings were passed down from his grandparents.

The glass table in front of us displays several lines of cocaine. As Candy snorts her first line I tell John I'm going to pass. John and I talk and talk, and it often feels like we're alone. Candy is totally out of it.

John tells me how fascinated he is with my skin color and that he once had the opportunity to teach a little girl who was black. I tell him I have ambitions to write a book but I don't know where to start. He suggests I start with poetry, so he grabs a pen and paper and we both write several short poems and then read them aloud to each other.

In what seems like no time, dawn is breaking. John pays us and promises to do this again.

I feel as though I'd just gone to sleep when I hear a pounding at my door. Thinking it must be John, I rush to the door prepared to tell him off, but I'm surprised to find Miss Huston. I talk to her with the door only slightly opened so that I can conceal my body, which is clad only by a bra and panties. The ninety year-old lady pushes the door open and tells me I'm going to be late if I don't hurry. I retreat as she barges in.

Miss Huston is an English woman I've been seeing for bible study on Wednesdays, but for a few weeks now I haven't been to church or bible study. She rummages around my kitchen and makes coffee as I get myself dressed. I usually tell Miss Huston pretty much everything about my life, but for some reason I can't answer her truthfully when she asks me what I was up to last night. As she drives me to church I'm longing silently to return to bed.

Church is good, a very enjoyable service. Usually I love going to church.

It's where I feel most at home because I was brought up in church, both in Jamaica and later in Canada. I stand in the alcove near the entrance waiting for Miss Huston to drive me home, but because she's a church elder she has to meet and greet the congregants as they depart. *God, it's taking forever!* I listen closely and then realize she's inviting everyone to join "us" downstairs for a potluck luncheon. That means I'll be here for another two hours! Thank goodness I learned from a young age to respect my elders and be patient because I'm actually seething mad! This is more than I bargained for. *I just want to go home!* I feel totally wasted and exhausted – and it's pathetic to have to walk away from people because your breath smells of booze!

After what seems like an eternity, Miss Huston drops me off at home. Soon I'm as one with my bed and I know there's no way I'm going to do a night shift. After a long, deep sleep, I wake up and glance at my alarm clock. It's six in the morning. I've slept for over twelve hours!

I hit the gym and make my way to the club for the day shift. Once I'm on the floor I go to sit down with the usual group of girls, but something seems different today. No one's drinking and they're all speaking in hushed tones. *Okay what's going on?*

I overhear one of the girls saying, "We don't even know if he's alive." "Who?" I ask.
"Paul," she answers.

"Of course he's alive," I insist. "He's probably just running late. Are you expecting him?"

"Oh my god!" another girl exclaims. "I guess you haven't heard."

"Heard what?"

"Paul was rushed to the hospital yesterday by ambulance. He was here when it happened…"

"What happened?" I ask.

"He was in the back with Emerald and just after he came out he started to walk funny and then fell over a few tables," interjected another girl. "It's like he was falling in slow motion. By the time I rushed over he was on the floor, unconscious. The waitress called 9-1-1 and the ambulance came and got him. It was scary: one second he was fine and just a few minutes later he was strapped onto an ambulance gurney shaking like a leaf."

"Has anyone called to see how he is?"

Another girl answers: “I did but there was no answer. I tried a few times.”

“Wow, that’s what I get for taking a day off,” I say. “I missed all the excitement.”

“It wasn’t exciting at all,” she replies. “It was just sad – and boring. Everything got fucked up. No customers came in for a long time ‘cause of the ambulance and the cop cars outside. Even after Paul was taken away, the cops hung around for a while asking a lot of stupid questions. They really messed up our shit! I wish I’d taken the day off.” The other girls nod in agreement.

Days turn into weeks, the weeks into months, and no one asks about Paul anymore.

It’s getting harder and harder to make money during the day shift as fewer guys are coming in. Not only have that, but the old customers always seemed to be going after the new girls. My novelty seems to have worn off for many of them. The owner is charging the girls higher freelance fees to try to compensate for his declining beer and liquor sales. As I continue to immerse myself in this subculture, I’m drinking more, not to mention smoking too much. Fortunately, I have several regular customers I can depend on.

After work, I often go out with my regulars to eat at fine restaurants and shop. This is one way to keep them interested in you. It creates a sense of companionship and intimacy, even though I always make it clear that sex is out of the question. But as much as you try to entertain them and keep them interested, you still end up losing most of them eventually if you don’t give up the punani. It's regular as clockwork: they meet you in the bar, they invite you out, and then they try and try to get into your pants.

A regular customer will often try to play one girl off against another. He'll show up when you and the other girl are both working the same shift and encourage catfights over whose customer he is. Then the game really starts! He'll ask you out to get the other girl upset. To keep him as a customer the other girl will go as far as sleeping with him – anything to get him back into her fold. I watch this play out a million times. Most often the girl who sleeps with the customer loses out because the challenge for him now is to get into *your* pants, and it drives him nuts! Now the hard-to-get girl – yours truly – has the upper hand. If I find out that a regular customer's slept with another girl, that's my golden ticket. If he asks for a date or to take me shopping, I say, "Oh, why don't you take your new girlfriend?" And then he turns into an innocent little boy, almost crying: "But I want to hang with you." So the chase is real and it never stops. And, in the end, I can often – not always, but often – wrap these guys around my little finger.

Picture this. I'm dancing for this guy who's about 55. He's heavy set, losing his hair, wearing old school glasses. His hair is unkempt, and he's wearing a suit that's at least a few years out of fashion. Oh, and he's a lawyer. For real, I'm sure he's wearing a Rolex watch. This is the kind of guy I don't mind talking to before I take him for a dance. Then I get into a VIP booth with him and all he does is cut up his wife. She doesn't *touch* him anymore, or all she does all day is *shop*. He goes on and on until I start to dance. I do my routine, getting on my knees to rub my breasts between his legs and bumping into his hard-on. This guy smells so bad that I bolt back up as fast as I'd gone down. The more he's spread his legs, the greater and fouler the smell filling the room. It burns my nostrils and makes me sneeze. I feel like vomiting. It's like there's a disgusting fish swimming in piss and shit between his legs.

This is when I get real with assholes like this. I say, "I know you're paying me to dance for you but I really can't continue. It just isn't worth it, because frankly *you stink*. Maybe if you take a shower your wife will touch you." *Yes you're mad at me, but can't you smell your own ass?* The funny thing is, he thinks he's insulting *me* as he throws down the money he owes me on the table and storms out.

I hear an announcement over the PA system. "All dancers report to the back office."

Because I've been telling guys off, I'm always thinking I might be in trouble whenever we get called to the office. But it hasn't happened yet. So all us girls are sitting or standing in the manager's office area, and everyone is silent as the club owner, Chris Rudan, walks to the middle of the room. This guy owns about five bars in a 60 km radius, monopolizing much of the strip club industry in the Golden Horseshoe area of Southern Ontario. But this club was his first and it remains his most profitable.

He's not looking happy.

"Okay you girls, I've been coming into this bar lately and hearing all this nigger music, all this rap shit. I don't want this nigger music no more. I don't care if it's

Michael fucking Jackson. No rap, no black music, and if I hear any nigger music, I'm telling you now, you might as well pack your bags and leave."

And that was it! *This guy's gone off the deep end.*

We all leave the room talking amongst ourselves in whispers. "What gives him the right to talk to us like that?" is the most common comment. But we know there's nothing we can do. Some of the white dancers feel they have to apologize to the black girls for this racist shit.

Suddenly, Rudan grabs my attention and calls me back into the office. He asks who I am, and I remind him that we've spoken before and that my name is Linda Lee. He stares blankly at me but I'm feeling cocky, so I ask him to remember this moment so that I won't have to reintroduce myself to him again and again.

I'm upset and I just want to leave, but my five hours aren't up yet, so I sit at the bar. I'm not paying attention to the guy sitting to my left. All of a sudden he says to me, "Can you move? I don't want you sitting next to me." "No way buddy, this is not the day to get on my bad side, alright?" "Bitch, you don't get it. I stopped here to have a drink, not argue with strippers."

"Fine have your drink and shut up, I wasn't talking to you."

Then the guy sitting with this jerk comes up to me and asks me for a dance.

I say no, but he whispers that he just wants to talk to me. He takes my hand and leads me to a VIP booth.

"Okay, what's the problem with your friend?" I ask.

"He's a good guy, really, but he has a problem with your color. You see his father was visiting New York City and two black guys mugged him, took all he had down to his running shoes but they weren't satisfied. I guess there was a struggle and they killed him. So since that happened, he's developed a hatred for black people."

I shake my head. "Well you're white and he's white and you don't see me asking him if his fucking forefathers enslaved my people, right?"

"Of course, you're totally right about that, but he's got this big hang up. I'm not saying it's right, but I thought you should know where he's coming from."

"Yeah, and it's a very *racist* place," I insist.

As we walk back to the bar I see a black girl talking to the jerk. He spits in her face and then gets up to exit the bar. As she's wiping her face clean, I take off one of my heels and throw it at the scumbag from behind. It moves through the air like a boomerang and collides with his head. Cursing and spewing racist garbage, he pivots around and lunges at me as his friend restrains him. After a few minutes, they leave the club, but not before complaining to a bouncer.

The black girl and I are sent to the office for punishment, because club policy is "the customer is always right." I get off with a warning, but the girl who got spit on is accused of "provoking the incident" and suspended from working in the club. I walk with her up to the change room as she tears up.

"I drove two hours to get here hoping to make some decent money," she cries. "How am I going to pay my babysitter? And my mortgage payment is due tomorrow! There's no place else for me to work and make decent money. Maxine's is dead." She cries and cries. "I have to work there for a month before they'll let me work here again."

I tell her to go back and explain her situation to the manager. Regaining her composure, she says, "No. I guess I should count myself lucky to be allowed to come back at all." I ask her why.

"The owner doesn't give a shit about us. If we didn't pay him money to work here, you think we'd be allowed in here? Let me tell you about this guy…. Back in the day, he only allowed two black girls maximum to work in any of his clubs at any given time – that's it. Two black dancers in a club full with over 60 to 80 girls."

"What?" I exclaim. "He had a *quota* for black girls?"

"Yeah. If you see him in the bar, just stay away. If he's on one side of the room, you stay on the other side. Okay? Just trust me."
"Really?"
"Yes really! This guy gets away with everything. He beats up girls. I even saw him hit his wife, okay? He put out a cigarette on a girl's leg, and because she wanted to keep working here she did nothing about it. Look, he got a stripper pregnant, the stripper had a baby girl, and since then his wife has moved out and she's trying to divorce him." "Can't we report this to someone?" I ask.

"Like who, the police? That's a joke girl. I think he was charged once for beating on girls but he got off. He's got much too much money, and money runs the world. Plus he's got connections.... How am I going to pay my babysitter and buy gas to drive home?"

I'm feeling really bad for her, so I give her 100 dollars. "Maybe you should just bite the bullet and go to the other club."

"Thanks for the help. I'll try to repay you when I can. And you're right – I haven't got much choice. This is by far the busiest club. I'll put in my month at that shithole, and I bet I won't make in a month what I can make here in one night. That fucker should just close that stupid club! But he needs girls there, so even though it's dead and he knows it, he always finds ways of forcing us to work there. Any excuse will do. And that shit gave him one today."

I run downstairs, and pay my twenty-dollar fee for quitting early. The girl and I leave the club together.

I can't sleep that night... all the lights are on in my house. Curled up on my couch, I'm drinking tea after tea thinking about every detail of that nightmare day. Dominating my thoughts is my fear of *him* – fear of his power and his unknown connections.

I hear a rap on my door. A chill runs down my spine and I freeze.

After a second knock, I look out my bathroom window and see John getting into his car. Five minutes later, I drive over to his house and confront him at his front door.

"I told you not to come to my house!"
"Well your lights were on."
"Wait a second – you knocked on my door because my lights were on? What if I'd had company, what then?"
"At two in the morning?"

"John, stop playing the fool."
"I got you a gift today, and I couldn't wait to give it to you. Please wait!" He goes into his house and returns with a really nice gift bag. I pull out a hundred year old bottle of scotch and a beautiful sweater with a $280 price tag still on it.

It's hard for me to stay mad now, so I thank him with a smile and he invites me in.

"It's nice that you've given me these gifts, but you're going to pay me for my time, right?" He nods his agreement.

John reveals that he's also bought himself the components of a new "toy" at the local hardware store. I sit and watch him put together this "toy." He attaches two copper-colored pipes and then puts a piece of aluminum foil over the end of one of them. After poking holes in the pipe with a pin, he carefully takes the ashes from an ashtray and packs them in the foil area. I've never seen this done before, so I'm curious to see what he's up to. Then on his glass table he pours out a small pile of little white diamond-shaped rocks. Some are bigger than others but they are all evidently too big for his purpose. So he uses a knife to cut them into smaller pieces. A couple of them go flying off the table and onto his plush rug, and he scrambles after them. It's hilarious to watch this fat, older man on his knees sweeping the rug with his hands to find his lost treasure. After a

minute or two, he finds them and he lets out a jubilant cry. "Yes!"
He pours me a drink and rolls me a joint, explaining he doesn't like to smoke weed because, to him, it's a downer. Every time he smokes a joint he falls asleep. I spark up my joint and my thoughts turn to writing. Before I'm done smoking he places a writing pad and pen on the table in front of me. I watch him put one of his white rocks in his pipe and light it. A surprising amount of smoke wafts upward from this little rock as he brings the pipe to his mouth and sucks the smoke deeply into his mouth and lungs. He lights and re-lights the rock until nothing remains but a cinder.

Holy shit, how this man loves to talk! He talks and talks about everything from his wife moving out, to what it was like living in this house when he was a little boy, to how great a schoolteacher he was. Then the best thing comes out of his mouth: "Why don't you write me a poem. I don't care what kind of writer you want to be, it's always good practice to write poetry." I'm excited by the idea, but I remind him I'm not good at spelling. He offers to help. I'm embarrassed to show John how illiterate I am but as I write, I often ask him to spell words, even simple ones, and he does so with great patience.

After about ten minutes, I stand up and recite my poem. He expresses amazement about how good it is. "I'm not saying this to be kind. I don't believe in that. I really think you have a natural talent. You should keep at it. Never stop writing. You should make the most of your gift."

So we continue drinking, smoking, and writing and we have a blast till dawn starts to break. I ask him for the money he's promised me but he doesn't have it. He starts to put his shoes on to drive to the bank, but I know he's in no shape for that, so I tell him "next time."

Of course when I get home I'm in no condition to work, plus I don't feel like going in after all the bull I put up with yesterday. I sleep all day and am awakened again by John. So I go over to his house for another one of his "parties." This time he has some books for me to read on poetry. He smokes his crack, and I stick to drinking wine. He has to write and print something for his church, so I help him with that. Then I write some more poetry and he critiques it. Daylight breaks and as I'm leaving I ask for my money. He's forgotten again. He tells me not to worry – he'll drop it off to me at work.

I sleep most of the day and rush off at six to work the night shift. As I sign in the manager asks me to wait a minute, so I stand there as five other girls are ushered into the office. He explains that he needs a favor from us: he needs girls at the owner's other club in London. The club is two hours away; we'll be driven there and back. I tell him I'm expecting a customer. He just frowns and says, "If you don't go, you can't work here anymore, you decide."

On our way to London I notice that our driver is drunk and smoking weed. He's speeding like a maniac and sometimes nods off, so we have to yell at him to stay on the road. After this ride from hell, we eventually arrive at this club in downtown London. I do four stage shows for no pay. Most of the time, I sit in a corner, since I'm not impressed with this place and I'm in no mood to talk to anyone. Our driver sits at the bar and knocks back drink after drink during the five or so hours we're there. *Fuck I'm pissed off! We still have to get a ride back with this loser.* We get out of there around 2:30 and drive another two hours back to Niagara. I get home around six in the morning. Once again the day shift is going to be a right off for me.

I show up later that day for the night shift and the manager immediately corners me and asks me to go to another of the owner's clubs, one that's notoriously dead. I tell him no. I explain I'm tired and I'm only planning to work a few hours because I've made arrangements to meet a customer. In his thick Serbian accent, he thunders: "No? You have the nerve to say no to me!!! *Why* no?"

I say, "I'm tired, please try to understand. I just can't do a seven-hour shift. Plus I need to meet my customer."

"Okay, you go," he says. I misunderstand him and walk toward the change room, but he yells after me, "No… you go home! You can't work here tonight."

I'm fuming mad at first, but once I'm back at my car I feel proud that I didn't give in to that shithead's bullying. It'll cost me, but it still feels great. *Enough is enough!*

With my evening now free, I decide to drop in at a Future Shop store where they sell computers and other electronic stuff. I stand out amongst the customers, to say the least. I'm dressed in a miniskirt, six-inch heels and a tight sweater that I've tied in the back to expose my midsection and belly ring, a winged unicorn. I spend quite a while with this cute young salesman who finally succeeds in selling me a desktop computer. I then drop in at the nearby Chapters store to find a book that can teach me how to use the damn thing. I select a book entitled *Computers for Dummies*.

I set up my new toy at home and I remain totally absorbed with it for the rest of the evening. Instead of making me feel stupid, *Computers for Dummies* makes me confident I can really master this amazing machine.

For the next few months, all I do is work the day shift and learn everything I can about computer technology. The Internet becomes a source of fascination for me. After checking out many websites I'm inspired to build one of my own. So I return to the bookstore for another *Dummies* book. I get into buying domain names for web sites I'd like to build. I have all kinds of ideas but to actually build a site is still too much of a challenge for me. One day I receive an email from a guy in Switzerland who wants to buy one of my registered domains. I ask him to make me an offer and he does: *Eight thousand U.S. dollars!* I almost fall off my chair. *You've got to be kidding me! I only paid seven dollars for it!* I counter his offer with a demand for $10,000 and he agrees. *How crazy is that?* For the next few weeks I devote myself full time to my new vocation. I end up owning over 30 domains and immerse myself in the mysteries of computer technology when I'm not haggling over the price of my domains with would-be buyers. Soon my friends are asking me to fix their computers. I'm now able to solve many software and even hardware problems. I feel ready to start a web based business of my own.

It's a day shift and, surprise, surprise: after all these many months, Paul is back and surrounded by a bevy of doting girls. *So the old pervert's still alive and kicking!* I keep my distance, focused on making some money. *I'll get the low down about Paul from the girls later.*

Soon my customer John shows up. I'm excited to see him because he still owes me from months back and I need the money. I give him a big hug and drag him into the back room. He doesn't want to party though. He says he stopped in because he saw my car in the parking lot, but he can't spend any money just now. He's on his way to the bank. I ask him if he's going to stop back after the bank, and he grimaces in a way that makes me wonder if I'm going to have a problem collecting my money. His body language is nervous and uncomfortable as he mumbles, "yeah, probably."

John exits the VIP area, and I'm just a few steps behind him when a blonde girl yells out to him. They sit and order drinks, and then he takes her into the back. I'm furious, but I know I have to abide by that damned unwritten rule.

So I wait and wait and they're back there forever. Meanwhile, I take two or three customers for dances and each time I'm in the VIP area I see the blonde still with John. *No money, eh John?*

While I'm waiting to talk to John, I accept an invitation from a customer to have a drink. He's a tall, good-looking, well-dressed bald man who seems more interested in conversation with me than in going in the back. He can tell that I'm upset about something. Without naming any names, I tell him about my problem with John. I say, "I don't care if it takes me all year, I'm getting the money that that fucker owes me."

No sooner than those words come out of my mouth than I realize this is a customer I'm talking to! *What are you doing girl?* I immediately snap back into stripper mode.

This man is funny. He keeps me laughing through a couple of rounds of drinks. He's telling me he's great at basketball, which just happens to be one of my favorite sports. I tell him I used to play high-school B ball and I can kick his ass one on one any day! He says, "you're on – don't be fooled by my white skin. I can play ball with the best of them. So just name the time and place." I sit back and think, *shit, this guy is pretty tall – he could be in the NBA. Who is he? Damn if I know!* We share a few more laughs and he tells me has to go. As he rises from the table he hands me his card and says,
"When you want your ass kicked, give me a call." I look at the card and *he's a lawyer! I ain't calling this fool any time soon!*

At the end of my shift, I get dressed and head down the stairs as John's blonde chick is coming up. So I ask her if John is still around and she says,
"No, he just left." I turn around and follow her back into the change room. I ask her how long she's known John, and she says only a couple of days.

"He's a fun guy. I love dancing for him when he's stoned because he always overpays me…. He's so fucked up right now – really fucked up. We did blow all night. I didn't even get to bed…. Neither did he," she laughs.

I just smirk. "Really?"

"Yeah, he's gone to see his dealer and then he's coming back to pick me up in half an hour. What are you doing later? This guy gets more than enough to treat an army."

"Thanks," I answer, "that's not my thing. But can you do me a favor? Tell him to drop off my money before ten tonight and not to come to my house ever again after that."

"He owes you money?"

"Yes," I reply.

"Why didn't you come back and collect it before he left?"

"Because you were with him and I didn't want to intrude."

"Girlfriend, I would have had no problem with that. He's an asshole for doing that to you."

"Well, just deliver my message please."

"I'll make sure he pays you doll," she assures me. She raises one of her legs onto the counter and checks her crotch in the mirror. As I head back down the stairs, I hear her mumbling, "No way, why would John do that to her?"

I go about my usual routine and finally relax to watch a movie at home. I hear a knock at around 9:30 and I rush to the door ready to give John a piece of my mind. But it turns out to be two little girls in Brownie uniforms selling cookies. As I'm about to ask them why they're out so late, I notice an adult in the background. They explain they are in a competition and whoever sells the most will win a prize. I ask them to wait there as I grab my wallet; they have one box of cookies each. I ask if they have more, and the adult male standing behind them asks me how many I want. I say twenty.

"Twenty!" he exclaims. "I'll have to go home to get some more."

Minutes later they return with a big package with twenty cookie boxes. I give the girls money and one of them hugs me around my waist. That little hug puts me in a much better mood. I go to bed after midnight. John has failed to show up.

The next day the dayshift is dead and I'm feeling a little depressed and tired. My only customer is Paul who takes me to the back for two songs. Afterwards, we have a drink. Paul turns out to be a great listener. Without mentioning John's name, I tell Paul about my situation and how I'm having a hard time getting the money he owes me. Paul expresses his sympathy and says he can't believe the guy is being such an ass to me. He gives me his number and tells me to call him.

It seems Paul has come to his senses about me. Since his medical emergency, he seems to have learned that he can't get his way with me the way he does with some of the other girls. I leave his company and join Cherry at the bar.

"Cherry, what's up with Paul?"

"I dunno, what do you mean? He was in the hospital for six months after his stroke. Now he's back and he's the same old Paul."

"But he seems nicer now," I suggest.

"No, he's still the same perverted Paul who wants everything… Were you in the back with him?"

"Yes," I answered.

"How was he?"

"He was fine. I had no problems with him"

"Probably because he was with you, and he knows your limits… I was with him too and one of my breasts is still hurting from his squeezing and biting."

A cute customer walks in and comes straight over to me and asks what I'm drinking. I tell him a wine spritzer and he orders one for each of us. Many of the girls are drooling over him as we sit close to the stage. He asks me if I remember him. I tell him yes because his face seems familiar even though I can't recall his name. We chat for a few minutes and then a light bulb goes on in my head. It's the CEO freak that craves punishment!

We have some fun in the back and he keeps me till the end of my shift. He's made my day. He asks if I would like to join him for dinner, assuring me he'll compensate me well for my time. As much as I want to go, I ask him for a rain check because I'm not properly dressed for a fine restaurant. I'd worn a tracksuit to work so that I could go straight to the gym afterward.

When I arrive home, I find a beautiful arrangement of flowers left at my front door. I read the card and it's from John, apologizing for his behavior. *But no money!* Furious, I drive over to his house and toss the flowers on his driveway without stopping.

Later that night, around three, my doorbell rings. It's Candy. She tells me to get dressed and when I ask why, she says "just trust me." "No Candy, you're high, and I'm not just going to jump because you're telling me to."
"Okay, okay… John was in, we partied, and …"

I interrupt her: "You woke me up because of that fool?"
"No, I'm on my way to his house. All night all he talked about was you. He begged me to bring you to his house."

"Okay Candy, just tell him I want my money. That's it… I'm not going. Whenever I hang with him it fucks up my days. Sorry Candy."

"Come on," she implores.
"I'll make him pay you. The way he's acting I don't see a problem, really!"
"Candy, I'm not in the mood to watch you and him do your stuff. I just want to get my money and then go. Okay?"
I don't get dressed. I remain in my night gown and drive behind Candy to John's house. He answers his door and I demand $2300. He says he doesn't have it but he'll get it in the morning. *Promises, promises!* I return home and slip into bed.

Same shit, different days! As months go by, I collect some great customers who always tell me in advance when they'll be back. I'm now able to count on a minimum guaranteed income based just on my regulars showing up, and I'm budgeting accordingly. Other customers are gravy. As the money flows in, my debts are vanishing.

And yes, John finally coughs up what he owes me.

Paul is back in full swing. One day, I'm at work after taking a few days off and one of the girls passes along a message for me to call him. I tell her I've lost his number, so she looks it up in her cell phone and gives it to me. That night I call and ask him what he wants. He says he wants my company. I tell him he's got the wrong girl. He can have my company for a fee but he shouldn't expect sex from me. To my surprise, he agrees to my terms. He tells me that he has a car but that he's lost his license and never gets to drive it. So he wants me to drive him around in it. I ask him how he knows I drive and he explains that he often arrives at the club fifteen minutes before it opens and has seen me pulling in. I'm surprised because I've never noticed him in the parking lot.

I emphasize that the reason I hadn't called him before is that I know what he's like in the VIP room and no amount of money is going to get me to change my position. Sex is out of the question. He says, "no, no, I just want you to drive me around and spend some time with me watching TV. And I'll pay you for that." He asks me how much for an hour. I tell him 300 an hour. He says fine, and he asks if I can come today. I agree.

We arrange to meet at his house in Port Colborne, an hour from my place and a good half hour drive south of the club on the shores of Lake Erie. When I get there he's dressed and sitting in his car in the driveway. He wants me to drive and run some errands with him. So we go out for a little over an hour. He tells me everything about his "best friend" who's now dead and buried in his back yard! Turns out he's talking about his pet dog!

Paul seems to know a lot of the girls I work with, but some of the names he mentions I don't recognize and I can't identify them until he describes how they look. Besides going to the club for his sexual exploits he clearly enjoys the on-going communication he maintains with several girls. He tells me he has all kinds of girls calling him. If what he's saying is true, he must spend much of his days on the phone when he's not at the club. I'm very careful about what I tell him about myself, because he's coming off as a gossip king. I could care less whether his stories are true or not.

At the end of our sojourn, he asks me to call him later, which I do in the evening. We talk, I just had to get off the phone and he asks me to call him back later. *This is becoming a pattern: no sooner do we end a conversation than he's asking me to call him back! This is one needy dude!* Eventually, we set up a time for our next meeting.

Talking to him on the phone can be a challenge because he can be hard to understand. He often sounds like he's gargling water. I try to look beyond his weird physical appearance and to forget his outrageous behavior in the back of the club. When I do that, it's easier for me to see him as just a nice but lonely guy. During our first meeting outside the club, he obeys my rules. He doesn't so much as touch me – not even a handshake. This arrangement looks like it could work.

The next day I return to work and the old fucker is back at the bar and up to his old tricks. He wants to take me for dances, but I'm busy and so I successfully avoid him. Before he leaves that day I'm in a VIP booth with a customer, and Paul, who's not exactly strong in the club etiquette department, pops his head in to say good-bye. I actually wish that he'll ask me for a dance because I want to be saved from the customer I'm with – but he doesn't, and I'm left to fend for myself.

Most often when I dance for a guy I get "up close and personal," but with this guy I'm standing as far away as I can. He doesn't smell, but earlier when I got down on my knees to run my hand down his leg, I felt this cord, and I quickly pulled my hand back. I thought this guy might have a cock pump. Not that I know what that feels like, but this object, whatever it is, is freaking me the hell out. Then, during the last dance, he confesses to me that it's been years since he's had a dance, and he apologizes for frightening me. "I'm wearing a catheter and a colostomy bag," he confides. *What the fuck is my world coming to!!!*

Curious, and not really understanding what he's talking about, I ask: "What do you mean *bag*, what bag?"

"I have a bag strapped to my leg near my ankle," he explains, with just a hint of a smirk. I quickly change the subject and we start chatting about other things. It turns out this guy has a great sense of humor, and both of us are laughing up a storm as he admits, "I'm pissing right now!" I sit with him for some time, and I truly have never laughed so hard in my life. I tell him he's missed his calling as a comedian. He could be "the comic with the colostomy bag"!

After work, I enter a quaint little restaurant and in the corner of my eye I see an old customer of mine sitting with a lady who looks to be his wife. He looks me straight in the eye and freezes as a "fear of God" expression spreads across his face. I avert my eye and pay him no attention, but now I'm certain that he's my customer. I glance at him from time to time, and I swear to God, I've never seen anyone eat his food so fast. I can only imagine what's going through his head. It's too funny! Does he really think that I might walk over and go: "Hi wifey, excuse me, but I know your husband from a little bar down the road that he frequents, and just to let you know, he pays me very well on a regular basis to see me naked." What the hell is he thinking!

For weeks after this, I watch out for this guy to turn up at the club so I can explain to him that "what goes on in the club, stays in the club," but he never shows.

I work all day and sign out as usual without a problem. I rush upstairs to change as I hear my name being called out over the PA system. "Shit no! They're probably going to ask me to work the night shift." I ignore the page and leave the club quickly. The following day, just before my shift was to start, my name is again called over the PA system and I make my way to the office. The manager tells me that they know I ignored the call to the office yesterday and that, as a punishment, I'm going to be sent for a few days to Maxine's, one of the owner's clubs in Fort Erie.

My heart sinks! No dancer wants to go Maxine's. It's the worst of the worst. A total waste of time – no customers, meaning no money! It's a bit of a mystery how and why the place is kept open. But whatever the reason, it's a dead bar from the point of view of us girls. Basically, we're used as unpaid props to maintain the illusion that the fucking place is a viable business. I pretend to agree to the punishment, but there's no way I'm going to that shithole!
I pack my bags and decide to try out a new club up north.

I enter the new club, show my I.D., and I'm hired without a problem. What blows me away is how nice the staff is. The club isn't nearly as busy as the Sundowner. Most of the guys here only go for one dance at a time, whereas I'm used to five, ten or even more with each customer.

After hours of sitting on a stool alone, watching the other girls idle their time away on those stupid game machines, I join the only customer there, a guy sitting with teased out hair and a big round bald spot on the back of his head. As I sit down, he uncrosses his legs and I immediately ask him for a dance.

He smiles in an encouraging way but doesn't reply directly. This club doesn't have a V.I.P. area but it does have a space for lap dances that's open for all to see.

Oh my God! This guy is wearing a white suit and a white linen shirt with a few buttons open by his neck. One of his hands is inside the shirt, apparently massaging his nipple. I watch this pervert as he plays with himself and glares at me. Then he says, "So darling, how about slipping out of that dress and showing me your underwear – I want to see that nice round ass of yours covered only by a g-string and those ripe boobies of yours in a sexy bra." I don't know whether to laugh or run!

I tell him: "Sorry, but I can't oblige with the bra, 'cause I'm not wearing one." So he says he'd like to take me lingerie shopping. He goes on and on about this as if he's some kind of expert. As I start to dance for him he removes his hand from his tit and takes hold of my hand and guides it toward his chest. He then exposes his own hidden treasure. Turns out this weirdo is wearing a padded bra! I pull my hand back abruptly, slightly nauseated. I blurt out, "Are you kidding me? You're wearing a bra!" He gets up and places his payment on the table and leaves. Maybe I was a little loud, but the way I see it, the music just happened to stop when I asked.

This whole experience is putting things in perspective for me. I can't allow myself to go into voluntary exile from the Sundowner and its crappy satellite clubs. There are just no good alternatives. Not for me anyway. Chris Rudan knows he's sitting on a gold mine – for every girl who gets fired, there are at least two replacements. He knows – he KNOWS – he can treat his girls like slaves, because the girls will do whatever they need to do to work there.

Working at Maxine's for a few days as punishment is nothing. I know that some girls have given blowjobs to the powers that be so they can stay on or get into the Sundowner. The crazy world of hoodlum rats!

And so I leave my northern exile, and return to do my three days penance at the dreaded Maxine's. I don't make a single dollar working there but it nevertheless costs me in gas and DJ fees. The bar makes money off my ass, but I don't.

It's nice, finally, to be back at my familiar stomping grounds at the Downer. One of the girls passes along a message for me to call Paul, and I'm pleased to see a few of my customers. A regular has a friend with him and the three of us get into a conversation about current events, agreeing and disagreeing about different things. But the bottom line is I'm here to work, and so I ask my regular for a dance. To my surprise, he says no, a first for him, but he does give me forty dollars to dance for his friend. So I take this guy to a VIP booth and start to dance for him. Turns out, he's a pig, a *serious* pig – but not in the usual ways.

This man tells me he wants me to pee on him!

I laugh nervously and reply that I can't do that because I'd wet the floor and smell up the whole VIP area. "How about an extra hundred bucks for your trouble?" he asks. I make an excuse and tell him I have to go to my locker and that I'll be right back. I rush up to the change room as fast as a woman running in heels possibly can. I can't wait to share this with the few girls who are getting changed.

"Guys, my customer wants me to pee on him in the back!"
"Golden showers!" shouts one of the girls. "What fun!"
The shocked look on my face prompts another to say:
"Don't tell me you've never heard of this before?"
I shake my head as another girl proceeds to advise me:
"Take off your shoes and stand on the couch, one leg on each side of him and then just piss all over him. It's easy!"
"I don't know if I can do it," I reply.
"For the right price I'll do it!"
"Really?"
I ask in a serious, matter of fact sort of way.
"Yeah, really!
I've done it lots of times. I bet I even know him. How much is he paying you?"
"He's offered me a hundred."
"Tell him your pee is golden and he needs to pay more."
"But the VIP area will stink…" I exclaim.
"And it doesn't stink now?" chimes in another girl, as everybody breaks out laughing.
"So, seriously, what do I do?" I ask.
"Just piss on him!" reply the girls, almost in unison.

I rejoin my customer, and I'm holding onto the hundred and forty I've received in advance as I start dancing for him. I don't want to have to return any of the money, but I'm dreading the thought of performing the requested "service." After two songs he asks me if I'm going to do it, and I say yes. As the fourth song ends, he grows impatient and asks, "when?" I reassure him it'll be soon. During the fifth song I take off my shoes and stand up on the couch naked, my pussy just inches from his head. I glance down at him just as he's looking up. The dim lights and shadows in the booth are creating an eerie effect, and his face looks positively demonic. His eyes are scaring the crap out of me and I reach a breaking point. I jump off the couch, and offer an apology: "Sorry, I just can't do that nastiness." Without saying a word, he rises angrily and storms out of the booth.

I sit there in a bemused state just wondering how any girl could actually piss on a guy. As I get dressed I notice the same customer walking by with one of the girls who had advised me. They enter the booth next to mine, and I sit there and observe the scene in the mirror, as she wastes no time standing on the couch and doing her thing. Disgusted, I leave my booth.

I call Paul, as promised, and he tells me to call him back because he's waiting for another call. I can't believe this guy doesn't have call waiting in this day and age. I walk around the club and watch as the pisser goes back to "work as usual." I sit at the bar next to a dancer with an unusually deep voice. She looks like a giant, her legs and hands big and thick. She reminds me of a man, so I walk over to Diamond and ask her if she thinks she's a man.

"Yes," she says.
"Well, not any more. She's a tranny."
"How does she get away with it, her face is so manly."
"The men don't see it the way we can – they can't see beyond the make-up. Plus think about it, most of the customers have a few drinks in them before they go for dances."

I watch as a man walks up to the tranny and starts chatting her up. As they talk, the customer is rubbing her leg. She uncrosses her leg and his hand moves closer to her g-string line. I glance at her crotch area and it looks flat.
"Diamond," I exclaim,
"She has no dick."
"Of course not, there's no way she could work here with a dick. She's had the full operation."
"You mean she had her dick turned into a vagina?"
"No, she was born with both and she had the dick cut off. Stop staring her down, she's one of the nicest girls here."

A guy walks by me and stops dead in his tracks. Leaning over to me and gesturing toward the tranny, he says, "I think that's a guy." Without missing a beat, I protect her by saying, "I don't know any guys with no dicks and with breasts as fine as those."
"No," he insists.
"That's definitely a guy."
"Okay, you go tell her she's a guy…"
"Baby, I'm not saying shit to her. I'm leaving that one alone."

My day is almost over so I call Paul again. We talk for just a few moments, as he's still waiting for another call.

As usual, he asks me to call him back. I tell him I'll call him tomorrow, but he insists I call him back shortly.

Exasperated with him, I decide to wait till the next morning to call him again.

Over the next few months, I start to visit Paul frequently as a paid companion and chauffeur – and a big part of the gig involves going along with his never-ending requests that I call him at home. He really enjoys chatting on the phone and feeling like he's the center of attention. I think it makes him feel wanted. He even asks me to call him first thing in the morning so he "can hear that sexy voice at the start of my day." Comments like that make me uneasy, but he's turning into a great customer, and I need the money. I try to keep the long-distance phone calls to him as brief as possible, because they can really run up my bill. All the same, I know I'm being well compensated, so I'm happy to humor him.

This gig with Paul is like a breath of fresh air. I don't have to tussle with customers, I don't have to deal with the Sundowner managers, and I don't have to pay any fees. And my earnings are guaranteed! What girl in her right mind would turn down this gig?

Although I'm not much for gossip I often find Paul's stories about his escapades quite entertaining. He can actually be a fun guy. I even enjoy his rants, and his extravagant compliments. One of the reasons I like him is that he makes me feel special. He'll make up stories and put me into them. He tells me I'm so beautiful I should be a model, "like Naomi Campbell." He even advises me which designers I should model for and what I should wear, right down to the color of the clothing. Sometimes he tells me I should be a movie actress:

"You'd be way better than the ones they have out there." Paul makes me feel good because he's a dreamer, and I love that about him.

When I get together with him in his hometown, we visit Tim Horton's and other local hot spots, but we almost always end up at his bank so he can withdraw cash to pay me and cover his other "expenses." It's clear to me that those expenses are mostly related to his main interest in life – cavorting with attractive young women.

Paul speaks often to me about a girl he sees from Niagara Falls and another one from St. Catharines. He tells me he's even paying the rent of the Niagara Falls girl. I assume they must be fuck buddies. Sometimes, he tries to bribe me into having sex with him, but I treat his propositions as a joke, and we just laugh it off. He seems to accept that it just ain't gonna happen between us, but even so, he keeps on trying, even while rubbing my nose in the fact that he has the sexual morals of an alley cat.

My most fun and longest-lasting "date" with Paul happens when I drive him to Burlington so he can look up a new girl he wants to hook up with. All the way there I'm thinking, *why would any girl give this guy her home address? I sure as hell wouldn't! I don't even trust him with my phone number!* Of course, the address she'd given him turns out to be bogus. *What a surprise!*

Paul enjoys boasting about what a generous sugar daddy he is to his girls. He withdraws money from his bank frequently to buy them stuff and even travel tickets. One time, he tells me that his Niagara Falls "girlfriend" needs to fly home to New Brunswick to visit her family, so he's footing the bill. "She's coming over tonight to pick up the cash," he says with a devilish twinkle in his eye. Half jokingly I tell him to be sure to wear protection, and he shoots back, "I'm not worried – if she has something, I must have it already too."

At the club Paul has asked most of the girls he sees regularly to go on trips with him; as far as I know, none have accepted. I certainly won't, even though it's an attractive prospect in some ways. He usually proposes a weeklong trip to Jamaica, all expenses paid plus payment for time and companionship. So let's do the math: seven days with at least five paid hours a day. That's pretty tempting, especially during the winter months when business at the Downer slows down, and the tropics beckon. The reason most of us don't take Paul up on his offer is that many of us have boyfriends who definitely wouldn't like the idea. For sure, Paul knows all about mine – including the fact that he's away on business most of the time.

Months go by. I'm working and now seeing Paul almost twice a week. My life feels almost hectic because he's always demanding so much attention. He wants to travel in the States so he's working on getting his driver's license back. He asks me to drive him to St. Catharines a couple of times so he can go to the government's motor vehicles and licensing office and look into the matter. Nothing comes of it though.

Some other driving jobs involve taking him to get his passport picture taken and later to submit his passport application. On both occasions he requests I take him to the bank and he returns to the car with envelopes stuffed fat with cash. He flashes the money at me and tells me that if I'd only sleep with him, all that money can be mine! *OOOhhhh, ooohhh, I'm good with hanging with you, but the thought of sleeping with you makes me want to barf!* Once again, I turn him down.

I'm getting dressed for work in the change room and I ask one of the girls a question about the appearance of my hair. For some strange reason, she doesn't answer me. I call her by her name but instead of answering, she seems to look straight past me, as though I was invisible to her, and then she looks away. *What's her problem?*

Later, on the floor, I receive similar treatment from most of the girls I know best. *Why are they ignoring me?*

Something very strange is going on here, and I haven't the faintest idea what it could be. Brushing it aside, I try to tell myself: *You shouldn't let this bother you. You're here to make money not friends.* But I'm not doing a very good job convincing myself.

This uncomfortable situation continues for about a week. In the meantime I'm talking to Paul and telling him about how the other girls are all treating me like I'm carrying the bubonic plague. "They're just jealous," he says reassuringly. I thank him for being so kind as to say that, but his reading of the situation isn't very convincing either.

Finally, I confront one of the girls and demand to know why I'm being shunned by so many of them. She tells me that the girls are mad at me because I pretend to be a "goody-two-shoes" even though I'm not.

"I don't think I'm a 'goody-two shoes'!" I protest. "Now, tell me what this is really about."

She doesn't want to tell me but I insist and she finally agrees. She reminds me of an incident a few months earlier. It was early in the night shift, about seven o'clock. I had just hooked my first customer and we were heading to a booth in the VIP area. I passed by a booth with a girl who was very young looking, certainly no more than 19. She was wearing a Catholic school uniform and she was down on her knees performing oral sex on a customer. I stopped and watched. Either she didn't notice I was there or didn't care. Ditto her customer. I left my own customer and went directly to the office to report what I'd seen. The manager returned with me and saw what she was doing for himself. He pulled her up onto her feet, as her embarrassed customer quickly zipped up his pants. The man rushed out and the manager ordered the girl to his office.

I continued to a different booth with my customer and the first thing out of his mouth was, *how much would it cost for that?* I responded: "For my big luscious lips to be wrapped around your dirty dick? Priceless!" I only got one dance.

Addressing the girl who reminds me of this event, I say:
"So I was wrong to report her?"
"No," she replies,
"but how can you be such a hypocrite and report her when you're having sex for money too?"
"What? Who do you think I'm having sex with for money?"
"We all know it's Paul."
"Not old Paul, the guy who buys us drinks? You mean two dance Paul?"
"One and the same," she replies.
"No way. That is a lie!

Are you really telling me you think I'm having sex with *Paul*?"

The girl calls over a few other girls and they come to her defense. I feel like I'm being ganged up on.

Then another girl, one I respect, drops a real bombshell: "Yes Linda Lee, you pretend to be so prissy but we know you don't practice what you preach. Paul was bragging about how you two are sleeping together."
"No way – Paul told you that?"
"Yes, and there's more. I'm actually scared for my life because, after Paul told me he was sleeping with you, he said he'd kill me if I said anything about it to you!"

The floodgate has been opened and now all the girls are piling on saying things like "I don't need any crazy customer going nuts in here with a gun. I have kids who depend on me."

Totally shocked, but also enraged by what I'm hearing, I let out a shout in as deep and clear a voice as I can: "Listen up you guys, I did NOT sleep with him. I'm NOT having sex with him, not here or anywhere else. If he told you I am, then he's a fucking liar. He paid me to drive him around and spend time with him, that's it. You know very well I've been offered big money for sex by a lot of guys who are much more appealing than Paul, and I've always said no. Sleep with Paul? You've got to be kidding me! If I tell you half the stuff he tells me about you guys, your heads would spin! You can't take anything he says at face value."

I'm so mad I can't walk fast enough to get to my phone. I take off my heels and start running up the stairs to the change room. A few girls follow behind me. I pull my purse out of my locker looking for my cell phone, and then remember I left it in the car. I ask if anyone has Paul's number and a girl gives it to me. I call him from the club's payphone. His line is busy and he doesn't have call waiting so I get dressed and run out to my car to get my phone. I call him again, and this time he answers.

"Paul," I shriek, "why did you tell the girls I was having sex with you?" "I didn't say that, they're lying," he replies. "You didn't threaten them and say that if they told me, you'd kill them?"

"Lies, lies, all lies! I'd never say anything like that."

"Listen to me you piece of shit, don't talk to me, don't look at me, just get fucking lost."

"I'm sorry, let me come and explain."

"Go fuck yourself and get lost."

"Listen, that's all lies. I Never. I've never said that."

"Really!" I exclaim, not believing a word coming out of his mouth. I end the call abruptly, wishing I'd been able to use the payphone to bang the receiver down on him and maybe break the asshole's eardrum.

I get a few hugs and apologies from the girls. Fuming mad, I light up a cigarette and smoke it half way down just as the manager is walking into the change room. I'm so lost in my thoughts, I don't even think to hide it. He asks me why I'm smoking in the club. His words fail to sink in until he knocks the cigarette out of my hand. He shouts about the by-law and the total ban on smoking in the building. I apologize and tell him I'm having a bad day as tears stream down my face. His demeanor changes and he points to a rarely used small room that has stairs leading to the outside. "Okay, go in there if you need to smoke. No one can enter from the outside using that door." I enter the room and smoke my cigarette before getting dressed and paying the fee to leave early.

I take a few days off and enjoy myself in the outdoors. I go bicycling and hiking and I hang out with Candy whenever possible. As always she's very supportive and lends me a sympathetic ear when I tell her what I've been going through with Paul and the day-shift girls.

When I finally return to work, I learn that Paul has been in the club a few times looking for me, and that, oddly enough, he hadn't gone for any dances. He'd only left messages for me to call him.

I decide to do a double shift to make up for my time off. At around seven o'clock in the evening Paul shows up and wants to talk to me. He follows me around the floor saying he's sorry and begs me to sit down with him. I ignore him completely. The very sight of him sickens me.

Feeling stressed, I go up to the change room to escape the lying weasel. Then I enter the little room where the manager told me it was okay to smoke. As I'm about to light up, a bouncer confronts me. "You're smoking!" I admit that I was about to, but I haven't lit the cigarette yet.

"Smoking's not allowed in the club," he says.
"I know, but the day manager said I could smoke here."
"Really, is that so?" he replies.
"Yes, really."
"It's a twenty buck fine for smoking up here. Pay me and we'll forget about it."

"I'm not paying you a cent. Go extort some money from someone else."

This three hundred pound bully comes right up and yells into my face: "You pay me the twenty bucks right now, or we're going to have a big problem."

I'm in no mood for a shakedown, and I'm fed up with all the intimidating tactics used by the male staff in the club against us girls. So, in a loud voice to make sure others can hear me, I tell him to back off and leave me alone. He starts pulling my arm, threatening to take me to the office if I don't give him the twenty bucks. I try walking away from him. When he grabs me again I shout: "Don't touch me, you're picking on the wrong bitch today … I saw what you did to that girl the other day."

The girl had been drunk and she'd argued with him. So he'd tossed her out of the bar in her underwear.

I tell the asshole to take his hands off me. I'm yelling, "Get the fuck out of my face." Then he asks, "And if I don't, what are you gonna do?" He keeps taunting me, "What are you gonna do?"

I manage to turn on the recorder of my iPhone without him noticing. We're now yelling so loud at one another that we can be heard below in the office. The night manager, Milan Kalkan, who's in his late twenties, appears and separates us physically.

"What's going on?" he asks. The bouncer tells him I've been smoking. I counter by admitting that I was about to smoke but hadn't started yet – and besides, the other manager had told me I could smoke in that space.

Looking me straight in the eye, the young manager says: "Okay, I'm increasing the fine from twenty to fifty. Pay it or go home."

I turn my back on these idiots and re-enter the change room. Everyone knows about this corrupt little racket, except maybe Rudan, who has little to gain from it. To make some extra bucks, the bouncer circulates among the girls working the night shift and "fines" as many as he can for breaking little rules, as well as for "insubordination" if they protest. Then he splits most of the loot with the night manager.

After getting dressed to leave, I go down to the office. "Listen to this," I tell the manager. I play back the recording of my argument with the bouncer and the subsequent exchange involving him. Then I ask him, "Does this sound to you like I was treated fairly and properly?" The manager's eyes open wide as he realizes that he and the bouncer have been caught red-handed. Their little extortion racket is in danger of being exposed.

The next day I'm called into the office to speak to the day manager, the one who'd given me permission to smoke. He's not concerned about the smoking issue or even about the argument with the bouncer. He's angry that I'd recorded the incident. So, to punish me, he sends me off to work at Maxine's, that dead club 45 minutes away in Fort Erie. I'm to work there for seven days. His instructions are very specific. I must work there from 4 p.m. till 2 in the morning, and I must punch in and punch out for a full week.
Before I'll be allowed to return to work here again, I'll have to give him the time cards that prove I've followed

his instructions to the letter. I'm really upset and just about to leave when a waitress walks over to me and points to a guy sitting at the back of the bar. She tells me he wants to talk to me. As I approach him, I realize I've never seen this guy before. He's wearing suit pants with a tucked-in formal shirt and a winter jacket. He looks up at me and identifies himself as a police officer. He asks if I'm Linda Lee and I say yes. He then asks me to sit down. Do I know a man named Paul? Yes, a few in fact. He starts to ask another question but I interrupt him and ask him for his card, because I've got to go. He hands me his card and asks me to call him when I have more time to answer some questions.

In my car I do a Google search for a lawyer in the area. I locate one and head right over to see him. I show him the card and tell him a policeman gave it to me at work and that he wanted to question me about a customer. I'm mad at Paul, but I'm also scared that he might have gone crazy and done something stupid like commit suicide or maybe even killed one of the girls he'd bragged to about sleeping with me. I don't want to tell the lawyer that I'm a dancer, but I know I have to answer the lawyer's questions as truthfully as possible.

After consulting with the lawyer, I call Paul. I'm relieved when he answers the phone.

"Did you call the cops on me?" I ask.
"I didn't," he replies. I explain to him that a cop came to the club and was asking me questions about someone named Paul. Again, he denies it.

I spend the rest of the day racking my brains, trying to remember customers' names. Although I'm good at remembering faces, names are hard for me. Could another Paul have called the cops on me?

Late in the day, the lawyer calls me back and tells me he's spoken to the cops and I shouldn't worry. I ask him if he has any more information about this "Paul" that the cop was asking about. The lawyer says, "His full name is Paul Dagenais." The last name means nothing to me, so I ask the lawyer if he found out where he lives. "Port Colborne," he answers.

I feel like I've been punched in the stomach. Now I know the truth – "Paul" has lied to me, again. I call the lying bastard and ask him forcefully for a second time if he'd called the cops on me. Once again, he denies it. "Paul, I just talked to a lawyer who spoke to the cops on my behalf, and he said that you called the cops on me – you, Paul Dagenais of Port Colborne.

So, why did you do that, and why are you lying to me?" He hangs up.
I call back and I can hear someone in the background as he's holding the phone, but he says nothing and then he hangs up on me again. I call the lawyer back and ask him if there's anything I should do. He suggests I should just get on with my life. I go home, clean my car and pack my bags, because I've decided against serving my time right now at Maxine's. Just before I take off for a club that's almost two hundred miles away, Candy shows up at my house – she's heard that the cops had come in looking for me. We sit down over coffee and I give her the full story about the cops and Paul Dagenais. I also explain that I've been exiled to one of Rudan's dead "detention" bars and how that came about.

"Wait a second here, Chris and I get along pretty well. I've been in trouble with the club before Why don't you let me talk to him for you?"

"I don't think that's a good idea," I reply. "The last thing I want to do is piss him off and get you into trouble. The managers and bouncers are bad enough, but that guy is really bad news.... Listen Candy, I don't want either one of us to end up in an 'accident' like his wife."

Rumors had been swirling for months that Rudan's wife had filed suit to divorce him after one of the girls ended up pregnant with his child some years back. She was going after a big cut of his business – hotels, restaurants, and a few strip clubs. Next thing you know, he's away on a trip and while he's out of the country there's a gas explosion in her home. Two maids escaped with minor injuries, but his wife was killed. The incident was later ruled an accident by the authorities.

"Please don't talk to this man about me, period. For your sake as well as mine."

Candy nods her agreement.

"So, after I get back, I'm just going to take my black ass to that shitty bar Maxine's and work and do my time at that dead hole, and punch that clock. Fuck, how I hate the way they treat us, and nobody gives a shit!" Candy mentions a group that puts up some posters on walls inviting girls to call them if they have a problem. "My friend's pimp beat the crap out of her and then forced her to work with a busted face. When she called that number, there was no answer. So she goes to their office and they were closed down. Really useful stuff!"

"Like I said, nobody gives a shit."

Here I am again, just another temporary exile from the Sundowner.

I'm ready to go to work at this new club when I notice a printed Internet news article from the "Global Post" on the manager's desk. It catches my interest, and I ask the manager if I can borrow it for a few minutes. "Sure." I order a drink and sit down to read it.

The headline reads: "**Strip clubs offer girls money for tuition, rent – Clubs in Canada desperate for dancers after government rule change."** It's by a guy named David Trifunov, and it begins with the question, "What do you think?"

The article reports how the Conservative federal government is stopping Immigration Canada's long-time practice of giving foreign workers visas after receiving job offers in strip clubs or massage parlors. Supposedly, this is about protecting vulnerable, foreign women from ending up in the sex trade. But, according to Tim Lambrinos of the Adult Entertainment Association of Canada, the decision was creating problems for strip clubs, because about eight hundred of Canada's 38,000 dancers are foreign strippers dependent on these special visas. "This situation has left a lot of the girls frustrated and stressed out," Lambrinos is quoted as saying. "They are living day by day and don't know if they will be allowed to stay in Canada." The industry is warning the government that the change will force women underground. But it's also having another, unintended effect. To make up for a shortage of girls in the industry, some clubs are going on a recruitment campaign, offering Canadian girls university and college "scholarships" if they're willing to become exotic dancers.

The question was: "What do you think?" My answer is: the Canadian government has gone completely crazy! I can't stop thinking about this article and the issues it raises. Should foreign-born women working in strip clubs have any rights at all? Apparently not, at least none that are recognized by the club owners or the federal government! To me, the government's stance is not just unjust; it's also incredibly hypocritical. They're changing the rules to supposedly protect "vulnerable women" from "ending up in the sex trade." But the real effect of the change is to empower the government to deport women who entered Canada under the old rules or force them underground!

Let's get real. Governments in Canada are doing practically nothing to protect the rights and security of exotic dancers, Canadian-born or not, who are being exploited and mistreated by club owners in the most callous of ways. Personally, I think if politicians want to "protect" women in the sex industry they need to begin by *listening to them*. But these "respectable" men in suits show no interest in doing that – and certainly not in curtailing the abusive practices of those "legitimate" club owners who are really just pimps masquerading as "businessmen." It's much easier for Canada's "leaders" to target the women who are the prey of these vultures, and then present themselves to Canadians as guardians of "public morality" and even "women's rights." It makes me sick!

These thoughts keep running through my mind, and I want to act on them. But I have to keep my focus. The struggle for day-to-day survival has to come first, and I desperately need to earn some money to make my mortgage payment….

For hours I sit scantily clad in this near-dead, under-heated bar, often shivering from the cold. I strike up a conversation with a really pretty but extremely pale girl who offers to buy me a drink. It's a kind gesture on her part, but I suspect she's sick of me asking when the bar's business will pick up. "Later," is her reply, "just wait." We move over to a warmer area of the bar, and I ask her a few questions about herself. I learn that she's just 16. I ask how it is she can be working here when the legal drinking age is 19 and she tells me that her mother signed a consent form.

I'm shocked by her reply. "So your *mom* signed the consent form?"
"Yes, sometimes she even comes and watches me on stage."
I burst out, "No way!"
"I think it's her way of checking up on me. I tell her almost everything about my drug use, my partying, but she hates my boyfriend so that's off topic…."

She asks if I'm African, and I answer "Jamaican." Excitedly she says: "My boyfriend is Jamaican too. I love his dark skin – I love yours too. One day I want to go to Jamaica. Is it beautiful there?" "You'd never want to leave," I answer. As I describe the lush beauty of my native country, she jumps around in her chair like a little girl.
"I can't wait to go …. I'm gonna dry that country out of pot."

Moments later, a tall well-dressed, good-looking black man approaches her from behind. My guess is he's in his early forties. I melt with every step he takes toward us. As he gets closer, his face seems to be shining with sweat. Then, without warning, he slaps the girl hard on the side of her head – so hard that even I wince out of empathy. She jumps up as her eyes connect to his, and then she falls backwards.

"Look around," she says, "It's dead. It's not my fault. I just thought I'd make a friend."
"You're not here to make friends," he replies as he gives me a menacing glance. "Go sit over there!" She rushes off to a different table and he follows behind her. They sit facing each other. I can't hear a word they're saying, but he's pointing his finger in her face and waving his hands wildly. Her head remains down. She's like a scared dog with its tail between its legs. My heart aches for her, and a tear drop forms in my eye. I can't wait till he leaves so I can go talk to her.

After his departure a few minutes later, I rush over to see if she's okay.

"Fuck off," she says. "Just fuck off!" I do as she says, suspecting her "boyfriend" pimp might be coming back soon. A few guys come in and I get busy, but my mind isn't at peace because I can't stop thinking about what this poor girl is going through. The more I think about it though the more I realize that there's really nothing I can do for her. I decide to keep my distance from the girl.

The money isn't nearly as good here as at my regular club, but I'm able to make enough to cover my hotel bill, buy gas for my car and still leave with at least two hundred.

At the end of the night my young friend is sitting in the change room and gazing outside as the wind blows snow against the window. I ask her if she wants to talk and she says no. Then I ask her if she's able to call her mother, and she says yes.
"Why don't you call her then?"
Slurring her words, she moans: "I'll never go home. You'd have to kill me."
"Why?" I ask.
"What's the point? You won't believe me either," she replies. "Try me."
She's about to fall off her chair. As I reach out to steady her, she finds her balance.

"My stepfather has been raping me since I was 9. It continued until last year, when I was 15…. You know what?"
"What?" I ask.
"I couldn't hurt my mother, I couldn't tell her. But one day – it was the first time I did cocaine in my room – my mom walked in on me. She went nuts yelling at me and she even brushed the coke off my dresser. So I got pissed off and I told her. I yelled it out … I screamed it out, and it felt good to finally tell her. To let her know why I was so fucked up, why I needed drugs. But she didn't believe me! She said I was lying and blamed everything on the drugs. And she's still with him! So fuck them!"
She gets dressed slowly. I make my way to the front. I'm looking through the bar's glass doors wondering if I should take a cab to my hotel and leave my car in the lot. Another dancer approaches me and says: "You

know that girl you were talking to? She's really fucked up – she takes more pills and drugs then fifty doctors can prescribe." She then exits the club, her laughter trailing off behind her.

I drop my bag and ask the bouncer if he can watch it. I run outside to start my car. As I sweep the snow from the windows, a white Cadillac pulls up at the front of the club and I observe the young girl getting in. I go back in for my bag and then leave the club for the night.

I return home to Niagara and the very next day I notice an official looking envelope on the front landing of my house. It looks like court papers. I call the lawyer I'd consulted with and I read him what I'm holding. He says he's a criminal defense lawyer and it sounds like I need an attorney who specializes in civil suits. I ask him if he can recommend one, and he does so.

I call the lawyer he recommends, whose name is Zijad, and I read him an "official court notice" that indicates an impending deadline for me to reply. When I'm done, Zijad tells me that Paul Dagenais is bringing a lawsuit against me for one hundred and fifty thousand dollars! He says I'm lucky to have returned home in time to address it or I could have lost the suit by default. He adds that we still have time to prepare a formal response. He's going to be busy for a week, but he tells me not to worry. He suggests I go back to work and that we get together in a week's time to deal with it.

Over the next few days, I finish out my deferred sentence at the dreaded Maxine's. I then return to work at the Sundowner so I can start making some real money. I give the day-shift manager at the Sundowner the punch cards that prove I've put in the required number of shifts during my exile. I'm happy to see the girls again, and my floor hustle is in high gear. The only thing driving me is anger. I ask every guy for a dance. For every three or four "no's," I get one yes. I have a new appreciation for how great it is to work in a club with loads of customers. I know I need to make some big bucks to pay the lawyer a retainer fee, so I work a double shift and leave only when the bar closes.

The next morning I finally meet face to face with my new lawyer. Zijad Saskin is a fairly tall, good-looking young white man. After reading the document prepared by Paul's lawyer, he asks me if there is any truth to the allegation that I borrowed money from Dagenais.
"None," I reply.
"He paid me! I worked for every dollar."
He asks if I ever signed an IOU statement from him.
"Absolutely not," I insist.

I then tell him the whole story about my dealings with Paul and our eventual falling out. After explaining the legal issues to me and how we need to proceed in response to the court summons, Zijad reassures me that there is no way Dagenais can win this lawsuit without evidence and that the case will come down to "credibility."

I decide to retain Zijad as my attorney because the summons deadline is approaching fast. During our conversation Zijad mentions that Chris Rudan is also one of his clients. I'm a little taken back by this, because the last thing I want is for that fucking guy to find out about my legal troubles. But Zijad assures me that I'm protected by attorney-client confidentiality and that he won't breathe a word about my case to anyone outside his firm.

Despite my apprehensions about his connection to the Sundowner, I insist that he not mention anything to the Sundowner boss about our discussions or the case. He reconfirms that it would be unethical for him to do so and that he certainly won't.

"If you see me in the club, don't even acknowledge me," I stress.

"Don't worry – I won't even say hi."

More to reassure myself than to make a point to him, I add: "Good. I've never seen you in there before, so why would I see you now?"

He mentions he can't remember the last time he was even in there, and explains that he's about to get married. He speaks to me with such affection about his fiancé that my heart warms toward him. I immediately retain him and return the next day with a cheque.

I feel much better now that I have a sense that my legal situation with Paul is being taken care of. Having a lawyer in my corner is giving me a sense of security and my focus can now be on working and paying my bills. I reunite with some of my old customers and go out with a few of them to restaurants and the casino and shopping. During my spare time, I start working out again at the gym. I'm in generally good spirits, but knowing that a legal battle lies ahead is a source of recurrent worry.

After a few weeks my lawyer updates me about the unfolding legal process. The case is starting. He advises

me that a date has been set for an "examination for discovery" session. This will be a meeting where my lawyer and I will meet with Paul and his attorney along with a neutral recording secretary. He explains that the lawyers for each party will ask the other party questions pertaining to the case, but there'll be no judge present. After answering all of my anxious questions, he tries to calm me down by advising me not to worry. He goes over a few questions with me, but one question he keeps returning to is how many times I drove Paul around. I keep telling him, "I don't know. I'm not sure."
"Well, was it ten times?"
I insist I just can't remember exactly.
"Was it 20 times?" he asks. I indicate it was probably less.
"Let's just say twenty times." I can only shrug my shoulders and wonder why he wants to settle on that particular number.

I start working double shifts on a more consistent basis, as I need to make as much money as I can. Not only do I have to pay my regular bills, but Revenue Canada is also breathing down my neck for unpaid GST. And I have no idea how much the legal battle with Paul is going to end up costing me.

The day before the "discovery" meeting with Paul and the lawyers, something really strange happens. I'm working a slow day shift and a guy I've never seen before comes over and sits at the bar beside me. He asks to buy me a drink and I accept. Minutes later we enter the VIP room. As I'm sitting with him waiting for a new song to start he explains that he's picked me because I look very fit and have strong-looking legs. I mention that I used to run track, and he compliments me by remarking "it shows."

As I stand up to begin my dance, he asks me to please sit down again. I tell him I've already sat through half a song, but he says not to worry and that he'll pay me for the song. I tell him I've heard that story before and that I'd like my money up front. He gives me sixty dollars and I sit down to hear what he has to say. He explains he's just got out of a long marriage and he's looking for some help. I explain to him I'm not a prostitute if that's the kind of "help" he's looking for. He assures me it's not and asks me to hear him out.

"I own an optical store close by. Perhaps you know it?"
"Yes, I've been in there to get my sunglasses fixed. It's a nice store."
"Thank you, yes it is nice. But now I'm losing my customers to my ex-wife. She's opened a new store and she's stolen the contact info for all my customers. I wish she wasn't there, you know what I mean?"

I look at him with an open mouth, not liking the direction this is taking.

"I think so…." I say awkwardly.
"You know what I'm looking for, don't you?"
"Not really," I reply.
"I'm looking for someone to go over there and lay a beating on her. I want to see her put in the hospital for months."
"I don't know people like that, I'm sorry…."
"I was thinking maybe *you* could do it. You look like a strong girl, and I'd make it worth your while. How does five grand sound to you?"

Speechless and scared, I just sit there waiting for the guy to leave. He gives me his card with his contact information and then assures me he doesn't want his ex-wife killed, just badly beaten. He gets up and asks me to call him later.

I rush upstairs to the change room and blurt out that this fucking asshole of a customer wants me to beat up his ex-wife for five thousand bucks! The girls offer a bunch of suggestions:
"Call the cops."
"Call his wife and warn her."
"Mind your own business and never talk to the guy again."

But what I just don't get is why he would approach *me* to do this. One of the girls suggests it's because I look strong and muscular for a woman. But I'm not buying it. I'm not tough looking, and I don't come across as a criminal type. And this guy never even met me before. I wonder if I'm being set up in some way. One thing's for sure: I'm not getting involved with this guy in any way. I want to forget the whole incident even happened.

After hanging out for a few more hours and making no money, I decide to hang up my G-string for the day. The night shift girls are making their way in, and I have a big day tomorrow. I don't really know how to prepare for the "discovery" meeting. I go on line but I can't find anything to help me. After going to bed, I can't sleep properly because my mind is racing with anxious thoughts of what's in store for me. Finally, around six o'clock in the morning, I fall asleep, but I'm soon awakened by my alarm at eight. Sleep deprived as hell I rush to complete some chores and get myself ready. I

arrive at the address that Zijad had given me for the "discovery session."
It's an office building in downtown St. Catharines. As I enter the foyer, my lawyer waves at me with a smile, as though we're meeting there for a fun event. Several feet away, I see Paul standing with a woman who appears to be in her seventies. I greet Zijad but say nothing to Paul.

We go upstairs to an office space and enter a room with a large table and half a dozen chairs surrounding it. There are five of us: my lawyer and I, Paul and his lawyer, and a medium-built lady who's facing us. Using a Bible, she swears Paul and me in with the standard line about telling "the truth, the whole truth and nothing but the truth."

My lawyer starts the meeting off by asking Paul a series of questions pertaining to his allegation that I'd borrowed a hundred and fifty thousand dollars from him. Most of Paul's answers are incoherent and rambling, so much so that the lady presiding over the meeting asks him to just answer the questions directly and to stop addressing me. I can't believe what's coming out of his mouth. It's just one lie after another. There's one important issue that we can agree on though. When he's asked if he's ever had sex with me, he tells the truth for a change and says: "No, nothing like that, never."

Then it's the turn of Clark Peddle, Paul's lawyer, to interrogate me.

Q. Can you state your full legal name please?
A. Thelma Angela Vassel.
Q. And do you go by any other pseudonyms?

A. Ah, Linda Lee.

Q. Linda Lee?

A. Stage name.

Q. Okay. And, ah, where do you live? Ah, do you want me to call you Angela?

A. I'd prefer, yes.

Q. Where do you live, Angela?

A. I live in Niagara on the Lake. 6 Firelane 11A.

Q. Okay. And how long have you lived there?

A. Ahm, you know what, ah probably 10, 12 years.

Q. Okay. And do you own that property?

A. Yes?

Q. Okay. And, ah, are you a Canadian citizen?

A. No.

Q. Okay. Where were you born?

A. Jamaica.

Q. Okay. When did you come to Canada?

A. '82.

Q. 1982

A. Mmhmm.

Q. Okay. And your parents, what are their names?

A. Brandon Vassel, and, ah Monette Sutherland.

Q. Okay. And. Ah, do they live in Canada?

A. My dad lives in Canada.

Q. Does he live in Toronto?

A. Yes.

Q. Okay. And where's your mother live?

A. Ahm, my mother died, ah, when I was seven years old.

Q. Okay.

A. Kingston, Jamaica.

Q. Okay. So you and your dad came up from Kingston.

A. That's right.

Q. ...in 1982.

A. ...And he did remarry.

Q. Oh, okay.

A. Yeah, my stepmother.

Q. But that's not your natural mother...

A. No.

Q. ... that's a different woman. Okay. And you said, ahm, Linda Lee is your stage name. What do you mean by that?

A. I dance at the Sundowner, and all the girls get a name to protect themselves.

Q. Okay. And how long have you dance there?

A. I've been there for numerous years – a few years. At least five, six.

Q. At least five, six?

A. Yes.

Q. Have you always been an exotic dancer?

A. Ahm, no, I worked at IBM.

Q. Okay.

A. Ahm, I had my own business, Ahm, and so forth.

Q. When did you work at IBM?

A. Ahm, it's got to before – over ten years ago.

Q. Okay. How old are you?

A. I'm 40.

Q. Okay.

A. I'll be 4 - - yeah.

Q. So you were So you were born in 1970?

A. '69.

Q. 69?

A. Mmhmm.

Q. Okay. Ahm, and so you worked at IBM, and before that you had your own business?

A. Yes.

Q. And what kind of business was that?

A. Ahm, I used to run beauty pageants.

Q. Okay.

A. Ahm, have, ahm, events, parties.

Q. Okay.

A. Yeah.

Q. Now, so you've been dancing for – you said about five years?

A. Yes.

Q. Just roughly. Okay. And you've lived in Niagara on the lake all this time.

A. Yes.

Q. And you've only danced at Seductions?

A. Ah, I never danced at seductions?

Q. Ah, sorry. Ahm, Sundowner.

A. Yeah.

Q. You've never danced anywhere else?

A. Ahm, I've done (sic) for years, but, I mean, live, ahm, for the last five years it's been the Sundowner.

Q. Okay, where did you dance prior to that?

A. Ahm, prior to that, Ahm – maybe I did something else, schooling or something. But it's been the Sundowner as long as I can remember.

Q. But...

A. And I'm estimating five years.

Q. Have you danced anywhere else is what I asked you?

A. Ahm, Anywhere else? I've danced many places after – before five years.

Q. Okay. Can you just give me a brief description where those were?

A. Ah, I can't even think. Ahm....

Q. You can't remember?

A. Not really, 'cause I dance, I quit, and I danced...

MR. SASKIN

Maybe I can undertake to provide that information?

A. ... and I quit. It's been – yeah.

MR. PEDDLE

Q. Sure, if you don't mind.

SASKIN

Okay.

A. Yeah, it's been a long time.

MR. PEDDLE

Q. Okay, are you married?

A. No.

Q. Okay, do you live alone in Niagara on the Lake?

A. Yes.

Q. You have any children?

A. No.

Q. Okay, do you have any relationships with biker gangs?

A. No, don't know anybody.

Q. Don't know anybody...

A. Not one person.

Q. ... in a biker gang? Okay. So if I called Tim Panetta tonight he's not – he's going to tell me he's never heard of you?

A. Don't have a clue who that is.

Q. Okay, that's fair. When did you meet, ah Paul?

A. I've known Paul for three, four years.

Q. Maybe three, four years?

A. Yes.

Q. When exactly did you meet him?

A. I met him at Sundowner when he asked me for a dance.

Q. Okay, and, ahm, did you guys develop some sort of relationship after that?

A. Ahm, Paul really likes a lot of the girls at the Sundowner.

Q. Okay.

A. Yeah.

Q. So your relationship with him wasn't anything special or different?

A. My relationship—no, wasn't special or different because– yeah.

Q. Okay, and, ah. Did you ever visit him outside the Sundowner?

A. Yes, he would come to the Downer frequently and ask me to call him. And sometimes I would, and he would ask me to come over.

Q. How many times would you have gone to his house?

A. Ah, numerous times.

Q. Okay, how many is numerous.

A. I can't count on my fingers.

Q. Okay, use your fingers and your toes.

A. Ah, you know what, I don't know exact. Ahm...

Q. No, no, just give me a rough estimate?

A. Ah, quite a few times.

Q. Would you say 20 or more?

A. Maybe less than 20

Q. More than 15?

A. Ah, probably more than 15. I'm not quite sure.

Q. Okay, and would you call him from your cell phone.

A. Ahm, yeah.

Q. Okay.

A. I think so.

Q. Are you prepared to give me the records indicating these calls, or showing these calls?

A. Ahm,

Q. And is there any reason they weren't produced as part of your affidavit of documents?

MR. SASKIN

I – I don't think there's ways to go back six months previously and get actual...

MR. PEDDLE

Q. Oh no, you...

MR. SASKIN

...calls.

MR. PEDDLE

Q. ...can go back and get them for up to 10 years. Your – your bills will show all incoming and outgoing calls, especially cell phones. They are very detailed.

MR. SASKIN

Do you still have your bills.

A. I...

MR. SASKIN

...dating back?

A. ...think so, yeah. I think so.

MR. SASKIN

If you have them—if they're in her possession we'll undertake to look for those bills and provide 'em.

MR. PEDDLE

Q. Okay, and if you can't find them you'll give me your consent for me to make inquiries on your behalf?

MR. SASKIN.

To the phone company?

MR. PEDDLE

Q. Yes, just...

MR. SASKIN

Yes.

MR. PEDDLE

Q. ... to the phone company...

MR. SASKIN

Yes.

MR. PEDDLE

Q. ...of course.

A. Okay.

MR. SASKIN

But we'll make the, ah...

MR. PEDDLE

Q. No, absolutely.

MR. SASKIN

Yeah, well...

MR. PEDDLE

Q. If you can't obtain them ...

MR. SASKIN

Yeah, if—if we can't obtain them you can get a chance to...

MR. PEDDLE

Q. I can attempt to try...

MR. SASKIN

Yes.

MR. PEDDLE

Q. ... on your behalf, okay.

MR. SASKIN

Get a chance to...

MR. PEDDLE

Q. Okay.

MR. SASKIN

And if you do try they would have to go through me first...

MR. PEDDLE

Q. That's fine.

MR. SASKIN

... because there are going to be other phone calls there that have nothing to do with this case.

MR. PEDDLE

Q. No. I understand that.

MR. SASKIN

Okay, sure.

MR. PEDDLE

Q. Yeah, I trust you to review it and...

MR. SASKIN

Of course.

MR. PEDDLE

Q. ... black line whatever you want. Is it normal practice as an exotic dancer to visit a client's house up to 20 times?

A. Well, the thing is, ah, Paul is persistent and he was, ah—he was a nice guy and he would come and ask numerous times. And I said okay. He'd say come and watch; I believe it was, Hercules. So I did, yeah. And hang out, yeah.

Q. Okay.

A. And I didn't hang out because it was – he asked me to, yeah.

Q. Okay, that's fine. If you went there 15 or 20 times, what did you guys do all the time?

A. Well he asked me to drive him to different, ahm, locations and stuff like that. Like, he wasn't driving and he wanted me to drive him to the park, to the bank of course, to ahm, to get his, ah, pass port. Ahm, to get, ahm –just the coffee shop. Stuff as such, yeah. To, ah— there's a place in, ah, the pen centre— behind the pen centre. He wanted to get his license. He had to write some tests. So I drove him around there to try to find the location and stuff like that.

Q. Okay, how many times would you say you took him to a bank?

A. Ah, whenever he asked me to.

Q. Okay, but how many times would you say that is?

A. Ahm, I'm not sure.

Q. 5, 10, 15, 20, 25?

A. Maybe 10.

Q. Maybe 10 times.

A. Yeah, maybe more, I'm not sure. Whenever he asked. I never kept a record.

Q. Yeah, but you must have—this is over a short period time I assume. How long were you hanging out with Paul?

A. Ah, mmm...

Q. Would it be fair to say about March...

A. Well, there's...

Q. ...09...

A. Many times ...

Q. ...to...

A. ...he asked me to come and I just simply don't go so.

Q. No, I understand that. I'm looking at time frame.

A. Yeah.

Q. So would it be safe to say about March of 09 up to maybe January of 2010— or'10?

A. March of – no, it started way before that.

Q. Would it be March of '08?

A. Ah, I think before that, because I think something happened at the club and the ambulance had to be there. And after that we had, ah—most of the girls had a little bit of pity, so that's when it really started.

Q. A little bit of what?

A. Pity. Like, we felt bad for him. Yeah.

Q. The ambulance came to get who?

A. Him.

Q. Paul?

A. Yeah, Paul.

Q. And what was that about?

A. I'm not sure.

Q. Okay, but you do know the ambulance came to pick him up?

A. I believe so, yeah.

Q. You don't recall when that was at all?

A. No. We all found out about it, so...

Q. So you weren't...

A. ... I have to look into it.

Q. ... actually present, you heard about it?

A. The next day I found out about it yeah.

Q. All right. So you can't tell me at all in terms of a timeline how—how long you knew Paul?

A. Roughly, three years.

Q. Roughly three years.

A. Yeah, I'd say so.

Q. So you knew him back in 08?

A. I can't remember—recall it. It hasn't been like this last year, it's been some time yeah.

Q. Okay, are you aware of any other dancers who went to Paul's house?

A. Ahm, well, he told me of a few girls, yeah. I'm not sure of the names, but I know that he flew one to Halifax. And that one he was having sex with. Ahm.

Q. And—who told you this?

A. He did.

Q. Okay. But you never spoke to a girl who told you that.

A. No, he did.

Q. Okay.

A. Yeah.

Q. And you don't know her name?

A. Ahm, he knows her name. He mentioned it to me.

Q. But you don't know her name is what I said...

A. No.

Q. Okay, and was she dancing at the Sundowner?

A. Ahm, when he told me about this I asked him and he wouldn't tell me. Like, her stage name or anything, so.

Q. But she was dancing...

A. And I know what...

Q. ...at the Sundowner?

A. I believe so, yes.

Q. How many girls dance at the Sundowner on most nights?

A. Oh Jesus, I don't have a clue. Quite a few.

MR. SASKIN

45 to 55

MR. PEDDLE

Q. You know that from personal experience, counsel? Okay, so there's a lot of girls there. And you don't know all of them is what I'm saying.

A. No, I don't.

Q. Okay. Is the Sundowner your only source of income?

A. At this time, yes.

Q. Okay, back in, ah, July through to January – July of 09 to January of 2010, was that your only source of income?

A. I believe so, yes.

Q. Okay. And you file your tax returns?

A. Yes, I do.

Q. Do you have any objection to providing me with your tax returns for the year of 09 and, ah 2010?

MR. SASKIN

No.

MR. PEDDLE

Q. You'll...

MR. SASKIN

I mean, we'll – we'll provide those...

MR. PEDDLE

Q. ... provide them, okay.

MR. SASKIN

...yes. No objection in my...

MR. PEDDLE

Q. Sorry. And where do you bank?

A. Ah, CIBC.

Q. That's the only place you bank?

A. Ahm, no. I did also bank at the Royal.

Q. Where is the CIBC? Which branch?

A. Niagara on the Lake.

Q. On highway 58 or 55. Whatever it is?

A. 55.

Q. Yeah, okay. And the royal is where?

A. Ahm...

MR. SASKIN

Where's the branch. Niagara falls, Niagara on the Lake, St Catharine's?

A. Which is—that—oh sorry, it was TD. 'Cause Royal is like nine year ago.

MR. PEDDLE

Q. Okay, so TD.

A. TD Canada Trust.

Q. Okay, where-which branch is it?

A. And that's on Lakeshore.

Q. In St Catharines?

A. Yes.

Q. Did you ever deposit large amount of money in any of those accounts? Cash?

A. Ah, I've deposited money, yes.

Q. Have you ever deposited any more than two thousand dollars on a day in—in any of these accounts?

A. In a day? I have.

Q. Do you have any problem with providing me with your bank statements from the period of, ah, January 09 through to, July 1st, 2010?

A. No problem.

MR. SASKIN

Say that's... January 09 to...?

MR. PEDDLE

Q. July 1st of this year?

MR. SASKIN

July 1st of 2010. Okay.

MR. PEDDLE

Q. Have you ever – well, since July 22nd, 2009, have you gone out and purchased any item who's – value more than two thousand dollars with cash.

A. No.

Q. Okay, have you – have you—since July 22nd, 2009, have you loaned anybody, ah, amounts over one thousand in cash?

A. No.

Q. Now, all the times you went to Paul to the bank, did he tell you why he was taking out money?

A. No, not in detail.

Q. Well, what did he tell you?

A. He was a flashy guy and brag and told me that if I would have sex with him I could have a lot of money, and I – I just couldn't do it.

Q. That's fine, but he was taking out significant amounts of money...

A. And that's fine...

Q. ...daily.

A. ...his business.

Q. But he didn't tell you what it was for?

A. No, he did not.

Q. And you didn't receive – I'm going to show you exhibit 4....

A. MmHmm.

Q. ...which you probably already looked at. Its amount of cash totaling a hundred and six thousand. (106,450.00)

A. mmhmm,

Q. Did you received any of these funds?

A. No.

Q. Not one dollar?

A. Not – well, when I drove Paul, 'cause I took time from work, he did pay me for my time.

Q. And what...

A. Different times.

Q. ...what would he pay you for your time?

A. Between three to five hundred.

Q. And aside from a few occasions where he paid you to drive him.

A. Mmhmm,

Q. ...you never received any of these other funds at...

A. No.

Q. ...are outlined here

A. No.

Q. And you have no idea what Paul did with that money?

A. No, he had many girls.

Q. What's that?

A. He had many females that he would go to the club frequently and see.

Q. So you're suggesting to me he could have spent a hundred and six thousand dollars over a period of, ah...

A. I was not his favorite.

Q. Okay, who was his favorite?

A. He had many.

Q. Well, who was his favorite?

A. There was a few girls.

Q. You just told me you weren't his favorite. Who was his favorite?

A. He had many girls.

Q. Okay.

A. There's girls come and go.

Q. Name three of them for me?

A. I can't, ask him.

Q. I'm asking you?

A. And I just...

Q. You said you were not his favorite. You saw him go with many girls. Name some of them for me.

A. Well, I just said you can ask him because girls come and ...

Q. No, you don't get to decide who asks who. I'm asking you specific questions. You have to answer me.

A. Okay, but what I'm saying, girls come and go.

Q. I understand that, but ... Okay. ... what are – what were the stage names...

MR. SASKIN

Can you – can you...

MR. PEDDLE

Q. ...of the girls?

MR. SASKIN

Q. ... name any three girls that he would get in addition to you to dance for him? Can you name any other three girls?

A. Ahm, I know the two girls. One girl she quit.

MR. SASKIN

What was – do you know her name?

A. I can't remember her name.

MR. SASKIN

Okay.

A. And ahm...

MR. SASKIN

Can you remember any of the girls' names?

A. Ah, just stage name. Ah, Dakota is her real name, but I can't remember her stage name. And there's other girls.

MR. SASKIN

There's Dakota, but doesn't remember her stage name.

A. No.

MR. PEDDLE

Q. And you don't remember her last name, I take it?

A. Oh, they don't...

MR. SASKIN

They don't ...

A. ... know my last name either.

MR. PEDDLE

Q. Okay, did you ever have a movie that you were going to shoot in Toronto or LA or Vancouver or...

A. What do you mean a movie?

Q. A movie?

A. That I was actually invo – no.

Q. No. Were you ever involved in the production of any movie, or anything like that?

A. Absolutely not.

Q. Did you ever borrow money to have your car fixed?

A. Absolutely not.

Q. Okay. Again, you have no association with any biker gangs?

A. Absolutely not.

Q. Okay, what does your dad do for a living?

A. Ahm, he's retired. He's an active preacher and ahm—or involved with the church heavily and, ah, he just retired.

Q. What church is that?

A. Ahm, I'm not sure what church he's going to now.

Q. What denomination is he?

A. Ah, mostly Pentecostal.

Q. Okay, were you born Pentecostal and raised Pentecostal?

A. Yes, but I practice seven-day (sic) Adventist now.

Q. Oh, okay.

A. And everybody in my church knows I dance. I don't hide it.

Q. Sorry, know you what?

A. They know I dance.

Q. Oh, no, no, no.

A. Yeah, I don't hide it.

Q. I'm not threatening you.

A. Oh. Oh.

Q. Don't get that impression.

A. No, I'm just saying. Like I don't hide...

Q. No, no.

A. ...what I do.

Q. No, no, I understand.

A. Though my pastor tries to get me to – I don't hide what I do.

Q. I don't hide what I do either, but sometimes I wish I did.

A. Yeah.

Q. Okay, now, so your dad is a preacher. So, ahm, I think...

A. Ah, he was active in the church I would say.

Q. Okay. Let's just say he's heavily involved in the church.

A. Yes.

Q. He doesn't hang out with biker gangs, does he?

A. No.

Q. Have you ever known him to hang out with a biker gang?

A. Absolutely not.

Q. Okay. That's what I'm asking.

A. Yeah.

Q. I noticed you borrowed a couple hundred thousand (200,000) off of Home Trust or something...

A. Mmhmm

Q. ...this year? What was that for?

A. How did you get that information?

Q. What was that for?

A. I remortgage my house.

Q. What for?

A. Because I paid Revenue Canada.

Q. Oh, you owned them money?

A. Yes.

Q. They audited you?

A. Yeah.

Q. How much did you owe them?

A. Ahm, I think sixty-six thousand (66,000).

Q. Okay, How much is your property worth down there?

A. Ahm, maybe three hundred thousand (300,000), four hundred thousand (400,000).

Q. Is it a condo or a house?

A. It's a little house.

Q. Okay. And you drive a Mer – BMW?

A. Yeah, it's a friend's.

Q. What do you mean it's a friend's?

A. It's a guy I'm dating. That's his vehicle.

Q. Don't you have one registered in your name?

A. No, I do not.

Q. When was the last time you had one registered in your name?

A. Ahm, it's been some time.

Q. Really?

A. Yes

Q. Okay. How long have you been dating this boyfriend?

MR. SASKIN

I don't know how that's relevant.

MR. PEDDLE

Q. Well, I just want to see if she's supporting him financially?

A. Oh, no, he's got his own job.

Q. He does?

A. Yes.

Q. Okay and he's got a job sufficient to give you a BMW to drive around?

A. When he's in Canada he drives his vehicle. He lives in Arizona.

Q. Oh, what's his name?

MR. SASKIN

I don't know how that's relevant.

MR. PEDDLE

Q. It's relevant because I want to check to see if she's supporting him.

MR. SASKIN

Well, you can ask – but you have asked the question if she's supporting him and that was...

A. And I said no.

MR. SASKIN

... her answer.

A. And I said no.

MR. PEDDLE

Q. Okay, but what's his name? I want to know his name?

MR. SASKIN

Ah, we're going to...

MR. PEDDLE

Q. You're going ...

MR. SASKIN

... refuse that.

MR. PEDDLE

Q. ... to object to that?

MR. SASKIN

I'm going to object to that.

MR. PEDDLE

Q. Okay. The reason it's a directly relevant is because I want to know if she's got somebody close to her who had – potentially has a bank accounts that she's depositing funds in. or if she's supporting somebody else. Ahm 'cause I noticed the BMW has no lien against it. Which means it's owned free and clear by this individual. I mean, I can find his name that way, but I prefer you to give it to me. You're still going to refuse?

MR. SASKIN

Oh, you can find out the name based on the...

MR. PEDDLE

Q. I can.

MR. SASKIN

Yeah.

MR. PEDDLE

Q. Just rather save the expense.

MR. SASKIN

I mean, the – the question is whether or not she's refuse – whether or not she's supporting him, and she's given her answer that she's not supporting him.

MR. PEDDLE

Q. The fact is I can't make inquires to do my examination of him, or potentially call him in as a third party without knowing his name. If there is nothing to hide I don't understand what the problem is.

A. Bobby Alexmas.

MR. SASKIN

There's the name.

MR. PEDDLE

Q. How do you spell that? B-O-B-B-Y?

A. One "Y".

Q. Last name?

A. A-L-E-X-M-A-S.

Q. And he lives in Arizona?

A. Yes.

Q. Were you dating him over the period in which my client alleges he loaned you the money?

A. Ah, yes.

Q. This 06 BMW you're driving, the license plate is BAXX 393

A. Mmhmm.

Q. And it has Ontario plates on it.

A. Yes.

Q. Okay, but he lives in the United States?

A. And he's here, as well. He just moved there for work. He's moving back.

Q. Is he a Canadian citizen?

A. Yes, he is.

Q. Okay. Subject to the inquiries, which I will be making...

A. Pardon?

Q. I said subject to the inquiries, which I will be making, I have no further questions from you right now.

[End of transcript]

Thank God, the examination is over! But am I hearing this guy Peddle right? Is he actually threatening me?

I'm eager to ask my lawyer a few questions, so we go to a nearby Tim Horton's for a chat.

"Is all this information really needed, and is all this probing into my private affairs legal?"

Zijad replies that it's all perfectly legal and that while it's intrusive, we have no choice but to cooperate. He also tells me that I need to get a list of the places where I've worked in the past, as well as a record of my phone calls in the period in question, my bank account records, and copies of my tax returns for the last few years.

I can only sigh and throw up my hands in frustration. "As far as my bank records are concerned, I only have an account at CIBC and that's very recent. And my TD bank account has been closed because of Revenue Canada's actions." Zijad is reassured. He tells me it looks like we have nothing to worry about from either set of records. The CIBC records are outside of the time period relevant to discovery, and the TD account is closed. So, we don't have to worry. All this will be explained to the judge, he says. I'm relieved, but I confide to Zijad that I'm feeling threatened by Peddle. "The way he was looking at me and trying to intimidate me was unnerving. And why all the questions about the car? It was bought well before I started visiting with Paul, and it's still not even paid off." Zijad reassures me that everything will come out in court, and I shouldn't worry.

I ask him why he didn't question Paul about all the girls he's been involved with. He explains that it's not up to us to prove that he used the money in question for something other than loans to me; rather it's up to him to make a convincing case that he loaned *me* the money. I find this argument reassuring because the only money I ever received from Paul was for services rendered – dances in the club or time spent with him in Port Colborne or driving him around. Even so, something tells me that we should go on the offensive and expose Paul's free-spending ways. I suggest we hire a private detective to go to the club and make some inquiries so that we can prove his involvement with girls other than me.

Zijad rejects the idea. He tells me not to worry and puts his arm around me in a way that is momentarily comforting. But later in the day I recall a strange remark he made in response to my suggestion to hire a private detective. First, he dismissed the idea on the grounds that any detective's findings would be dismissed as "hearsay" by the judge, in the absence of direct testimony from any girls he interviews – so we would have to subpoena the girls. But then he said something about how a detective could find out where Paul's money actually ended up, adding "for all we know it could be in a bank account in Jamaica." He said this with a wry grin and a knowing glint in his eye, and then stressed once again that the burden of proof is on Paul and his lawyer, not on us.

I can't be sure, but Zijad's "bank account in Jamaica" comment might mean that he doubts my innocence. I don't know what to think, but I comfort myself with the thought that my lawyer nevertheless seems very sympathetic to my cause.

Over the next few weeks, I keep myself busy with work at the Sundowner.

One day I'm sitting at the bar waiting to make eye contact with a customer. Out of the corner of my eye I suddenly notice that Zijad is sitting at the far end of the bar with Chris Rudan. I avert my eyes in shock and then look again to confirm what I've just witnessed. Neither seems to notice me observing them. Their heads are somewhat bowed and their hands are animated, suggesting an intense verbal exchange. Suddenly Zijad looks up and our eyes lock. I don't know whether I should move away or remain where I am. My heart is racing, but I stay put as I pray my lawyer isn't talking about me. Suddenly Zijad is standing right in front of me with his hand extended towards me. I shake his hand as we exchange hello's and a few pleasantries. Upon his exit from the club I look over at Chris and we make eye contact briefly. Agitated, I get up and make my way to the change room.

The next day an incident at work gives me a welcome comedic distraction from my worries. I'm sitting in the change room redoing my makeup, because I just got off stage and I'm sweaty and hot. A girl enters and she's complaining loudly.

"This fucking guy called the manager on me and demanded his money back after I danced for him for a whole song."
I go, "What! Why?"
"For 'false advertising' … false advertising! Can you believe it?" she continues. "Yeah, he told the manager that when he first saw me he liked what he saw, so he went for a dance – and I gave him a good dance! But he was disappointed when I took off my bra. He said my breasts disappeared." "No! He didn't!" I laughed.

"Yes he did!"

She's standing in front of the mirror fixing her blond hair and then she removes her bra. I burst out laughing. Soon I'm laughing so hard that my whole abdomen aches and I'm eventually forced to bend over to ease the contractions. This girl is wearing a size C bra stuffed with padding that lifts the tops of her tiny breasts upward, creating the illusion of a full and ample bosom. But when she takes her bra off she's a size A … if she's lucky! She goes from "big boobs" to "tiny tits" in seconds! It's the funniest thing I've seen or heard in a long time.

"Fuck you too!" the girl says. "Nobody's ever made a big deal about my tits before." "A true 'breast man' would," I suggest, as I fold my arms across my aching tummy.

"Fuck them!" she says.
"Did you give him back his money?"
"No!" she huffs, storming out of the room.

I'm working a double and well into the night shift, around ten o'clock, I hear a list of girls being called to the office. After about the tenth name is called out, I realize that all the girls being summoned are black. A number of us begin to compare notes, trying to figure out what might be going on.
Eventually, our names are all called out. One girl says, "I'm putting on my recorder," and some others activate the recorders on their smart-phones before they enter the office.

As we stand in the office waiting for someone in authority to appear, I wonder *why aren't any of the white girls here? Out of about ninety girls in the club that night, why have the twenty or so black girls been singled out?* At that moment I feel isolated and scared.

Chris Rudan walks in and asks the white bouncer to leave the room. I have a sick feeling in my stomach. I move closer to the door so I can make a run for it if necessary.

Chris launches into a little speech in a stern tone. It's somewhat incoherent and made all the more difficult to understand by his thick Serbian accent.

"Since I've been in the business, I've never been prejudiced. I know a few of the black girls. There are good girls to work in my locations – in fact in all of my locations. Seems like now I might be that way. I'll tell you why.

You girls are taking a lot of advantage of being rough upstairs, banging on the doors, kicking doors. You have no fucking respect for my property! I have to fix it after you lose ??? Talking bad to white girls. Some of you have fucking pimps. I don't want to know. I don't want to accuse anybody. Mind your own fucking business, if you want to work with me.

"Clean, do your jobs, take care of business like everybody else. I hear shit right now. I'm going to, one by one, get [you?] the fuck out. Ok, give you a nicely…"

A bouncer walks in, and Chris tells him "to leave us alone here please." Then he continues.

"This honestly worries me. Don't be surprised if I have no job for you. I need a job; I need a job, bingo done. Once I close the doors, I close the doors. The door is closed no matter what, because I can't afford to fuck around here. The girls [in] daytime is doing dirty business. I'm not talking just the black girls – that includes white girls. I don't want that kind of business here either. I'm being honestly…."

He mumbles something I can't make out and then continues his rant. He ignores my hand held high waiting to ask a question.

"… work there is nobody around us, we are talking straight, honest true business, so don't have surprise – that's all I want to tell you. Banging upstairs, kicking the fucking door, 'fuck you this', 'fuck you this', 'fuck off', is not going to work here. I tell you very nicely and politely, okay. Think what I'm saying. Don't have surprise and don't come back and talk to me 'sorry Chris' – it's not going to work."

After he's done I feel sick to my stomach – like we've just stepped back fifty years in time. As we re-enter the bar a few customers stop me and want to know if we're ok. They ask what happened, but I'm too humiliated to say anything.

I'm in no mood to work so I go upstairs to the change room and find a few of the black girls discussing the meeting. The room is full of comments:

"He thinks the black girls have pimps, but it's mostly the white girls who do" and "what's he talking about anyway, he's the biggest pimp around."
"How come he didn't have no white girls there?"
"He's making a point; he's only going to fire black girls. We haven't had any problems with the white girls, so really, what was that meeting about?"

"*I was never racist but now I am!* … B.S, so long as I've known Chris he's been a fucking racist. He don't have to convince me that he's one now…. Nobody has been banging doors or kicking doors…"

"Something is very wrong with this picture. I'm selling my house and moving out of this town if I can't work here."

"Did you see him send the bouncer out? I thought I was going to be wacked. I'm still shaking."

Then it's my turn: "Seriously, he thinks he owns us, to treat us like that. I'm not going to pick cotton for that slave master. I can't move right now – I have to finish paying off Revenue Canada so I'm stuck here for a few years anyways…. Remember that black girl with the big bum?" "Yeah Natasha…" answers one of the girls.

"I can't remember, yeah, well one of the bouncers caught her dancing aggressive in the back, so he sent her to the office and now she has to work in the *Sensations* massage parlor next door. You know what they do there?
... Well, let's just say, the customers get a happy ending. She can only work here one shift and then she has to work there. I told her she didn't have to, but she's so young and impressionable – with her soft little voice, she said she *must* if she wants to get back into the bar. So *who's* the real pimp?"
Another girl adds: "Yeah, and what about when Chris asks you to go dance for one of his friends. They want the works in the back room and they think they're entitled because they're his friends. Fuck him! If I didn't have my kids to feed I'd be outta here so fast!"

Another girl begins to say she's going to call the Human Rights Tribunal, but she's interrupted by someone who says: "You want to die right now? You know this man is connected."

"I don't care. I'm calling," she says.

She's interrupted again: "Did you know that one of the few black guys who ever worked for him as a bouncer got murdered in one of the rooms upstairs? Did you know that?" "No way," she answers.

"Why that happened, I don't know – but I'd think about your kids first before doing anything risky."

For the rest of the night, I keep getting texts, from white and black girls alike, with comments about what had happened.

The next day I run around getting all the paper work requested by my lawyer, except for my phone bill records, which I'll need to order. After we discuss the various documents pertaining to my case, I mention the meeting Chris had with the black girls in the club. Zijad wants to hear more, but his inquisitiveness makes me nervous, so I decide to say as little as possible. I ask him if what Chris did was proper and he admits it probably wasn't, adding that no one is going to do anything about it. He explains that Chris knows lawyers and politicians from here to Ottawa, and without exactly saying it, he suggests that Chris is untouchable.

I get into work a little late in the day. I'm annoyed because I have to pay a twenty-dollar penalty on top of the usual floor fee, but I sign in because I have a few customers waiting for me. As I'm making my way upstairs, I hear my name called over the P.A system: I'm being summoned to the office. I don't want to go, so I sit down in the change room for a few minutes, collecting my thoughts. After I'm called a second time, I make my way to the office. I call a friend on my cell phone but there's no answer. As I disconnect, it occurs to me to turn on the recording app of my iPhone as I enter the office … just in case something bad is about to happen.

"Yes, did you call me?" I ask the manager.
He invites me in and gets right to the point.
"So you think you're smart recording the conversation."
Flustered I respond: "I don't know what you're talking about."

"Well we can't have you working here right now. You have to go do a month at Maxine's. Then you can come back here."
"But I have a few customers out there right now waiting for me."
"Too bad," he says.
"Do a month at Maxine's, then you can come back and see your customers."
"But why…?" I ask. "I haven't done anything."
"Why? Because Chris says so, that's why." "If it's about my argument with the bouncer, I wasn't wrong to record that.
He was trying to extort money out of me. It's not fair to send me away again for that."

"Sorry, I'm doing what I was told to do."

Once again I clean out my locker and exit through the back door. I call a friend and tell her about this latest setback. She says, "you know that's how they operate – just do the time, get back in, work hard and get the fuck out of that business."

"That's my plan," I reply. "I'm just starting to build my business website – I've registered my business name and now this! Fuck man! There's no money at that club. I'll be lucky if a single guy shows up. Why is it even open anyways?"

"Maybe it's a tax write-off…"

"Then if he wants girls there, he should pay them to work there instead of forcing them to work for nothing."

She shrugs and says: "Why would he, when he has a monopoly on the market?" *She's right of course. Chris will do anything that suits his interests. The man has no conscience whatsoever.*

As much as I don't want to go to Maxine's, I have no choice. This is going to set me back by months.

I go to work there, punching in and out nightly at this stupid club. Most nights I don't even make enough to cover my DJ fees and my transportation costs. One night I decide to skip Maxine's and try a club near Toronto, where I might be able to make some much-needed real money. In the change room, I run into one of the girls who'd been at that now notorious meeting with Chris. She's more mobile than I am, with no permanent residence, living in motels near the variety of clubs she works.

She's excited to see me and gives me a hug. She tells me the management here is so nice they actually care about the girls, suggesting that I should work here permanently. I explain I can't commute four hours every day, plus I have good customers at the Sundowner that I don't want to lose. She tells me she called the Ontario Human Rights Tribunal and reported everything over the phone about Chris's rant. They wanted to meet with her in person but she got cold feet and gave them a fake address.

As she tells me this story I consider the possibility that Chris got wind of a potential Human Rights Tribunal investigation into his behavior and now suspects that I blew the whistle on him! It would have been a simple "two plus two." He knew I was there for his racist rant and the day manager may have told him that I'd been suspended for recording my argument with the bouncer weeks earlier.

Is Chris trying to send me some kind of message with this latest punishment?

Later I get a text from one of the black girls at the Sundowner telling me that Chris had just met with a bunch of girls. He announced that he's going to reopen the Seductions club next door and that if any girls want to be waitresses or whatever in the club to talk to him. "Something is up," she says. "Why is he suddenly being so nice to us?" I tell her Chris must be feeling some heat – that he's trying to cover his tracks. All this reconfirms my suspicion that a Human Rights investigation might be underway.

I return to Niagara and serve out the rest of my month-long "sentence" at Maxine's. But when I try to go back to work at The Sundowner, after duly presenting my proof that I'd done my time at Maxine's, the manager informs me I'm still not welcome back. I'll have to work at another of Chris's slow bars, The Penthouse in Thorold, for an additional two weeks! *More bullshit! More bullying, arbitrary, infuriating bullshit!* I'm desperate to make some money, and I know the only club where I can do that is The Sundowner. That's where I have regular customers, and I can't connect with them until I return. I'm fit to be tied! But what can I do? This latest punishment brings to mind some previous events pointing to the complete powerlessness of us girls.

I remember the time when we were ordered by management to attend a meeting where a labour organizer made the case for us to band together in some kind of union. Apparently, Chris was legally required to cooperate with this effort. We were told that if we didn't attend the meeting we'd be barred from working at all of his bars. But we were also told to say nothing during the meeting. One of the girls was given a script to read, which basically amounted to a statement that we were all satisfied with the way we were being treated and didn't feel any need for a union. After the meeting, Chris's son Semo thanked us for our "cooperation" and said that if we ever had a problem at the club we should contact him. In a hushed tone, he told us that he knew full well that his dad could be hard to deal with.

Later that same year, we were rounded up like animals and transported to City Hall for another stage-managed meeting. Again, we were expected to present a common face and keep our mouths shut. The City was bringing in a new licensing system and the Lord of The Sundowner was against it. The meeting was supposed to be an open forum, but only Semo and his team actually spoke.

Yes, I remember all this as I decide to take Semo at his word and see if he can do something on my behalf about the shitty treatment I'm receiving. For days I try to reach him, with many messages left, but I never hear back from him.

I'm home in bed when I hear a knock at my door late one night. There's no way I'm going to open my door at 3:30 in the morning. I go to the bathroom without turning on any lights and look out the window. I see two people getting into a car. I can't tell if they're male or female. Moments later they speed away.

At 7 a.m. I call Candy to see if she'd been one of my visitors. She assures me it hadn't been her and that she hadn't even gone to work last night. I drive over to

John's house and find him partying with three girls from the Downer. I ask him if he'd stopped by my house. He denies it and one of his girlfriends says they haven't even left the house for three days – they've been "partying" the whole time!

On my way home I check my mailbox and find that most of the documents that my lawyer had requested have now arrived, including my phone records. I set up an appointment and meet with Zijad later that morning. I explain to him that my TD bank account has been closed because of lack of funds and that it's now in overdraft. I'd set up a payment plan with Revenue Canada to pay my back taxes, and the automatic withdrawals had left me in a situation where most of my recently issued cheques had bounced.

I bring up the idea of hiring a private detective, but once again Zijad shoots down the idea saying, "what good would that do? Any information a detective might obtain from the other girls would be seen as pure hearsay."

It doesn't seem to occur to him that, if and when our detective finds that they have information about Paul that can be used against him, the girls can be called as witnesses. When I point this out, he shrugs and says: "But will they be *willing* or *hostile* witnesses? If they're hostile, they can do a lot of damage to our defense."

Zijad seems determined to base our whole legal strategy on the flimsiness of Paul's evidence against me. Part of me wants to believe that his strategy will work, but another part is growing uneasy and wants to gather more information about Paul just in case we need to go on the offensive.

Later that day I speak to a few girls and they tell me that Paul had definitely been busy having dates with many different girls over a long period, including the time I was seeing him in Port Colborne. But none of these girls have any first-hand knowledge and none wants to get involved in any legal battles. One girl mentions that she has a friend who's been seeing Paul. For a substantial fee this girl had driven down from Toronto to see him on several occasions. She didn't know much about their arrangement, but the girl had actually mentioned her dates with Paul on her Facebook page. I ask her if she can send me a copy of that page, and she says she can. I immediately call and report this to Zijad, but once again he insists this information is of no use to us.

I have a great idea. *Forget about proving that Paul was involved with other girls.* I recall several of my co-workers telling me that he'd threatened *to kill them* if they told me that he'd been bragging about sleeping with me. I'm quite friendly with one of those girls, and I'm sure I can talk her into testifying on my behalf. *If I can get someone to testify, under oath, that Paul had actually threatened to kill some of the Sundowner girls, wouldn't that definitely help our case?*

I raise the idea with Zijad, and, with some reluctance, he agrees to interview her. I make all the arrangements and, after the interview, he tells me that he *might* call her as a witness, "if necessary."

After returning home, I take a long bath, read a few chapters of a book, and turn out the lights. I welcome sleep, but my conscious mind remains in overdrive. I toss and turn, but remain in bed hoping that I'll eventually drift off to sleep. About 3:30 in the morning, bright lights flood my driveway and seep into my house.

I rush out of my bathroom and peer through the blinds. A car reverses itself out of the driveway and then speeds away.

I'm now wide-awake and more than a little frightened. I wonder, *Who can that be? ... I've lived here for ten years and I've never seen this much activity late at night.* I live on a dead-end rural lane that is so narrow that two cars can't easily pass each other. I return to bed and eventually watch the sky wake up. I feel more relaxed as dawn breaks, because I feel safer when the sun is up. Around noon my conscious mind shuts down, and I sleep till 8 in the evening. I'm curious to find out if the event of the previous night had just been a random occurrence. Feeling stressed out, I go to the gym and walk on a treadmill for an hour.

I'm home around 11 p.m. My instincts tell me to park my car ten houses down the lane at my neighbors, and I do just that. At 1 a.m. I turn off all the lights in my house, but I keep going outside and checking the lane to see if there are any headlights coming in my direction. Nothing. At four o'clock I go to bed. A few minutes later I see headlights appearing in my driveway. I hop out of bed and rush to the window to see if I can identify the make of the car or who's in it. The vehicle turns around and leaves before I can gather any information. I stay up for hours afterward, but there are no further visitations.

I fall asleep midday but my neighbor knocks on my door and wakes me up to get me to move my car. I park it in my driveway and return to bed. I wake up in a panic realizing that it's now dark. But it's only nine o'clock. I decide to hide my car again.

The early-morning visitations happen repeatedly over the next few weeks.
After one of these incidents, I discover that my car tires have been slashed. I have to do something about this, so I decide to go to the St. Catharines police station.

I explain to the desk clerk what's been happening, but she seems indifferent and unmotivated to help me. She insists that there's nothing the police can do without a license plate. I explain to her that there's no street lights on my rural lane, so it's hard to make out much and impossible in the middle of the night to read a license plate from any distance. I ask her if she can take the matter up with an officer, but she's adamant that there's nothing the cops can do for me. Frustrated and angry, I just leave, but not before saying, "If I turn up dead, remember this."

That night I park my car in an out-of-the-way spot and hide out among some peach trees on the farm that's situated across the lane from my house. Like clockwork, the car arrives around 3:30 a.m., then turns around and drives away. Once again, I get nothing, even though I'm outside and closer to the vehicle. I just can't make out anything on the license plate, and I can't even see the make of the vehicle.

I return to the police station and explain to a clerk that I'd tried but had been unable to see anything worth reporting. Impatient with me, she says, "So, there's still nothing we can do for you."

The end of the month is approaching, so I have to get to work to make some money. I lock up my house and head out of town to one of the busier clubs in the Toronto area.

After returning home a few days later, I spend the next few months trying to get to the bottom of those nocturnal visits. I cover the face of my iPhone and turn the camera on to make a video clip of the vehicle, but when I review it I can see nothing but the headlights.

Eventually, Zijad calls and tells me *he's* going to court for a "pretrial hearing."

"You mean *us*?" I reply.

He advises me that my attendance isn't necessary, but that I can come if I want to.

Determined to show my interest in being as "hands on" as possible and on top of all aspects of the case, I dress up as nicely as I can, fully expecting to see the Judge. But upon my arrival, Zijad instructs me to just sit at a bench outside the courtroom doors. As I wait for Zijad to return, Paul's lawyer exits the courtroom first.

Finally, Zijad emerges from the courtroom looking like James Bond in a dark, tailored suit and with briefcase in hand, his hair slicked back.
A light breeze, caused by his brisk gait, moves his jacket gently, as if he were facing a fan. I rush over and he tells me with a confident grin that they have nothing on me and there's no way we can lose the case. None of this is news to me because I've been saying all this from day one. True, I've had some reservations about Zijad's strategy in the past, but in light of what he's saying now,

I'm feeling much better about things, and about him. On the other hand if looks could kill, you'd think Clark Peddle just committed murder.

We walk to our cars and I follow Zijad back to his office.

Zijad and I enter his office, and I catch him up on what's been going on. I suggest to him that Chris might be behind the mysterious nighttime events that have been freaking me out. He expresses skepticism and asks me why Chris would do that. I respond by saying, "I can't think of anyone else who'd be interested in scaring me that way." Zijad tells me he's going to talk to a police friend and get him to look into it. I tell him when the visitations usually happen, and suggest that if his police friend could come a little earlier and wait for them, he might be able to catch them red-handed.
Zijad asks me if I have a will, and I tell him I don't. He seems surprised, but I tell him I'm not concerned about that right now because, using a Jamaican expression, I don't have "a chick or child." Zijad goes on and on about it, but drawing up a will is the least of my problems. I leave my lawyer's office feeling better. *Finally someone's listening to me!*

That night I hide my car and wait outside hoping for Zijad's police friend to show up, but he fails to appear. The mysterious car comes and goes once again. In the weeks to come, I call Zijad repeatedly and ask him when his friend will be coming, but he always puts me off and admits that he hasn't yet gotten a hold of him.

I decide to ask for help from some of my neighbors. Without getting into the details of my situation I tell them about my concerns regarding the nightly visits to our quiet little corner of the world. My neighbors offer to let me do stakeouts in their cars if that will help me get a better look, and I accept their offers.

Later that night I'm able to observe two people in the stalker car, but I can't view the plates. The following night I run an extension cord across the lane to power my mobile phone, which I use to record the events of the night. But, as always, the recording provides a very unclear view of the vehicle and its license plate.

I keep calling my lawyer to ask him about his cop friend. Each time I call, he insists that he's been unable to reach the guy. But he always uses the occasion of my calls to ask me where I'm currently working. I like to give him the names of two clubs where I'm *not* working. Past experience indicates that when I tell him where I'm really working I often find myself kicked out of the club in short order. Maybe it's coincidence, but given Zijad's association with Chris and the long reach of Chris' influence in southern Ontario, maybe it's not.

Eventually, I decide that I need to feel out Zijad on a few matters and we arrange a face to face meeting. I complain again about the fact that he hasn't made good on his promise to enlist the help of his cop friend. I stress that the late-night stalking is taking a huge toll on me. I'm sleeping during the day and keeping an eye out for this fucking car at night. I tell him, "On top of all this, I can't understand why I'm not being allowed to return to the Sundowner. I need money desperately, man."

Zijad offers to talk to Chris on my behalf, but I decline the offer, telling him that there's nothing he can do to help me with my situation at the Downer. I ask him if I can sue Paul's lawyer for talking to Chris about me, because I'm convinced that someone did. My question is calculated: I want Zijad to know that I suspect there's a connection between my problems at the club and the lawsuit I'm fighting. And I want to see his reaction, because it's really him I suspect, not Paul's lawyer. He tells me I can't sue Peddle because he isn't representing me, and he can speak to anyone he wants to about the case. Then he says that, in his opinion, whatever hostility Chris feels towards me is all about my recording habits and has nothing to do with my legal troubles.

I point out that if Chris has issues with my recording his bouncers trying to extort me or any of the others girls, then he can solve that problem easily by banning cell phone use on the floor at work – it's that simple. My lawyer nods in agreement and he suggests we get back to the matter at hand – preparing for the trial.

I ask Zijad whether I should ask some of the girls to testify that Paul had threatened to kill them if they breathed a word about his claims to have slept with me. He tells me that, in his opinion, such testimony wouldn't be helpful to our case. Then I ask him about hiring a private detective so we can obtain the names of all the girls he was involved with during the period in question. Again, he shoots down the idea, insisting that our defense is straightforward and that we have little to worry about.

As we leave his office and he walks me to my car, he reassures me he'll get in touch with his police friend. He asks me if I'm going to work this week. I tell him I'm still looking for the right club, but yes, I owe him some money and I need to work. He asks me again where I might be working and I repeat that I'm just not sure yet.

I'm doing the best I can to keep my head above water. I've approached a brokerage company to refinance my house and secure a loan so that I can pay Revenue Canada and other creditors. I view my desperate financial situation as temporary, something that will soon be behind me. I have total faith in the judicial system to put an end to this nightmare I'm going through. It's just a matter of time before the case will be over and I'll be able to return to making some real money.

I used to love my home – it was my refuge, a source of peace and relaxation.
But I now associate it with anxiety and sleepless nights. I've established roughly what time the stalker vehicle comes to my home, but I'm very frustrated that I haven't been able to observe its plate number.

I decide to do a stakeout on the road that leads onto mine. That road has just one light, and I'm unable to see the license plate as I watch the vehicle proceed toward my lane. As I give up on the location, I try moving to a discrete spot on the main drag a short distance away. I pay close attention to each and every one of the small number of cars that pass by at that time of night. Eventually, I observe a car turning left off the main drag, then down the dead end street to the bridge and then over to mine. I lose sight of it for a few moments but soon see it re-emerging and heading back in my direction. When it turns back onto the main drag, it unexpectedly turns right instead of left – the direction opposite from where it originally came. I hold back for a few moments and then try to follow it down the road from a distance. But it's going very fast – it's as though the driver is actually timing something. I can't catch up. I'm already well over the speed limit and scared to go any faster.

Zijad calls again and I meet up with him. He wants to know when I can pay him. I explain that I'm not making money, and because of all the strange goings-on in the middle of the night, I'm not getting much rest. I ask him if I can recruit at least one witness to support me in court. He continues to insist I don't need one. But when I beg him to cooperate with me on this and I inform him I already have a particular friend in mind, he finally agrees to conduct an interview with her if I make all the arrangements. I call Eden and she immediately agrees to testify on my behalf and to speak to Zijad later that afternoon.

After the interview and Eden's departure, Zijad tells me that it's nice that she wants to help me, but that he really believes her testimony is unnecessary. He mentions in an off-handed way that she had told him that Paul had offered her money for sex. "Yeah, as I've told you, Paul's a busy guy with the girls!" We share a laugh. But I'm beginning to think that Zijad is sounding like a broken record about the other side simply not having a case.

"I know you're feeling confident, but please go along with me on letting her testify. I'll feel stronger going into court knowing that she'll be speaking on my behalf." Zijad gives me a fist bump.

I tell Zijad about my plan to hide at the auto-body shop on the main drag near my house to see where the "stalker car" will go if it shows up again that night. I want to see if it'll head off towards Niagara-on-the-Lake or towards Niagara Falls. "I hate to ask you again," I tell him. "But can you please try to reach your cop friend again and ask him to help me?" He hugs me and apologizes for his lack of diligence. He reassures me he will.

My troubles are accumulating, and I'm beginning to feel overwhelmed. My livelihood has been badly compromised; Revenue Canada is putting unrelenting pressure on me; I'm terrified by the nighttime visits of the stalker car; and I'm increasingly anxious about my upcoming date in court. The stress is taking its toll on me, physically, emotionally and psychologically. To make matters worse, it's becoming clear that I may never be able to return to work at the Downer. Whenever I call the manager, I'm told he's not there. But if I follow up the call with a text message to one of my friends at the club, I'm often told that the manager is sitting right there in his office. I decide that he's simply avoiding me.

One of my friends calls and tells me about a new meeting held the previous night. It was all about the dancers' cell phone use in the bar. From now on, if you're caught using your phone anywhere in the club, you can be fined an outrageous penalty. My friend is very upset about this because she has children and she needs to be able to check up on them.

I put down the phone, a feeling of nausea suddenly erupting in me. My mind is in overdrive as I recall my exchanges over the last year with my lawyer. *Can it be that he's reporting everything I'm saying to him to Chris? Why this sudden ban on cell-phones? Could it be that what I told Zijad in confidence about the iPhone recordings I'd made was the inspiration for this new policy? Is he telling Chris everything about me, about my legal problems? I recall him coming over and shaking my hand in the club on that one occasion, even though I'd told him to never acknowledge me there. Yet that's exactly what he'd done, and he'd done it in Chris's presence. Had he deliberately fingered me to Chris?* I analyze that and other flashbacks, over and over again.

That week I accept an invitation to stay with a friend, but I reveal nothing about what I'm going through. I'd like to remain there indefinitely but I know I can't overstay my welcome, so I return home after a few days. I've caught up on my sleep and I'm now able to think more clearly about my situation.

I'm more and more certain that Zijad is somehow behind at least some of my troubles. When he calls me to his office, I decide to secretly record our conversation. He tells me he wants to prepare me for what he expects will be aggressive questioning from Paul's lawyer.

He counsels me to only answer the questions that are directly posed to me and not say anything else. I suggest that maybe I should also try to get my side of the story across to the judge whenever the opportunity arises. In fact, I want to go on record about everything, including the stalking. But Zijad firmly rejects the idea, saying this will only muck up the case. When he asks me where I'm going to work that day, I just say "maybe London"

– because I know I won't really be going there. *The less this guy knows about my personal business, the better.* I'd fire him on the spot if I could, but I have no money to retain another lawyer. But as always, by the end of our conversation, no matter what my intuition might be, he always manages to draw me back in … to believe in him. So much so, I never even bother to listen to the recordings of our conversations, because I believe he's on my side.

Later that night I come up with a plan to learn more about the stalker vehicle. To get onto my dead-end lane, you need to cross a small bridge and only one car can do that at a time. I'm going to wait till the car enters the lane and then I'll drive down from the main road and block the bridge with my car on the other side. Then, I'll run as far away as I can into the adjacent vineyard and call the cops.

I go to the top of the main public road, Lakeshore Road, and wait in the parking lot of an auto body repair shop. A little before 3:30 a.m., a vehicle, coming from the west, turns off Lakeshore Road and onto the road leading to the bridge. It stops abruptly about half way down the road, about fifty meters away from the bridge. *This is unusual, they've never stopped like that before. Also, it's a black SUV, not a car I'm used to seeing.* The interior light comes on, and I puzzle over what the occupants might be doing. *Are they looking at a map for directions – or possibly readying a weapon?*

The interior lights go off and the SUV drives forward, turning onto my lane.
I'm shaking and I make a sudden decision to change my plan. I move my car a short distance to hide beside a

long rig that's also parked at the second auto-body shop on Lakeshore Road.

My new plan is to wait for them and see what direction they'll take, so that I can pass that information along to the cops. A few minutes later, I notice the SUV passing by me on Lakeshore Road. Suddenly its brake lights go on as it veers onto the shoulder of the road just ahead of me. I'm literally cowering behind my dashboard as I watch the SUV make a u-turn and then pass by me again. I sit upright in my car seat. *I don't like this!*

I pull out and turn around, believing that the SUV is gone. But suddenly, I see that it's actually been parked right behind me, concealed by a fence! *Oh my God, I'm pulling away just in time!* The SUV then makes a turn and follows behind me on Lakeshore Road. A VW bug is immediately at my rear. The SUV passes the bug and then starts to gain on me.

I'm now driving faster than I ever have in my life. The SUV is trying to overtake me, but I keep increasing my speed. I'm hoping desperately that a cop will appear and come to my assistance. The SUV continues to chase me right up to a canal lock, but then, suddenly, it disappears.

I speed like a crazy person across Niagara-on-the-Lake to St. Catharines and then onto the highway to Niagara Falls. I rush into the Niagara Falls police station and tell the clerk at the front desk about what's just happened. An officer listens to my story and takes a statement. I'm still shaking as I return home to get some sleep.

Later in the morning, having failed to get a wink of sleep, I go to the auto body shop where the dramatic events of a few hours earlier had occurred and I ask the proprietor if he has a video camera monitoring his property. He nods a yes, but my joy is immediately deflated as he tells me that it's not currently operating. I head over to the second auto body shop and ask if they have a video camera and they say no.

The police officer I'd spoken to in Niagara Falls said he'd check things out that night. I'm staked out, waiting for both him and the stalker vehicle to show up. To my relief, the officer arrives first and parks discretely. Minutes later, a car turns onto my lane. With his lights flashing, the officer stops it and questions the driver and a passenger – a white guy and blonde woman. On foot, I approach the scene, attempting to overhear the exchange. The intruders are telling the cop that they're just delivering papers. Moments later, without even inspecting their vehicle or asking for identification, he accepts the explanation at face value and lets them go.

Later, the officer asks me if I might have over-reacted and mistaken these people for someone else, someone with clearly sinister intentions.

"I don't know if it's them, but I know for sure what I just went through! And I've been going through this shit for months. That was no innocent paper delivery guy chasing me last night. The real paper delivery guy doesn't even show up until after dawn."

The officer nods and says: "Okay. If I were you, I'd go home and get some sleep. There's nothing more that can be done now, but don't hesitate to call us if you feel threatened again."

I head out of town to make some money.

Returning a few days later, it's about 4:30 in the morning as I near my house. I'm turning off Lakeshore Road onto the dead end stretch that leads to the bridge and my lane. I proceed cautiously and swing over to the far right to be able to see beyond the thick bush on the left-hand side of the road. I can't see very well at all but I notice a car parked not far from the bridge that crosses over to my lane. I stop and call the cops. They arrive a short time later and then question a couple of people who are soon allowed to go their own way. The cops tell me the couple said they were just waiting to see the sun rise over Lake Ontario.

I ask the officer: "Was it a blonde woman and a white guy?"

"Yes," he replies.

"They've been on this lane before several times and were questioned by another officer," I inform him. "They claimed to be delivering papers. I didn't believe that story then and I don't believe them now."

"Well, I can't very well arrest them for waiting for the sun to come up." "Officer, does this really make any sense to you? These same people have said in the past that they're here to deliver papers. Now, they're claiming to be here to see the sun rise, even though it's been raining and overcast for days! What kind of a sunrise are they expecting to see under these conditions? Why would you so easily accept such a story?"

"I'm sorry, ma'me, but I had no good reason to hold them."

I shake my head and wish the officer a good day. *Useless! These Niagara cops are only good for one thing – issuing traffic tickets.*

I'm getting lots of tickets because I'm spending more time in my car, and a black girl in a BMW is an automatic stop for lots of cops.

I go home just as morning is breaking. A neighbor a few doors down calls out a "good morning" to me. She tells me that another neighbor, during a late-night trip to the bathroom, had observed two men standing outside her house smoking. It had been around four in the morning.

A few days later a couple of detectives call on me. They interview me, but what is most interesting is their questions about Chris Rudan. The way they're coming at me, I feel inclined to trust them, but when they want to interview me on camera, I decline. As if to rub salt in my wounds, one of them then says: "Well then, all we can tell you is – have a good escape plan."

A fucking escape plan! They know I'm in danger, and cheap advice is all they're offering me!

I meet with Zijad and bring him up to date. Then I ask him, again, if he's spoken with his police friend. Somewhat defensively, he replies that he can't ask him to sit and watch my house all night. I tell him I'm not expecting any such thing. I can let him know the approximate time they're likely to come around.

He points out that the police think that I'm just all worked up over paper delivery guys. I don't know whether to laugh or cry. “The problem with that idea is I’ve lived there for over ten years. I know all about the comings and goings of the paper guy by now – and this has nothing to do with that. And why would a paper delivery guy chase me down Lakeshore Road?”

He abruptly changes the subject by saying we have to prepare for court. I ask him what I should wear, and he suggests a modest, conservative dress. He goes over a few details of the case with me and asks me to confirm that I’d driven Paul around approximately twenty times.

“I don’t think it was that much, but ok, as you say, it’s in the ballpark.”

I ask him if the pre-trial discovery info will be submitted, and he says that the judge will certainly be considering those transcripts in his deliberations.

“Are we going to call Eden as a witness?” I ask. He shakes his head and again tells me that it won’t be necessary.

I can’t believe my ears. “Come on,” I shout out, “you’ve got to be kidding me! I need someone on my side. Paul Dagenais is making truly outrageous accusations against me. I want the judge to get a glimpse of this guy’s dark side. Eden can give him that. I’m sorry, Zijad, but I disagree with you on this. I’ll contact her to see if she’s available.” Somewhat sullenly, he nods his head.

In the lead-up to my day in court, I’m spending every night trying to get the low-down on the stalker vehicle. There’s a new development. They’re now turning their headlights off as they make their way down my lane. Of course, I still can’t make out the license plate numbers.

The day before court I'm running on no sleep. In spite of Zijad's advice, all I want to do is tell the judge everything I've been going through. I'm more and more convinced that the stalking is connected in some way to my case.

As I'm getting ready to go to court on Friday morning, I get a phone call saying that my case has been "put back." *Shit, that's the third time this has happened.* I have to endure another weekend of intimidation before I can have my day in court. That weekend I'm on the lookout every night but nothing much happens. The stalker vehicle is nowhere to be seen.

I'm behind on my bills and I ask my mortgage company to wait, plus I need them to address my original complaints that no one wants to address. I explain that I have a big case before the courts. I assure them that as soon as it's over I'll be able to get back to work and catch up on all my overdue payments. A lot is riding on the court's decision. All too much… It's the morning of my court date, and I meet my lawyer at the courthouse. He advises me to keep my emotions under wraps as much as I can, and reminds me of some of the issues likely to be raised by Paul's lawyer. He warns me that the most potentially damaging thing about our case concerns the records of my numerous phone calls to Paul.

"But he was always asking me to call him," I remind Zijad. "He couldn't call me because I didn't want him to have my number. I don't think there was a single time when I said goodbye to him that he didn't say 'call me back'."

Zijad says he understands that perfectly well and that the pre-trial documents also establish that very well. The judge isn't stupid, he points out. If Paul really didn't want to talk to me, he wouldn't have been answering all those calls for six or seven months. It stands to reason that he would have called the police and complained about harassment if my calls weren't welcome, but he didn't.

"Zijad, please, please, highlight all of that to the judge, as well as the fact that cell phones often lose their signals in the Niagara region, so callbacks are common."

He nods his agreement.

I can hardly keep my eyes open. I'm seeing "rain drops" even though it isn't raining. But my eyes begin to clear as I enter the courtroom. An adrenalin surge suddenly energizes me.

Just before the proceedings begin, I whisper one last instruction to my lawyer: "Please talk about my house mortgage and Paul's other girls so the judge realizes that Paul's money hasn't paid my bills."

We're instructed to rise as the judge makes his entrance.

Monday, August 29, 2011

MR. PEDDLE [for the Plaintiff]**:** I would like to call my first witness Your Honor, the plaintiff, Paul Dagenais.

PAUL DAGENAIS: SWORN

EXAMINATION IN-CHIEF BY MR. PEDDLE:

Q. So Paul. How old are you?

A. Sixty-one.

Q. Okay, and where did you work during your lifetime?

A. I worked at the Robin Hood, I worked at the Inco; I worked 30 years for the St. Lawrence Seaway.

Q. And where did you live all this time?

A. 125 Johnson Street.

Q. And who did you live there with?

A. My mother, had everybody. Brothers, I had four brothers and five sisters.

Q. But today do you live there with anybody?

A. No.

Q. How long have you been in the house alone?

A. Oh, since three years old.

Q. No, how long have you been in the house yourself, just you?

A. Forever.

Q. Okay. But how long have you been there without anyone else living with you?

A. Oh - oh maybe five years now.

Q. And have you ever had a girlfriend, Paul?

A. I had a few. I took them out and that was it, eh.

Q. You ever been married?

A. Never.

Q. And have you seen any girlfriends in the last 10 years?

A. Yeah, I got one in Alberta and uh, she moved away and what do you call it...

Q. How would you describe your financial life?

A. It's not too good now.

Q. Okay but - okay, let's say prior to 2008?

A. 2008? It wasn't bad.

Q. Are you a big spender?

A. Never.

Q. Okay, what ...

A. I only spend what I - how you call it, what I need to use eh?

Q. What did you do with the money from your jobs? When you got paid from work, what did you do with your money?

A. Bank it. I paid board and I banked the rest.

Q. And what kind of a vehicle did you drive?

A. Hyundais, always Hyundais - old ones, new ones. Well they were all new but, how you call it - I kept on trading them in, eh; they'd get higher up, eh.

Q. Have you spent any money on your house?

A. Just the vinyl. Well the insurance paid for that, sorry.

Q. And how's your health?

A. Fine.

Q. Okay, did you have any medical problems a couple of years ago?

A. Oh, just a stroke, that's it.

Q. Just a stroke?

A. Pardon?

Q. Okay. How long were you in the hospital when you had your stroke?

A. Six months.

Q. And when did you meet Ms. Vassel?

A. In February, 09.

Q. And where did you meet her?

A. Sundowner.

Q. And what were you doing at the Sundowner?

A. Oh, just talk, mostly.

Q. Okay, and when you went there, how much money would you spend?

A. Two-fifty.

Q. And how many times a week would you go?

A. About twice a week, sometimes.

THE COURT: Sorry, how much did he spend - is it two - fifty? Is that right?

MR. PEDDLE: Two-fifty I think he said Your Honour.

THE COURT: Okay. Is that $250? Is that correct?

A. Yeah.

THE COURT: Okay.

A. Yes Your Honour.

MR. PEDDLE:

Q. Okay, when you were at the Sundowner, did you get lap dances from Ms. Vassel? You have to say yes or no.

A. Never, never.

Q. You never had a lap dance from her?

A. Never.

Q. But would you sit and talk to her?

A. Yeah, I would.

Q. And did you pay her for that?

A. Always - it seems the way they do it, its $20 a dance eh? Not a dance, but $20 after every song. But I never spent too much money with her; I used to go around, eh.

Q. Okay, so you would go to various different people is that what you're saying?

A. Yeah. Yes.

Q. Okay. Now describe your relationship with Ms. Vassel.

A. Well, I didn't like it when she was using me for my money.

Q. Okay, but just describe your relationship. Like...

A. Oh, she was all right.

Q. But I take it that it turned into more than just seeing her at the strip club?

A. No nothing more, just to talk, that's all.

Q. Right, but did you ever see her outside of the strip club?

A. Well she used to come over to my house.

Q. Okay.

A. ... all the time. I didn't expect that.

Q. When did she start coming to your house?

A. About a week after I seen her in February.

Q. And would she call you at your house?

A. Sometimes, but she would mostly come over on her own.

Q. Okay, and when she came over, what happened?

A. Oh, not much I'll tell you. Fooled around a little bit but never - you know, not really sex or anything like that eh? Just fooling around.

Q. Well were you boyfriend and girlfriend or ...?

A. No.

Q. And what - where would she park when she came to visit you?

A. Right on - right on the side of the road, on Elizabeth Street. You don't know it but it was - she never came in my driveway, she used to park in front of my - the next door neighbor's lot, you know, road. She never came in.

Q. Did you ask her why she never parked in your driveway?

A. Yeah, I told her - why don't you bring the car in the driveway? No, I don't want to. So I said, well leave it where you want.

Q. Did you ever have any dates with Ms. Vassel?

A. No dates.

Q. Did you ever pay her to go out with you anywhere?

A. No.

Q. Did Ms. Vassel ever promise you anything?

A. Yes. Should I tell you?

Q. Go ahead and tell the judge.

A. Well I loaned her - what was it - I loaned her money for her mother's funeral. I loaned her money for her father's funeral. I loaned her money to get the transmission fixed in her car. I loaned her money for her rent; she said she didn't have enough money to pay her rent so I paid that off, loaned it to her. And then she was going to make a movie in Toronto and I paid her - loaned her that money. She was going to get a Visa car - Visa, to get her citizenship to Canada, or they would have to deport her back to Jamaica, so I loaned her for that. And what else now. Oh yeah, her father borrowed $7,000 and that amount, so I loaned her that, to get her father out of you - you know, the - out of the jam he put himself in.

Q. Who was this jam with?

A. The bikers. She borrowed – he borrowed the money from the bikers and the bikers – she had to pay it back, so I loaned her the money to pay it back and they would ask for the percentage over the top of the money I loaned her. So, I had to pay the percentage. She would never make the phone call in the house. She said, I'm going to go to a telephone booth. She probably called them up on her cell phone, but I didn't know that eh, really. So if she went to the telephone booth it's two blocks, three blocks away from my house and she'd be back in a minute to tell me – strange.

Q. So, how did you go about the actual loaning of the money? I assume you...

A. Oh yeah, I ...

Q. Just wait until I finish the question.

A. Okay.

Q. I assume you didn't keep cash in your house?

A. No.

Q. So, what would you do?

A. I would go to the bank. She took me to three trust bank in – how you call it – in St Catharine's, which I never knew there was a branch out there. All I did was go to my bank in Port Colborne, the trust. She knew where they were, all of them. I never went there in my life, to them banks.

Q. And how did you get to the banks?

A. She drove my car.

Q. Did she ever drive her own car?

A. Never.

Q. Okay, and when you got to the bank, what would happen?

A. She would say, don't tell anybody my name, and I went into the bank and get the money and I said this is a loan. There's her – okay. So I gave her the money. Then she would go to another bank because you had to have two days, you know, to give them, clearance, to get the money. So I went to three banks and I took out $2,000 or $ $3,000 in every bank. And I said, don't forget, this is a loan. Here's here – oh, I'll pay you back, don't worry about it. Don't worry.

Q. And between July of 09 and January of 2010, how many times would you have gone to the banks and one this?

A. Can you repeat that please?

Q. Between July of 09 and January of 2010, how many times would she have driven you to the banks?

A. Oh, maybe 20 times.

Q. And would this happen – or how often a week would it happen?

A. Sometimes twice a week. Sometimes – well every time she'd come down, she needed money, she was crying for something, eh?

Q. I'm going to ask you to pick the exhibit book you have in front of you there.

A. Yeah.

Q. And just look at Tab 1, peel over the number one.

A. I've got it.

Q. And can you identify that to the court?

A. I have to get my glasses. Those are all the loans I made her.

Q. Well, can you identify what this is? Whose bank account this is?

A. That's mine.

Q. Okay.

A. My bank account.

Q. All right, and Tab Number 2, if you flip over, it's a Canada Trust account.

A. That's mine too.

Q. Okay. And Tab Number 3, that's a second Canada Trust account?

A. That's all mine.

Q. And Tab number 4. Are you sure you're at number 4 Paul?

A. Yes.

Q. This is a summary I think you and your sister prepared, is it not?

A. That's Desjardins. That's all mine.

Q. Okay, are you sure you are at Tab number 4?

A. Yeah, that's Tab 4.

Q. I'll just check with you to make sure. Okay. Just want to make sure we're on the same page. Okay, now can you tell the court what this is?

A. That's accounts from my Caisse Populaire, but now they call them Desjardins.

Q. All right, and it also has your Canada Trust on there as well?

A. Yeah, Canada Trust too.

Q. Now, did you and your sister prepare this?

A. Yes.

Q. Okay, And why did you prepare this?

A. Well, for the court.

Q. And what are you trying to show the court here?

A. That all the money lent off me, borrowed, loaned.

Q. And what's the total on page two? Not Tab 2, just flip the one page.

A. Oh. Yeah, that's $132,845.

Q. Okay.

A. That's the amount.

Q. Okay, can you flip to the next Tab now, Tab number 5? In here is a list here of one, two, three, four, five, six seven, eight, nine different TD. branches.

A. MmmHmm. She went to the one in Port Colborne, that's the one on Clarence Street. She went to the one in St. – three in St. Catharines. And Niagara Falls, Oh yeah, St. Catharine, St. Catharine, and even Welland she went to.

Q. So, are these the branches you went to?

A. Yeah. Yes sir.

Q. And did you normally bank at any of these branches?

A. I only bank on the one in Canada Trust on Clarence Street in Port Colborne.

Q. Okay.

A. And Desjardins is in Port Colborne too on Killaly.

Q. Now, between the period of July 09 and January 2010, did you make any big purchases personally, yourself?

A. No, not really.

Q. Did you take any trips?

A. Trips?

Q. Take any vacations?

A. No. she promised me to take me to Jamaica, but we never did go. She was supposed to move into my house, she never did it.

Q. So you made no purchases during that timeframe?

A. No.

Q. You have to say yes or no.

A. No.

Q. Paul, if I can get you to turn to Tab 9. Your Honour, that document didn't come out very well in the photocopy, so I'm just going to show you the original. How Paul ...

A. Yes sir.

Q. ... did you ever discuss with Ms. Vassel repayment of the loans?

A. Yes I did.

Q. And when did you have those discussions?

A. At my house. I even took a Holy Bible out of my room, the Statue, and gave it to her and asked her if she was going to pay back the loan. She said yes, you'll get everything back, and she was holding her hand on the statue.

Q. What is the statue Paul?

A. Pardon?

Q. What is it? What is the statue?

A. The Lord, the Holy Lord. It's about this high.

Q. Are you a religious man Paul?

A. Yes, I am.

Q. And this document that you've just looked at here, dated January 4th, 2010, can you tell what that is?

A. The 24th?

Q. At Tab Number 9 Paul.

A. Yeah, I got it. The first page or what?

Q. There is only one page I think.

A. Oh. Yeah.

Q. Do you have it there?

THE COURT: He is not on Tab number 9.

A. There's two pages.

MR. PEDDLE:

Q. No, no, Tab 9 flips the other way. Sorry my friend. You go to a Tab and you flip it that way.

A. Oh yeah, thank you.

Q. Okay, you're welcome. And can you tell his Honour what that document represents?

A. Yeah, that's was – I wrote this out on top. It was $151,000 regarding that. I did this before she even came to the house. I wrote that down – Paul Dagenais – I will pay back $151,000 to Paul Dagenais. And she wrote her name – it's got her name, but she crossed it all out.

Q. I see three ...

A. Yeah, three ...

Q. ... things there.

A. ... tries and she crossed them all out.

Q. Well why did she crossed them out?

A. I don't know.

Q. Well did you ask her?

A. She didn't want to see it. She didn't want me to see what was underneath it. You know what I mean; like I went to the washroom, everything was clear with her name on it and then I went to the washroom and she crossed everything out with the ink – with the pen.

Q. After January 4th, did you see or speak to Ms Vassel again?

A. January 4th? Well I got the police down there at the Sundowner.

Q. Okay, let's talk about that for a second. After January 4th, what did you do then to collect your money, if anything?

A. What year?

Q. Sorry, take your hand away from your face, I can't quite hear you.

A. Okay, what year?

Q. In January of 2010, just after this note was prepared.

A. Oh yeah. Well she sent a cheque that she got from the movies for $120,000 – she said if I could give her $5,000 of the money, she would use the rest for a loan, you know, to pay me back some of the loan. So, she took the cheque and she said, I've got to go to California to get the employer to sign the cheque. So, she was gone for about three days and she came back over. She always wanted money, that was her main objective.

Q. Did she bring back any of the money from California to pay you?

A. Never, nothing.

Q. Now you mentioned a few minutes ago something about the police.

A. Yes I – she was harassing me on the phone all the time, coming [sic] me up about five or six times about every two minutes, so I got – me and my sister went down to a lawyer's office and the lawyer told me to call the policeman and I sent him down to the

Sundowner. I told him where it was and everything. And the man said that was her false name and everything, you know.

Q. Well up until then, what did you think her name was?

A. Linda Lee. That's what we called her from. I never knew her name. I didn't even look at her driver's license to see; I never asked about that. If I would have knew from her driver's license. But the policeman found out, eh.

Q. Okay, and did you mention the money to the policeman?

A. Yes.

Q. And what did he say to you in response?

A. He said – how you call it? He says, I wouldn't loan her nothing, she's a scam – you know what I mean? A scam. Just to rip people off.

Q. Okay.

A. And he said that she went to Buffalo, the policeman said, and she wanted to break up a man and a woman.

Q. Okay, let's not get sidetracked Paul.

A. All right, all right.

Q. Let's just stay focused. Did the police charge her, to your knowledge?

A. They didn't charge her, but they give her a warning not to harass Paul any more.

Q. Did you receive a call from Ms. Vassel after that?

A. I received it first. She said, did you call police; and I told her no, at first. And she called me back and she said, you did call the police. Yeah, I did.

Q. And did she say anything about the money in the conversation?

A. Yeah, she said, I'm not going to pay you back no money. That's it, no loan, no money.

MR. PEDDLE: Your Honour, those are all my questions.

THE COURT: Thank you. Just hold on for a second please.

MR. SASKIN: Of course Your Honour.

THE COURT: Okay.

MR. SASKIN: Thank you Your Honour.

CROSS – EXAMINATION BY MR. SASKIN:

Q. Mr. Dagenais, you currently live alone, is that right.

A. Yes.

Q. Yes, and that's at your house in Port Colborne?

A. Yes.

Q. And you own that house?

A. Yes.

Q. And you said you live alone there, how long?

A. Since my mother went to the old age home. Five years.

Q. Never been married?

A. Never.

Q. You have no kids?

A. No kids.

Q. And your sister is the closest family you have?

A. Closest? I've got brothers and sisters ...

Q. Brothers and sisters, no kids, right?

A. Yeah.

Q. No wife. And you didn't work anywhere right now?

A. No, I'm retired since 2004.

Q. So you've been retired for about seven years now, eight years?

A. About seven.

Q. And you get a pension every month?

A. Yeah.

Q. And that's about $2,000 in total?

A. $2,000?

Q. How much is your pension every month?

A. About $1,821.

Q. Okay.

THE COURT: Sorry, what was that; $1,821 you said?

MR. PEDDLE: Yes Your Honour.

MR. SASKIN: Yes, $1,821.

THE COURT: Yes, okay.

MR. SASKIN

Q. And you have no other sources of income?

A. No.

Q. Is there a mortgage on your house?

A. No.

Q. If you could put a number on your monthly expenses, how much does it cost you to live? So, between your let's say property tax, food, car insurance, medicine, water, hydro; how much do you pay every month?

A. About $700.

Q. So between your pension of $1,821 and $700 in your expenses, you have about $1,100 of disposable income?

A. Yeah.

Q. Is that right, okay.

A. But for groceries too, about $200. I've got to eat.

Q. Of course, so is that including in the $700 you told me, per month.

A. No.

Q. So $700 plus $200?

A. That's right.

Q. So you have just under $1,000 to live every month?

A. Yes.

Q. Okay. Now, I understand you had some health issues in the past few years?

A. Yes.

Q. You had a stroke in 2008?

A. 2007.

Q. 2007 it was?

A. Yeah.

Q. All-right, and you spent some time in the hospital as a result of that – six months?

COURT REPORTER: Your answer.

A. Yes.

COURT REPORTER: Thank you.

A. Sorry.

COURT REPORTER: That's okay.

MR. SASKIN:

Q. Tell me in your own words, how has your stroke affected your life?

A. Well I got a bad arm. Well my hand eh? But the rest of it's all right.

Q. Other than that you're fine?

A. Yeah, but I could still use the hand eh, to use stuff.

Q. Now, you're familiar with a gentleman's club called Sundowner, right?

A. Yes.

Q. And you've been there before?

A. I've been in there.

Q. Okay and you would go there to watch women dance?

A. That's it.

Q. And that's where you met Angela?

A. Yes.

Q. And you've never met her before you went to the Sundowner, is that right?

A. Oh I met her before – well, yeah. No I didn't, I didn't see her before the Sundowner, yeah.

Q. And you would buy Angela drinks when you were in the Sundowner?

A. I bought her some drinks. But I used to drink water because I'm – three years I've been in alcoholics and I go every month, about ever two months eh, and I never drank for three – since 08 till now. August 8th till now.

Q. So when you were at the Sundowner, you would buy Angela drinks and you would buy other girls drinks too, is that right.

A. No.

Q. No, so you would only buy Angela drinks?

A. Well, she wanted a drink, so I bought it for her.

Q. And none of the other girls asked you for drinks?

A. No.

Q. And you would take some of the girls to the back room to have them dance for you?

A. Back room?

Q. You would go for lap dances, is that right?

A. I don't go – there was no lap dance in the back room. We used to talk and fool around a little bit.

Q. Well, you stated you paid $20. Per dance and at times you would spend about $200 at the Sundowner?

A. Yeah.

Q. On private dances, right?

A. Well, it wasn't a dance. I told you before; after every song they charge $20. So, it wasn't lap dances; we used to sit down and talk and just fool around a little bit.

Q. Oh, I see. So you would fool around with more than one girl per visit?

A. Oh yeah.

Q. Not just Angela?

A. No.

Q. Would you fool around with Angela?

A. A little bit.

Q. Now, you say you only started going in February of 2009 to the Sundowner?

A. I was there before.

Q. You were there before.

A. Oh yeah.

Q. Okay. So I'm going to suggest to you that you started going well before 2009.

A. Oh yeah.

Q. Oh yeah, okay. Now, I'm going to suggest to you that you met Angela about six years ago at the Sundowner.

A. Six years?

Q. Does that sound accurate?

A. I don't even know if she was dancing in six years.

Q. Okay, and you said you would go two to three times per week?

A. Oh, sometimes once a week, sometimes maybe I never go for a month.

Q. Oh, I see. Now, you would usually drive to the Sundowner?

A. Yes.

Q. Okay. But, I understand you lost your driver's license in August of 2008.

A. Yeah.

Q. Okay.

A. She was driving then.

Q. She was driving then, okay. So when would you drive to the Sundowner?

A. Sometimes take a taxi cab ...

Q. No, my question was, when would you personally drive to the Sundowner?

A. When I had my license.

Q. Okay, but you lost your license in August of 2008.

A. Yeah.

Q. And did you get your license back?

A. No.

Q. No, Okay.

A. I'm still waiting for them.

Q. And that was for impaired, is that correct?

A. Impaired?

Q. Okay,

A. Impaired what?

Q. Impaired driving. You were pulled over by the police for an impaired driving and that's why you lost your license?

A. Yeah, that's true.

Q. And just to make sure, that was in August of 2008?

A. 2008 – I don't know what time it was.

Q. Well I understand it's August...

A. I don't ...

Q. ...of 2008.

A. All right, that's good enough.

Q. Now, you still have your car, you just don't drive anymore?

A. Yeah.

Q. Okay.

A. It's in the garage.

Q. It's your evidence today that Angela would come to your house, out of the blue, and she would ask you to give her money?

A. That's right.

Q. And she knew where you lived?

A. Yes.

Q. And you never told her where you lived? Or did you tell her? How did she know where you lived?

A. Oh she could look up in the phone book just for my name; it's under my dad's name, I never changed it.

Q. I see. But, I'm going to suggest to you sir that you ask Angela to hang out with you and drive you around places and that you would pay her money, because you could no longer drive?

A. I didn't – I loaned her money; we only went to the banks, understand?

Q. Okay, well my [sic] suggest to you is that you asked Angela to hang out with you and to drive you around because you could no longer drive.

A. She only drove to the banks to get money, so I can loan her the money.

Q. Well I'm also going to suggest to you that you offer Angela between $300 and $500 to hang out with you and go on dates?

A. That's not true.

Q. Because you could no longer drive, you had trouble coming to the Sundowner, so you wanted to bring Sundowner to you?

A. No. I got my hand on that statue, I'm telling the truth.

Q. I understand that you put your hand there earlier. Now, let's get right to it. I'm going to ask you to turn to Tab number 4, which is the summary of the alleged loan you gave Angela. Now Mr. Dagenais, do you have any other bank accounts, other than what's shown here?

A. No.

Q. No, okay. Any investments?

A. I have a guaranteed investments. Guaranteed investments.

Q. Okay. Now, on July 22nd, you made cash withdrawal from your Canada Trust account for $1,200.

A. On January what?

Q. On July 22nd

A. Of what year?

Q. Of 2009. Have a look at Tab Number 4 ...

A. That was probably for ...

Q. ... you prepared this document.

A. ... her mother's funeral; for her mother's – she wanted to go to Jamaica to see her mother's funeral.

Q. Okay, so that was the $1,200?

A. Right.

Q. And you never got Angela to sign anything at that time?

A. No.

Q. And you never looked at her driver's license to make sure that you were talking to the right person ...

A. That was ...

Q. ... or what her name was?

A. ... that was her business. I didn't go through her purse to look for her driver's license.

Q. Well you are loaning somebody $1,200, sir?

A. I loaned her more than that. I loaned her $132,000, almost $151,000 to tell you the truth.

Q. Okay, well for the $1,200 that you say that that was for her to go to Jamaica for her mother's funeral?

A. And I gave her $1,800 to go see her father's death, and he was living in Toronto. And I gave her the $7,000 the man took out, her husband, was for a school kid to go to – how do you call it, for her son schooling.

Q. All right, we'll get to that.

A. All right, cool.

Q. We're going to go through these one by one. So, on July 22nd, you say that it was for a funeral and you never made Angela sign anything?

A. No.

Q. No, okay. And you thought her name was Linda Lee then?

A. Linda Lee.

Q. And she was practically a stranger to you?

A. Yes.

Q. Okay. So then on July – let me see, what was the next time you loaned her a big amount; that would have been July 31st of 2009, you say that you loaned Angela another $1,200?

A. That's true.

Q. Okay, and what was that for?

A. I don't know really, for something anyways.

Q. It must have been something, right? Okay.

(Q.) So on – let me see, when was the next time? On August the 4th, you made two withdrawals – one from one bank and then one from bank number two. And to looks like one was for $1,150 and then the other one was for $4,095. So that's a total of $5,245.

A. That's what I loaned her.

Q. Is it your evidence that Angela asked you for $ 5,245 ...

A. She asked me ...

Q. ... on that day?

A. ... for more than that.

Q. I'm talking about August 4th

A. Yeah, yeah, okay. She didn't ask me ...

Q. To the penny.

A. ... Yeah, she asked me, but I loaned it to her. She asked me about the money and I loaned it to her. She always used to ask for money all the time. I lent her $10,000 at one shot.

Q. Okay, when was that? When did you loan her $10,000?

A. When she was going to make a movie in Toronto.

Q. Okay, so show me where you took out $10,000 at one shot. What date was that?

A. Go back to the 6th.

Q. October the 6th.

A. Yeah.

Q. Okay.

A. And I paid her $10,000 to make a – get her citizenship too. That's $20,000.

Q. And at no time did Angela sign anything? At no time did you ask her to sign anything?

A. She said she would give me back my money.

Q. Yes, but my question was, she never signed anything.

A. She never signed, because I, I ...

Q. And she never – and you were never repaid the money that you loaned her initially, the first $1,200?

A. I never got nothing.

Q. And yet you continued, on each occasion, to loan Angela money?

A. She was crying all the time. She said, I'll pay you back Paul, I'll pay you back. That's all I heard out of her. Why didn't she pay something back?

Q. And you are – you are a frugal man sir; you worked all your life...

A. All my life.

Q. ... to save this money?

A. And I worked hard too.

Q. And yet somebody sheds a tear and you're spending your life saving on practically a stranger, is that what you're telling us?

A. Well she wasn't – I seen her a couple of times over there.

Q. Okay, now I'm going to ask you to turn to – in the book at Tab 1. Now let's go to an entry on September the 1st of 2009. Were you with Angela on September the 1st?

A. 2009?

Q. 2009, yes.

A. Yeah.

Q. You were with her on that day?

A. Well I don't know, I didn't know that – that's a long – we're talking three years here boy.

Q. But we're also talking about $130,000 here.

A. Yeah.

Q. So, on that day, you deposit $21,260 into your account.

A. Yeah, I got it from the – I had $40,000 in American money.

Q. Okay.

A. In the Desjardins. I took it from there and I put it back in my chequing account; $20,000 – I put some in my savings account, $20,000.

Q. So why were you cashing that in? Why were you putting that into your account?

A. Why not.

Q. You wanted to ...

A. I want it to grow.

Q. And I want it to grow?

A. Yeah.

It would grow in this account more than in another account; more than in a GIC.

MR. PEDDLE: Objection your Honour, I don't think the witness said it was in a GIC, he said it was in an American account.

THE COURT: An American account.

MR. SASKIN: Okay, I apologize.

A. Yeah, an American account, that's right.

Q. So September 2nd, were you with Angela?

A. Well I went from January of 09 to January '11 – '10.

Q. And you were with her every single day?

A. No.

Q. No. on September the 2nd, it shows that you made a withdrawal of $6,000. Were you with Angela on September the 2nd? You don't remember?

A. I couldn't tell you that.

Q. Well, if you took out $6000. And allegedly she drove you to – and allegedly she drove you to the bank, you must have been with her.

A. Yeah, I probably withdraw that and she would tell me I loaned it – she loaned it off me.

Q. So, it's your evidence that every single one of these cash withdrawals that's shown on the summaries were given – were loaned to Angela?

A. That's right.

Q. And it's your evidence that they were loaned on that specific day. That she's the one that took you to the bank?

A. All the time.

Q. On every single occasion here, on 30 some – odd occasions; including September the 2nd and September the 1st. because on your summary it states that on September 1st, you took out $5,500. So it's your evidence that on September 1st, Angela was with you, drove you to the bank and you gave her that money?

A. I didn't give it. I loaned it.

Q. You loan it, I apologize. And the same goes for September the 2nd?

A. Yeah, that's right.

Q. You took out $6,000 and you loaned it to Angela, because she was with you on that day?

A. I went to the bank and she loaned it off me.

Q. Okay, Now, I'm going to suggest to you sir that Angela wasn't with you on September the 1st or the 2nd?

A. Why?

Q. Because it was Angela's birthday on September the 1st ...

A. Oh, come on ...

Q. ... and she was not around?

A. ... what did she ever care about her birthday?

Q. Okay, I see.

MR. PEDDLE: Objection Your Honour, I think my friend is giving evidence as opposed to asking the witness a question.

THE COURT: Well, he put to him a suggestion; he can deny it or not. I assume that we will hear more about this later.

MR. SASKIN: Yes.

THE COURT: Okay.

MR. SASKIN: And just to comply with the rule in Brown & Dunn I would like to put it to the witness.

THE COURT: Yes I understand that.

MR. SASKIN

Q. Now sir, let's got to this envelope.

A. The first envelope?

Q. The envelope is at Tab 9 of your book...

THE COURT: Perhaps we should mark this as an exhibit separately.

MR. SASKIN: We can mark it as exhibit 2.

THE COURT: Exhibit 2.

EXHIBIT NUMBER 2: Envelope – produced and marked.

MR. SASKIN: Perhaps.

THE COURT: And he can see it. Just a second.

MR. SASKIN

A. Tab 9.

THE COURT: Just a second Mr. Dagenais.

A. Okay.

THE COURT: If you would give that to the witness please.

A. All right, thanks.

MR. SASKIN:

Q. Sir, this is your handwriting, correct?

A. That's my handwriting.

Q. So on January 4th, 2010, you tried to get Angela to sign this piece of paper?

A. Yes.

Q. That says, "I owe amount $151,000 to Paul Dagenais."

A. Dagenais.

Q. Dagenais, I apologize. Where does the number $151,000 come from?

A. From all her loans.

Q. Well, I understand that you claiming for $132,000.

A. I know, but that was the original one here.

Q. And it's your evidence that on January 4th, she refuses to sign this?

A. She put her name on it but she crossed it out when I went to the washroom.

Q. And she did this three times?

A. Three times. You don't know the way she works.

Q. So it's your evidence that she signed the name and then immediately thereafter crossed it out?

A. Yes.

Q. Three times.

A. Three times.

Q. So, on January 4th, it became apparent to you that Angela is not going to repay any of my money back, is that right?

A. Yes.

Q. So on January 4th, you knew there was going to be a problem?

A. Yes, that she wasn't paying anything back.

Q. Okay. Now, in your summary, and let's look at your Canada Trust account, you claim that on January 13th, 2010, you loaned Angela another $2000.

A. Canada Trust?

Q. Well let's have a look at ...

A. What Tab are you on?

Q. Let's look at Tab 4. Tab 4, second page. It says, "Account Canada Trust" all the way on the right side of the page. January 13th, 2010, the sum of $2000. So your evidence is, on January 4th, I knew that she wasn't going to pay me any money back and yet on January 13th, you take out $2,000 and loan it to Angela.

A. It must have been for something.

Q. It must have been for something else. Is that...?

A. No, no, no, I'm just saying.

Q. Well I...

A. She was always at the house crying for money, crying for money. I got sick of it, all the time, you know? She would cry tears for that money.

Q. Mr. Dagenais, I'm going to suggest to you that you never loaned any money for Angela?

A. And you're ...

Q. And I'm going to suggest to you that ...

A. I loaned her the money ...

Q. ... over the course of your relationship ...

A. ... I loaned her the money.

Q. And I'm going to suggest to you that over the course of your relationship, you paid Angela Approximately $5,000 to spend time with you?

A. I did not.

Q. To drive you around?

A. That's a lie. That's a lie.

Q. And I'm going to suggest to you that you were also spending money on other women?

A. I did, at the Sundowner; $ 200, sometimes three, a week – a month sometimes.

Q. I'm going to suggest to you that you were offering to take girls on trips?

A. No.

Q. Not just Angela but other girls as well.

A. Never. Never.

Q. I'm going to suggest to you that you paid another girls to go on trips.

A. Never. I've never been out of Port Colborne all my life.

MR. SASKIN: I have no other questions Your Honour.

THE COURT: Any re-examinations?

MR. PEDDLE: No re-examination your Honour.

THE COURT: I don't have any questions, thank you very much Mr. Dagenais.

A. Your're welcome Your Honour.

THE COURT: You can just leave the ...

A. Leave the book here?

THE COURT: That's right.

A. Okay.

WITNESS FELL WHILE EXITING THE WITNESS BOX. Every one gathered over him helping him.

MATTER ADJOURNED BRIEFLY

They called Recess.

UPON RESUMING:

MR. PEDDLE: If it pleases Your Honour, I will call my second witness.

THE COURT: Okay.

MR. PEDDLE: Denise Dagenais. She's just outside.

DENISE TAYLOR:

EXAMINATION IN CHIEF BY MR. PEDDLE :

Q. Okay, Ms. Taylor how old are you?

A. Seventy – one.

Q. Okay, and where do you live right now?

A. 53 Coronation Drive in Port Colborne.

Q. In relation to your brother's house, how far away would that be?

A. Oh, I would say about 10 minutes.

Q. Okay, and are you married?

A. I'm a widow.

Q. Do any kids live at your house with you?

A. No.

Q. And do you currently work anywhere?

A. Not presently.

Q. Are you retired?

A. I am.

Q. And where did you work before you retired?

A. I worked at the office of Davies, Ebert and Wilson, Barristers and Solicitors, where I was an estate secretary for 25 years. My husband passed away in 1994. I took a sabbatical for two years, then I went to work for West Street Medical Centre for a period of six years and then I retired.

Q. Okay. And what is your relationship to Paul.

A. He is my brother.

Q. Okay. And do you know Paul well?

A. Extremely well.

Q. Okay, can you explain your relationship with him? Do you see him every day, you see him once a month?

A. I speak with him several times a week. I take him grocery – I'm his transportation; for groceries, doctors' appointments and anything concerning driving I take him, and to visit his mother and everything, MmmHmm.

Q. Okay. Now Paul earlier testified he lived at home up until I believe your mother went into an old age home, is that accurate?

A. Paul lived with my mother all of his life. He's single. And eight – approximately eight years ago my mom came to live with me because she was ill and Paul – she was very dependent on Paul. Paul drove her wherever she wanted to go and he was loving and caring towards her, and he still is.

Q. Can you describe Paul's life?

A. Yes, Paul is – he lives a very simple life. Mainly his entertainment consists of watching programs on television; programs about – from 1950s on. He is frugal. He's – he lives – he just lives a very simple life, simple life. He – what else could I say...

Q. That's okay. When did you become aware that Ms Vassel was in Paul's life?

A. Well, Paul used to speak to – we always spoke on the telephone and Paul always – he mentioned her name, known as Linda Lee. And he would say to me that she would be coming over and as well – I became concerned – because she would frequent his residence and she mentioned – Paul mentioned to me that she was going to come and live with him and they were going to Jamaica together on a vacation. So I said, gee Paul, I said I think that I should meet this lady, you know, because he is my brother and I am concerned about him, but none of that ever transpired.

Q. When did you become aware of Paul's problems with his bank accounts?

A. Well, when – I received a phone call from my brother and he mentioned to me that he received a phone call from Canada Trust bank in St Catharines.

Q. Okay, you can't state what the bank person told him...

A. Okay.

Q. ... because that's hearsay evidence.

A. Okay.

Q. Are you saying that you became aware of it through your brother?

A. Through my brother. He telephoned me and mentioned that – and asked me if I knew that Paul was withdrawing large sum amounts of money because that was – that is not my brother.

Q. And what did you do when you became aware of this?

A. Actually. At the time, nothing.

Q. And after you did nothing, what did you do?

A. Well I became – I got involved when Paul showed me the – the statement – the note that he had written that she was to – they were loans and that he was going to be repaid. And so obviously he called me and said – Dee he said, can you come over, I have something to show you. And I did go over later on in the afternoon and he showed me the note and apparently she wasn't going to repay him. And so I said – then he showed me all his bank records. We looked everything over and I could not believe – because that was his life savings. And then we talked about, sat down for hours. Then I said, well maybe we should go and see a lawyer, which we did. And the lawyer advise us that it was a civil matter and to – you know, proceed with it.

Q. In front of you is an exhibit book, sitting right in front of you on the bench.

A. MmmHmm.

Q I'm just going to ask you to flip to Tab 1.

A. I'm just going to put my glasses on.

Q. Yes, that's fine. And before I ask you any questions, when you went to see Paul and you went through – you said his bank records, did you familiarize yourself with all these banking transactions and business?

A. I did.

Q. Okay, and at exhibit 1, there is a copy of a bank book.

A. MmmHmm.

Q. Are you familiar – can you identify that for the court?

A. Yes, I can. The first one is the Desjardins account. He only had one account there, in Port Colborne.

Q. And the second one Tab 2.

A. The second one, these are two bank accounts and these are – the second one is one bank account from Canada Trust and yes, I can verify that I've seen them and I've dealt with them.

Q. Okay, and the third one?

A. Again, that's his second bank account at Canada Trust, and Paul and I went through all of them – all the withdrawals, and I am familiar with that as well.

Q. Okay, and at Tab 4, did you prepare this summary of what purports to be the amounts that were withdrawn and loaned to Ms Vassel?

A. I did.

Q. And how could you distinguish these amounts from other withdrawals?

A. I'm sorry, I don't follow you.

Q. Well how did you and Paul come to realize that these were the amounts that had been withdrawn and given to Ms. Vassel?

A. Well, they were from his – withdrawn from his bank accounts.

Q. So you simply went through the accounts and looked at ...

A. Each individual item.

Q. And you can also identify the items he withdrew for his own personal use?

A. Yes, but they would just be very, very minute amounts. He would never withdraw a large amount of money, never.

Q. Previous to July of 09, did you see anywhere in his accounts where he had withdrawn large amounts of money?

A. Well if you wanted to call like $1,200 a large amount of money. I think that was – I think they commenced in July and then there was another $1,200 and then after that they just ...

Q. Okay, but what I'm asking you is, prior to July ...

A. Yes.

Q. ... did you look through his bank accounts – were there any large withdrawals from there?

A. No, no sir.

Q. And after January of 2010, were there any large amounts that had been withdrawn?

A. No sir.

Q. To this date?

A. No sir.

Q. At Tab 5 there is a list of some instructions here – actually it's nine branches of TD Bank, if you could turn to that.

A. MmmHmm.

Q. Did you create this sheet as well?

A. I did.

Q. And what did this reflect?

A. This reflects all the banks that Linda Lee drove my brother to, to withdraw the amounts of money.

Q. Was it common practice for Paul to use any of these institutions?

A. No. He didn't even know where they were.

Q. And at Tab 8, there is a list of some telephone calls made to Paul ...

A. Yes sir.

Q. ... from the defendant.

A. Yes sir.

Q. Did you compile this list?

A. I did.

Q. And is it a complete list?

A. Some of the – some of the telephone calls were missing ...

THE COURT: Sorry, which Tab, sorry?

MR. PEDDLE: We're at Tab 8 Your Honour.

THE COURT: Tab 8, sorry.

MR. PEDDLE:

Q. Sorry, what were you saying?

A. Some of the telephone calls were missing and then...

Q. Is that what you're showing in Tab 7, the missing dates?

A. Um. Yes they are.

Q. So these were the records you had not been provided with in terms of Ms Vassel's phone records, is that accurate?

A. There was – yes, yes Mr. Peddle.

Q. And of the ones that were provided. Tab 8 accurately reflects all of the calls made to Paul?

A. Yes.

Q. And were there any days that there were more than one call coming in?

A. Oh, yes.

Q. What is the maximum number of calls he would have received in any day?

A. Well, I know one – one – there was several phone calls – well basically all of the – there would be more than one phone call ever day.

Q. Looking at your record there, how many calls were made on July 30th, for instance?

A. July the 30th there wasn't anything made on July the 30th. July the 31st there were.

Q. Sorry, are you in Tab 8?

A. I am in Tab 8, yes.

Q. Okay, and scroll down to July 30th, 09 front page.

A. Yes there's numerous, numerous phone calls.

Q. Can you count them for me please?

A. One, two, three, four, five, six, seven, eight, nine, 10, 11, 12 phone calls.

Q. Twelve phone calls on the same day?

A. On the same day.

Q. Did you cross reference some of these telephone calls to the date of the withdrawals...

A. All of them.

Q. ... from the bank accounts?

A. All of them.

Q. And what did you – what conclusion did you arrive at?

A. I concluded that she would make those telephone calls the day before. The next day she would attend my brother's residence and then they would go to the bank to withdraw the monies.

Q. Did you personally notice any change in Paul's lifestyle from July of 09 to January of 2010?

A. No.

Q. He didn't buy any big ticket item or...

A. Nothing, he's a very frugal person.

Q. And in your examination of all his bank records, did you find that he had transferred monies elsewhere or ...

A. No, no.

MR. PEDDLE: I have no further questions for this witness Your Honour.

THE COURT: Okay, just a second. Okay Mr. Saskin.

MR. SASKIN: Thank you your Honour.

<u>CROSS EXAMINATION BY MR. SASKIN:</u>

Q. Good morning Mrs. Taylor.

A. Good morning.

Q. My name is Zijad Saskin, I'm going to be asking you a few questions on behalf of Ms. Vassel.

A. MmmHmm,

Q. Now, you stated you know your brother pretty well and you speak with him several times a week?

A. I do.

Q. Okay. Is it almost on a daily basis or every other day?

A. Oh, about three time a week.

Q. Okay. And what do you talk about?

A. What do you talk about? Well, let's see. The – mostly the programs that he watched on television and then he – I asked him if he needs any groceries, or does he want to go see his mother and just things in general.

Q. And you drive?

A. I do.

Q. And you – you're aware that Paul lost his license in August of 2008?

A. I am.

Q. And since then you've been driving him around to places where he'd want to go?

A. Yes, I've driven him to doctor's office – basically whatever – whatever transportation he requires I provide for him.

Q. So you are very well aware of Paul's life?

A. I am.

Q. And he would tell you everything?

A. Um, yeah he – yes. Yeah, he tells me about, you know when he went down to the Sundowner or when he – when Linda Lee would come over. Yeah, pretty much.

Q. And he would tell you about Linda Lee as well?

A. Oh yes.

Q. And he would tell you that she would come over?

A. Yes.

Q. Okay, and would he – he would tell you that he wanted her to come over or no.

A. Well sometimes he would mention when she was coming over. Sometimes she would just come over without the telephone call.

Q. At times he knew that she would be coming over?

A. Uh, yes because she would call him previous to that and then she would, she would come over the next day.

Q. And from your understanding, he was spending a lot of time with her?

A. Well, I don't know about a lot of time, but it seems from these records ...

Q. I'm talking about from conversations with Paul.

A. Yeah.

Q. ... he would tell you that – I'm spending time with Linda?

A. Yes.

Q. Okay, and did he seem to be happy to be spending time with Linda?

A. Well Paul's a very lonely person. So I would assume that he probably – I don't know, he never talked to me about that.

Q. And he mentioned to you that he wanted to go on a vacation with Linda to Jamaica?

A. Well, she's the – she brought over the brochures and took him for his passport and that – he said that yeah, she was going on a vacation with him.

Q. So you heard enough about Linda that you said, gee Paul, maybe I should meet this lady?

A. Yes, MmmHmm.

Q. And yet, you never met her?

A. No, It never transpired.

Q. Did Paul say – yes, I want you to meet Linda?

A. Yes, he did.

Q. And you never did?

A. And I never did.

Q. So this was obviously somebody that Paul cared about, otherwise he wouldn't have asked you that he wanted you to meet her?

A. Well, when somebody wants to move in to his house and take a vacation with him, of course I would like to meet her.

Q. So let's say towards the end of July – July 22nd, Paul allegedly went to the and took out $1,200 and gave – loaned it to Angela - - or Linda?

A. MmmHmm.

Q. At any time in July, did Paul ever say to you – I'm loaning her money?

A. I didn't know at that time in point that he was....

Q. The question is, did he say to you – I'm loaning her money.

A. No.

Q. Yes or no.

A. No.

Q. No, at any point in August, did Paul say Denise, I'm loaning her money?

A. No.

Q. So, it wasn't until when, precisely, that you learned that Paul was loaning, or allegedly loaning money to Linda?

A. Yes, September.

Q. In September. So in September of 2008 – or September of 09, you learned that Paul was loaning money to Linda?

A. Not – no. no, that's when I received the telephone call from my brother, in September.

Q. Okay and you did nothing about it?

A. No.

Q. You didn't go over to Paul – you were concerned about Paul, so you didn't go over to his house and said Paul, I received some news that you are loaning this lady money, whom I've never met; can I see what's going on?

A. I didn't know at that time in point that they were loans.

Q. But you knew that he was taking out large sums of money from his bank account?

A. Well, according to my brother, yes. Yes, I, I but that's his money. I mean he can do whatever he wants with it. It's not my – you know. Had I known....

Q. To the best of your knowledge, your brother did nothing either? To the best of your knowledge?

A. He did nothing ...?

Q. Did he go over to Paul and say – Paul, what are you doing?

A. Well again it was – really, it was none of our concern?

Q. But eventually it became your concern?

A. It did, yes.

Q. So what changed; how come it became your concern? It wasn't your concern in September, but it was your concern how long after?

A. Well until Paul notified me, because she wouldn't sign the note that Paul gave to her.

Q. Okay, and do you recall when that was?

A. Yes, that was in January.

Q. January, do you know precisely the dates, or no?

A. Well, January – well he signed that note July the 4th and then she was over ....

Q. Sorry, you said "July", is it ....

A. I'm sorry ....

Q. .... I believe it's January.

A. .... January the 4th, 2010.

Q. Okay.

A. And then after she wouldn't sign the note, then that's when he called me.

Q. So you said "he signed the note", what did you mean to say by "he signed the note"?

A. Sorry, She signed the note and three times he asked her to sign it and she kept crossing it out, crossing it out....

Q. Okay.

A. And then he became very upset because.

Q. And that's when it became your concern?

A. And that's when it became my concern...

Q. So you started ...

A. ... because that was his life savings.

Q. You started looking at his bank notes?

A. Yes I – his bank accounts, yeah.

Q. So on – and let me understand this; you sat down with your brother ...

A. MmmHmm.

Q. ... and you had gone through all of his bank accounts?

A. Yes sir.

Q. So what you did in this list is, you took a look at almost every withdrawal that he has made, which was in excess of $1,000, and you put that down as a loan that Paul allegedly made. How did you, how did you differentiate between what was a loan and what was not a loan?

A. Well, they were all loans.

Q. And that's what Paul told you? You have no independent knowledge to say – yes, they were all loans. You were not there on July 22nd; you were not at the bank when Paul took out the money, correct?

A. No, I wasn't but ...

Q. And you have never met Linda Lee, prior to maybe even today?

A. I met her at the pre-trial.

Q. At the Pre-trial.

A. Yes.

Q. Okay, so before this litigation started, you had never met Linda Lee?

A. No, no, no.

Q. So, independently, other than what your brother had told you, that he took out all of these series of large withdrawals from his bank accounts, you have no independent knowledge that this money was loaned to Linda Lee?

A. My brother would never take any large amount of money and just give the money away; because this was his life savings. And apparently the monies were loaned for – he – Paul mentioned to me what these loans were for.

Q. Again, and that's exactly what I'm saying. Independently, you have no other knowledge. It's only what Paul had told you?

A. Yeah, exactly.

Q. That's it, okay. And you say that he's a very frugal gentleman?

A. Yes, He is.

Q. It's not like him to loan out large sums of money?

A. No, no. To withdraw any large amount of money out of his bank account, no.

Q. And I believe you even said Paul would never do that.

A. Well, if – if - he must have – he had reasons, I guess, why he took the monies out. She must have given him valid reasons to – for him to withdraw the monies, or else he wouldn't have withdraw those amounts of money at all.

Q. I understand. And you are aware that Paul was going to the Sundowner?

A. Yes.

Q. And you're aware that he was spending money there?

A. Well that's obvious, I guess.

Q. Did he ever tell you how much he would spend?

A. No, no, he didn't.

Q. Did he tell you how often he would go?

A. Yeah, he – we talked about it and I told him – I was honest with him and I said, It's not a place to go.

Q. Yeah, You didn't think it was a good idea.

A. No.

Q. ... for him to keep going there ...

A. No.

Q. ... and spending money? So, just to be clear, from July 22nd, 2009 to January 4th, 2010, you had not met Linda Lee?

A. Only – only at the pre-trial.

Q. Only at the pre-trial, okay. And you state that on or about January 4th or 5th, Paul called you and said – she refused to sign this note; theirs is something I need to tell you?

A. MmmHmm.

COURT REPORTER: Excuse me. Your Answer?

A. Yes.

MR. SASKIN:

Q. Yes or no please.

A. Yes, I'm sorry.

Q. And then on January 13th, 2010, you had gone through the bank accounts and you noted that on January 13th, 2010, Paul took out $2,000. If we take a look at Tab 4, the second page of Tab 4. You created this document, is that right?

A. I did.

Q. Bases on information that Paul gave you and based on looking at his bank records?

A. Tab 4?

Q. Tab 4, second page of Tab 4. There are two entries for January 13th, for a Canada Trust account on the far right side of the second page. It says January 13th, $2,000.

A. Okay, MmmHmm.

Q. Isn't it odd to you that Paul would loan someone $2,000 after the fact – after the fact and told you – she's refused to sign the note.

A. Let me take a look at the book here. January the 10th. January the 10th, here we are.

Q. The 13th, January 13th, 2010.

A. This is not very clear here on my sheet. Are you looking at the – Yeah, it's not very clear on my sheet here.

Q. Okay, give me one second.

A. At all.

Q. Well, let's look at Tab 2 in front of you.

A. Okay.

Q. Look at Tab 2.

A.	MmmHmm.

Q.	And go to the last page of Tab 2.

A.	Okay.

Q.	There are two entries for January 13th.

A.	Okay, you said Tab – sorry.

Q.	The last page of Tab 2.

A.	$2,000....

Q.	$2,000 on January 13th.

A.	Yes, that's correct, MmmHmm.

Q.	And that's after the note was allegedly not signed by Angela, correct?

A.	Yeah, the note was signed on January the 4th – well he tried to sign, or maybe it was – the note was dated January the 4th.

Q.	Okay.

A.	So ...

Q.	And the note said, the sum of $151,000, is that correct?

A.	Correct.

Q.	Now, when you went through all the bank records and the bank accounts, what is the number you came up to?

A.	About $132,000.

MR. SASKIN: No further questions Your Honour.

THE COURT: Re-examination?

MR. PEDDLE: I'll be brief your Honour.

RE –EXAMINATION BY MR. PEDDLE:

Q.	If I could have you turn to Tab 8, sorry Denise.

A.	Tab 8, MmmHmm.

Q.	It's the last page of Tab 8.

A. MmmHmm.

Q. Where there calls from Ms. Vassel after January 13th?

A. I'm sorry?

Q. Were there telephone calls to Paul from Ms Vassel after January 13th?

A. January 14th there was, yes.

Q. Okay.

A. There was two. And I was there for one of them. I had just brought Paul back from grocery shopping. The telephone rang and it was Linda Lee, also known as Thelma. And at that time in point we had notified the police and the conversation was...

Q. What date was that on?

A. January the 14th.?

Q. January the 14.

A. Twice, there was two phone calls. And she – and I asked Paul to hand the phone to me, I would like to speak with her. And she must have heard me say that, because she hang up. I went home and then about six o'clock or 6:30 that night, she called back again, the same night – the same day.

Q. The note that's at Tab 9 is dated January the 4th.

A. Yes.

Q. 2010. Do you have any idea what date Paul tried to have Ms. Vassel sign that note? Do you have any idea what date he actually asked her to sign it?

A. I – well yes, because she called – she called – it must have been the – she called on – just a second here. I don't want to say something that – I know she called – she called twice from Brantford on January the 4th. And that's when Paul prepared the note because he knew that she was probably going to come down to borrow more money. And so that's when he sat down and he took an envelope, which is Paul, and wrote down that note. Now, whether she came down the same day or whether she came down the day after ...

Q. In fact, she could have come down at a later time.

A. She could have, yes sir.

MR. PEDDLE: Thank you. Your Honour, that's the plaintiff's case.

THE COURT: Okay, just one moment please. If you could just stay for a moment please. So, the two calls you were just referring to in your evidence, they are the two calls from Brantford on January 4th, in Exhibit 8, is that what you are referring to?

A. Yes Your Honour.

THE COURT: And what about these later calls after January 4th, do you know what they are? You weren't present for those, I take it?

A. No, no.

THE COURT: Okay.

I was just ...

THE COURT: Okay, that's fine. Just on January 4th okay. I have no other questions for you. Thank you very much.

A. You're quite welcome.

THE COURT: you can step down.

A. Thank you'

MR. PEDDLE: That's the plaintiff's case Your Honour.

THE COURT: Okay, you can stay in the court room if you wish.

A. Okay.

THE COURT: Mr. Saskin.

MR. SASKIN: Yes Your Honour. I would like to call my first witness, Angela Vassel.

THELMA ANGELA VASSEL: EXAMINATION IN CHIEF BY MR. SASKIN:

Q. Angela, you have already stated your name for the record. What is your date of birth?

A. September 1st, 1969.

Q. And what is your address?

A. 6 Firelane, 11(a), Niagara on the lake.

Q. Is that a house?

THE COURT: In Niagara on the lake.

A. ...Niagara on the lake.

THE COURT: Thank you.

Q. Is that a house?

A. That is a house.

Q. Do you own it or rent it?

A. I own it.

Q. And how long have you been at that house?

A. Approximately give or take 10 years.

Q. And Angela, what do you do for work?

A. I work at the Sundowner and I have a small business, I'm starting a small business.

Q. And what do you do at the Sundowner?

A. I dance.

Q. And how long have you worked there?

A. Approximately six years.

Q. Okay, and can you tell me, what does an exotic dancer do?

A. An exotic dancer takes a fee for dance in a private area.

Q. Okay. And on average, can you tell the court, how much money would you make on an average night?

A. Average – about three, four, five hundred, roughly.

Q. Anywhere from $300 to $500?

A. Yeah, average.

Q. Okay. Angela, do you know Mr. Paul Dagenais?

A. Yes, I do

Q. And where did you first meet Paul?

A. I met Paul at the Sundowner.

Q. Okay, and when did you first meet Paul?

A. Approximately six years ago.

Q. Okay, and what would typically happen when you saw Paul at the Sundowner?

A. Typically Paul, he'll buy a few of his favorite girls drinks and we sit with him and one by one we go for dances.

Q. Okay, and did he spent any money on you?

A. Yes.

Q. How much, on average?

A. A hundred dollars.

Q. And did you see Paul dance for anyone else ...

A. Yes.

Q. ... or dance with anyone else?

A. Yes.

Q. Okay, and is it normal for a dancer to give VIP dances for free?

A. No.

Q. Based on your observations, how many other girls would dance with Paul?

A. Four to five.

Q. Okay, was he drinking while at the club?

A. Before his stroke, no. Before his stroke, yes – after his stroke, no.

Q. Okay, did he ever buy you drinks?

A. Always.

Q. Okay, what about anyone else?

A. Yes.

Q. Was he a good customer?

A. Yes.

Q. Was he a regular customer?

A. A regular customer, Yes.

Q. Was he your best customer?

A. No.

Q. Now, was there a time that Paul was noticeable absent from the Sundowner.

A. Yes.

Q. And do you know what happened to him?

A. Our understanding was he was – he had a stroke.

Q. Now Ms Vassel, do you see clients outside of the club.

A. Yes.

Q. Okay, now how dose that work?

A. Usually I either meet them at the club and we leave for a fee, but there is no sex involved, and they usually –well, they know that in advance.

Q. Okay, and do you get paid for this?

A. Yes, I do.

THE COURT: Could you hold on just a second.

MR. SASKIN: Yes, certainly. I'm sorry Your Honour.

THE COURT: I am behind in my notes here.

MR. SASKIN: Sure.

THE COURT: Okay, go ahead. Sorry about that.

MR. SASKIN:

Q. And my next question was, how much do you charge for – let's call it a date?

A. Three to five hundred; it depends on the time.

Q. It depends on the time?

A. Well I don't usually charge by the hour, but if I am there for like three hours, I will say three hundred in advance. If I go for dinner, and we're having dinner and we agree on three hundred, but if it goes beyond that, say another two, three hours, usually two hundred more.

Q. Okay, now what happens on a date, typically?

A. I usually do whatever they want to do, besides sex.

Q. Did you see Paul outside of the club?

A. Yes, I did.

Q. Okay, and when did that start?

A. That started roughly a couple years ago.

Q. Okay, and how did that come about?

A. Paul would come to the club and ask numerous times if I would come visit him.

Q. Okay, and did you make arrangements with Paul?

A. Yes.

Q. And what were the arrangements for seeing Paul outside of the club?

A. For a fee, if I come over, he would pay me and I'll do whatever – drive him around, whatever he wants to do.

Q. And Paul agree to this?

A. Yes, he did.

Q. And would you charge the same price to Paul that you would for your other clients?

A. Yes, I did.

Q. So let's backtrack just a little bit. Since Paul started coming to the club, how much money would you say that he spent on you inside the club, between VIP dances and drinks, overall, if you can estimate?

A. It would be in the thousands?

Q. Five thousand, does that sound accurate?

A. Yeah, it would have been like five thousand.

Q. Okay, now let's talk about outside of the club again. How were the arrangements made to see Paul outside of the club?

A. Well, usually I call him and then he'll tell me what time. If I don't call him, say in a week's time he shows up at the club and ask somebody for me to call him.

Q. Now, tell me, what was a typical date like with Paul? What would you do?

A. Well sometimes I would go to his house and we would watch Hercules, which was one of his favorites. Or we would sit there and just talk about whatever he wants to talk about. Sometimes I would drive him to the park, we would go to the park and hang out and talk. We'd go to Tim Horton's. We'd go to the bank. We went up to Burlington a few times. We went-we did stuff.

Q. Okay, so what would you do at Paul's house? You said watch Hercules, what else?

A. Watch Hercules. We talked a lot about the bible.

Q. Okay.

A. He would show me things like awards that he got at work or things – just things he achieved and stuff like that.

Q. Now, you also said you drove Paul to the bank?

A. Yes.

Q. Why would you drive him there?

A. Because he asked me to.

Q. Okay, and when you drove Paul to the bank, did you go inside the bank with him?

A. Never.

Q. Which bank did he go to?

A. Canada Trust and I can't remember the names of the other ones.

Q. And was there anyone else with you at this time?

A. No.

Q. So you stated that Paul would go inside the bank himself?

A. Yes.

Q. Now, what would happen when he would return to the car?

A. He was a boastful person, just like he is in – comes into the club. He likes people and you know – he was boastful. He would tell me if I was to sleep with him, I would have all this money. I didn't know exactly what was in his – I didn't know what he had in his envelope, but he would say that to me.

Q. But he would show you an envelope?

A. Yes.

Q. And what was your reaction to seeing the envelope?

A. I would be like – I'm fine with whatever I get, my pay, but he could go and get who he wants; which he usually – in the club he usually gets a few girls that he spend a lot longer time with, because he like more action.

Q. Okay, and you personally witness this?

A. Yes.

Q. You witnessed this yourself?

A. Yes.

Q. Okay. How many times did you see Paul outside of the club?

A. Mmm, I'd say approximately maybe two dozen times, under that.

Q. Okay, and did Paul pay you on each occasion?

A. Yes he did.

Q. Okay, how much?

A. Three to five hundred.

Q. Did he never not pay you.

A. No.

Q. Can you estimate, overall, how much money did Paul give you for your dates?

A. Approximately five thousand.

Q. Okay, and was it your understanding that this was a loan?

A. No.

Q. Okay. Now, have a look at Tab number 4, in front of you, at exhibit 1. Prior to this litigation, have you seen this document before?

A. The – withdrawal re loan to Thelma Vassel page?

Q. Yes.

A. No.

Q. Okay, now Ms. Vassel, this is a list of loans that Paul alleges were given to you. Now outside of the $5,000 that we know about, did you receive any of this money from Paul?

A. No.

Q. Now Ms. Vassel, have a look at Tab number 9, which was also made an exhibit, as Exhibit 2 I believe. What can you tell me about this envelope?

A. This envelope – Paul had shown up in the club once with an envelope and stating for me to sign it and I said no.

Q. Okay, and why did you refuse to sign it?

A. Because I do not own him $151,000.

Q. Do you own Paul – do you own him any money?

A. I do not owe him any money.

Q. When did you stop seeing Paul?

A. I stopped seeing Paul because he started to create problems at work for me.

Q. What kind of problems?

A. The girls didn't want to tell me but I realized they were being a little bit standoffish with me and finally a couple girls told me that Paul had came in there ...

MR. PEDDLE: Objection.

MR. SASKIN: That's fine.

THE COURT: Yes, you can't ...

A. Oh.

MR. SASKIN:

Q. Now, Ms. Vassel, you phoned Paul on many occasions?

A. Yes.

Q. Why did you call him?

A. He was a good customer and most often a lot of times I would get text or email that he was in the club looking for me, asking me – asking for a phone call. I would call him because he's a very good customer.

Q. And why would you call several different times in one day?

A. It depends on where I am, the location. Sometimes if I'm by the lake, I get cut off and I would call him back. Sometimes it's very hard for me to hear him, and I'd tell him- because of clarity – I'd tell him I'll call him back or you know – basically it communication.

MR. SASKIN: Those are all my questions Your Honour.

THE COURT: Just a second. Thank you.

MR. SASKIN: Of course.

THE COURT: Thank you.

MR. SASKIN: Thank you Your Honour.

THE COURT: Mr. Peddle

CROSS EXAMINATION BY MR. PEDDLE:

Q. Ms. Vassel...

A. Yes.

Q. ...I take it you're not sexually attracted to my client in any way, are you?

A. No.

Q. And how would you describe your friendship from July of 09 to January of 2010.

A. With him, it was good. Can you make clarification as to what you are asking?

Q. Well, I'm just asking you to describe it. What was your relationship?

A. I do not discriminate, he is a nice man.

Q. Okay, you said you made calls to his phone and you were often cut off and you had to recall, etcetera?

A. Yes.

Q. If I could get you to turn to Tab 6 and have you go to page number two in there.

A. Pardon me?

Q. Go to page number two, Tab 6. These are your phone records, I understand.

A. Yes.

Q. Did you produce all of your phone records to me Ms. Vassel?

A. Yes.

Q. There weren't gaps in the phone records you provided?

A. I gave you everything I got from the phone company.

Q. Was there any reason that there were significant months that were missing?

A. I don't understand what you are asking me. What I received I gave right to you.

Q. Right, but there were significant months that were missing. Do you know why that is?

A. I gave you what I received, so I don't know.

Q. Okay, on page two, if you go down to the very last line...

A. MmmHmm.

Q. ... it's a call made on July 25th. What is the duration of that call?

A. A minute forty – four.

Q. Okay, flip over. You have a bunch of calls here, it looks like eight or 10 each, and the duration of those –some of these are for three minutes...

A. MmmHmm.

Q. ... and some are for six minutes. Why would you be calling Paul 12 times a day and speaking for that length of time?

A. I can't recall the moment, but usually we speak and then I would call him back.

Q. All right, I understand that's been your testimony ...

A. Get disconnected.

Q. Your records that have been produced, even though it's not all of them, show substantial amounts of calls to Paul over six month period.

A. He was a very good customer and if he asked me to call him back in a couple minutes, I would.

Q. He was a good enough customer that you were basically calling him every second or third day, four or five times?

A. Oh yes, because he would also come to the club looking for me if I didn't call him.

Q. Right, but your evidence before was, you would call him back. Why would you call him so many times?

A. If I'm by the lake and I got disconnected and Paul loves to talk. It's hard to understand him, but when I'm on the phone with him, we do talk. Whatever he wants to talk about –Hercules, what's his plans; whatever.

Q. Okay. Well a lot of these calls do come from your home in Niagara on the lake. A lot of them also came from Niagara Falls and St. Catharines, is that accurate?

A. MmmHmm.

COURT REPORTER; Excuse me...

A. Pardon me?

COURT REPORTER: ...Ma'am – excuse me, Ma'am I'll just ask you, you must answer yes or no, out loud, you can't ...

A. Oh, I didn't hear what he said though.

Q. My question was, a lot of these calls do come from Niagara on the lake but a lot of calls also came from Niagara Falls, St. Catharines, Grimsby: is that accurate?

A. If it states so, yes.

Q. And I assume on those occasions you didn't lose any signal?

A. I'm on a cell phone as well.

Q. Correct.

A. Yeah, so sometimes you can.

Q. Do you usually lose your signal in St. Catharines?

A. Yeah, it depends yes, on the location, yes.

Q. Would you call him while you driving or would you be stationary?

A. I would call when I drive, sometimes.

Q. What kind of a vehicle do you drive?

A. I am driving my boyfriend's car.

Q. What is it?

A. It's a BMW.

Q. Where does your Boyfriend live?

A. He's in Arizona.

Q. How many times would you say you took Paul to the bank, over the period from July to January?

A. Whenever he asked. I'm not sure of the exact time because every time I get in his vehicle it wasn't only to the bank, so...

Q. But you took him to the bank a lot?

A. Yes, I did.

Q. And how come you never wanted to go in?

A. Because it was not my place to. He wanted to go to the bank; I didn't have to walk him to the teller.

Q. But you would go to the park with him, correct?

A. Yes.

Q. You would go to Tim Hortons with him, correct?

A. Yes.

Q. Why wouldn't you walk into the bank with him?

A. Well, when we went to Tim Horton's as well, we would go through drive – thru and we'd sit there and we'd talk, so I didn't go into Tim Horton's with him. When we went to the park, we went to the park, we stayed parked in the car and we'd look around. So...

Q. Do you have any witnesses at all to your dates?

A. He's a witness.

Q. Any other witness to you dates?

A. No.

Q. And did Paul give you any indication what he was doing with this cash he was withdrawing?

A. Well I know there was one lady friend that he had come over a few times that he flew to

Halifax – I can't remember, Alberta – there was a lady that used to go and visit him frequently as well.

Q. And I assume you heard this from who?

A. Paul.

Q. Okay. Do you have any Idea how he would have spent $130,000 in six months?

A. I don't have a clue.

Q. His lifestyle was not extravagant, was it?

A. It was in the club though.

Q. I understand what he said he spent in the club, but I don't think it differs that much from yours. But to get from $5,000 in lap dances to $130,000, you will agree with me is a big jump?

A. Well, he had a couple of favorite girls in the club, so I'm ....

Q. A couple or a couple of dozen?

A. No, just a couple.

Q. During the time in Question here in July of 09 to January of 2010, is it accurate to say you didn't even operate a bank account?

A. Revenue – I did operate one but revenue Canada got involved, yes.

Q. Okay, so for several months though, you did not use a bank account?

A. Correct.

Q. So you just dealt in cash transactions, I take it.

A. I work in a cash business.

Q. You never deposit that cash?

A. No.

Q. Where does it go?

A. It went to pay Revenue Canada and my bills.

Q. Dose any of it go to Arizona?

A. No.

Q. Why is revenue Canada in your life?

A. Because you have to pay taxes.

Q. So you've been audited, I take it?

A. I have been.

Q. And you were shown to have been inaccurate in your filings?

A. Actually my accountant does the paperwork so ...

Q. Yes, but revenue Canada did audit you and find that you did not pay proper income tax, it that accurate?

A. Well actually, the problem that – the latest problem that I had with them was my GST. I didn't know that on exotic entertainment you had to pay GST.

Q. And how much GST did you owe them?

A. I believe with interest, $50,000.

Q. Fifty thousand dollars?

A. Yes.

MR. PEDDLE: I have no further questions for you.

A. Okay.

MR. SASKIN: The court's indulgence Your Honour's, just to speak with my friend.

THE COURT: Yes sure, go ahead.

MR. PEDDLE: Your Honour, my friend pointed out that he had sent a letter to me in December with the missing phone records. I never received that, it's not in my file. But, that being said, in term of the evidence with respect to the missing phone records, we take no issue with it.

THE COURT: Okay, thank you.

MR. PEDDLE: Thank you Your Honour.

THE COURT: Do you have any re-examination?

MR. SASKIN: No re-examination, thank you Your Honour. You may step down.

A. Thank you.

MR. SASKIN: You Honour, I have one more witness. I don't think I'm going to be more than five, 10 minutes with her.

THE COURT: Okay.

MR. SASKIN: So unless – subject to Your Honour's discretion when you want to take a break your Honour.

THE COURT: No, that's fine. Please call her now.

MR. SASKIN: Okay, call Harlow.

HARLOW (SWORN):

EXAMINATION IN CHEF BY MR. SASKIN:

Q. Good afternoon Ms. Harlow. Can you tell the court, where do you live?

A. Niagara Falls.

Q. And what is your address?

A. 165 Bellbaiy.

Q. And what do you do for work?

A. I'm an entertainer.

Q. Please speak loudly so the record can pick you up.

A. Okay.

Q. And where do you work?

A. Sundowner.

Q. And how long have you work there?

A. Eight years.

Q. Okay. And do you still work there?
A. Yes.
Q. Ms. Harlow, do you know Paul Dagenais?
A. Yes. I do.
Q. Is he the gentleman who is sitting to my right?
A. Yes.
Q. And when did you first meet Paul?
A. 2004, roughly, when I started working at the Sundowner.
Q. Okay. And is that where you met him?
A. Yes.
Q. And how often would you see him at the Sundowner?
A. Twice a week.
Q. Okay, and did Paul spent money on you?
A. Yes.
Q. How would he spend money on you?
A. Cash, taking me for dances.
Q. Okay, and where would you take Paul for dance?
A. In the VIP room.
Q. Okay, and was he a good customer?
A. Yes.
Q. So how much money would he spend on you, on average?
A. Sixty to a hundred bucks.
Q. Okay. And did Paul ever mention Angela to you?
A. Yes.
Q. Okay, what would he say about her?

A. Um, that he liked her a lot, he was looking for her in reference, and things like that.

Q. Okay.

THE COURT: I didn't catch what – your last statement.

A. That he liked her; he came in specifically looking for her on occasion.

THE COURT: Okay, came in looking for her, okay thanks you.

A. Yes.

MR. SASKIN:

Q. And how often would he come in looking for Angela?

A. A few times.

Q. Okay. Did you ever tell Angela that Paul was looking for her?

A. Yes.

Q. Okay, Did Paul ever offer you money for sex?

A. No.

Q. Okay. Did he offer to see you outside of the club?

A. Yes.

Q. Okay. And did you ever see Paul dance with any other girls?

A. Yes.

Q. Okay, Okay, and in or about January 2010, did you recall any specific conversations you had with Paul?

A. Um, one specific conversation I had with him, he said that he was waiting for Angela. I asked him for a dance and he said he was going to wait for because he really liked her and he said he was sleeping with her and he told me not to tell no one or he'll kill me.

Q. Okay, and did you tell Angela what Paul told you?

A. I did, but I didn't tell her right away, because I did not want to be involved in it. But, he had said it to a few other girls too, so it did eventually get out. So then we did have a conversation about it, yes.

MR. SASKIN: Okay, thank you. I have no further questions.

THE COURT: Okay, thank you. Could you just – thank you. Mr. peddle starts, I just want to finish my notes here. Okay, Mr. peddle.

CROSS EXAMINATION BY MR. PEDDLE:

Q. Sorry, you spoke to fast. I didn't catch your last name. What is it?

A. Harlow.

Q. Harlow. Ms. Harlow, the adult industry – well let's just take the Sundowner right now. All the girls, they know each other well, correct?

A. Yes.

Q. And it's got to be like any other place you work; rumors go around, swirl, is that accurate?

A. Yeah, it can be accurate.

Q. Okay, and you guys basically all know what each other is doing and who you are seeing?

A. Not necessarily.

Q. No?

A. No.

Q. If they come to the club though?

A. If somebody comes to the club, you could see certain things that go on, but every – you don't work the same shift with the same people every single day...

Q. No, no, I understand that.

A. ... so there's a lot of things that go on that you would not know about.

Q. I understand that. You never went on trip to Jamaica with my client, did you?

A. No.

Q. To your knowledge, did any other exotic dancer at the Sundowner go away with him?

A. I don't know, I can't speak for them.

Q. No, but to your knowledge?

A. I don't know, I don't think so.

Q. And to your knowledge, my client never purchased any gift for any of the girls?

A. I don't know if he's purchased gift for them.

Q. Okay, to your knowledge, you don't know of any?

A. I don't know.

MR. PEDDLE: I have no further questions Your Honour.

THE COURT: One moment please. Any re-examination Mr. Saskin?

MR. SASKIN: No Your Honour.

THE COURT: Thank you. I have no questions, thank you very much. You can step down. Any other witnesses Mr. Saskin?

MR. SASKIN: No more witnesses, that's the case for the defense Your Honour.

THE COURT: Okay. Well why don't we adjourn for lunch now and then we will have submissions after lunch; does that make sense?

MR. PEDDLE: Fine Your Honour.

MR SASKIN: Yes.

The judge calls a recess.

We leave the courtroom and I go outside for a smoke. I don't have any money for lunch so I return to my car only to find a parking ticket on the windshield. *Great!* I remove it, nestle into my front seat and set my phone alarm for fifteen minutes. I fall asleep right away but am awakened by that nerve-wracking buzz after what seems like just a minute. I hurry to the courtroom for the closing arguments.

Peddle's closing presentation is so vile I feel like vomiting. He finishes up saying something about how, since his client stopped talking to me, there have been no further withdrawals from his bank account, mentioning the dates from June to January. *Yes, now that I'm no longer in his life, Paul Dagenais has become a perfect angel.* I want to throw up in Clark Peddle's ugly face.

It's now Zijad's turn. As he starts, my stomach sinks. Everything seems to be moving at a very fast pace. As he moves on to each new sentence, I'm still hanging onto his last, trying to analyze it. I'm feeling more and more nauseated as I realize that Zijad's closing argument is, on so many levels, pathetically weak and incomplete.

The court adjourns for the day. The judge will render his decision the next morning.

That night is no different from others of recent days. I keep a nightlong vigil but no strange cars or SUVs appear. After returning to my house around six a.m., I set my alarm for seven so I can make it to court on time.

At the courthouse, I catch a glimpse of myself reflected in the glass doors. Except for some red lipstick, I have no makeup on, but I can see that that I'm looking really hot! Bystanders are staring at me as if I'm a celebrity.

I join my lawyer who's sitting on a bench outside the courtroom. He greets me with a hug and remarks that I'm looking very good.

"Really? I got almost no sleep." He just smiles. "Zijad, I still can't get over Peddle's closing statement. I want to get a copy and read it carefully, because there's something very wrong, and very revealing, about what he said."

He shrugs and tells me that it doesn't matter now. All that matters right now is what the judge is going to say.

"I'm worried the judge is going to make a big deal about my phone calls to Paul. He seemed to take a lot of interest in those calls, even though I tried to make it clear that Paul was always asking me to call him. Plus there were other reasons for my repeated call backs."

Zijad reassures me that I handled myself well and that I'd explained it very clearly. I'm pleased to hear him say that. I'm thinking, *with my testimony and the discovery information, the judge should have no difficulty in seeing the truth.* I cross my fingers and enter the courtroom behind my lawyer. As I take my seat beside him, I fix my eyes on the door to the judge's chambers and wonder if I'll be able to read anything from his demeanor when he finally appears.

As he enters the courtroom, I rise to my feet in anticipation. I'm aware of an irregular heartbeat as I sit down again, take a deep breath and await his judgment.

Superior Court Judge Lococo greets the court with a "good morning" and then reads his prepared comments.

“REASONS FOR JUDGMENT”

OVERVIEW

Paul Dagenais is a 61 year old retiree and life–long bachelor. He frequented a strip club called the Sundowner Gentlemen’s Club. During the period July 2009 to January 2010 he withdrew a total of $132,845 in cash from three bank accounts. According to Mr. Dagenais, he loaned the money to Thelma Angela Vassel, an exotic dancer who worked at the Sundowner. There was no promissory note or other written acknowledgement of any loans by Mr. Dagenais to Ms. Vassel.

Ms. Vassel denied that Mr. Dagenais lent her any money. According to Ms. Vassel, she knew Mr. Dagenais as a good customer at the Sundowner, whom she also saw professionally outside the club for “dates”.

She acknowledged receiving money from Mr. Dagenais on a fee for service basis, both at the club and outside the club, but claimed that the total amounts received were nowhere near $130,000. Ms. Vassel estimated receiving a few thousand dollars, perhaps $5,000 over the years she knew Mr. Dagenais, for dances in the private VIP area of the club, and a further amount totaling approximately $5,000 for dates outside the club. She claimed to have no knowledge where Mr. Dagenais would have spent over $130,000 in less than six months in 2009 and 2010.

In January 2010, Mr. Dagenais asked Ms Vassel to sign a statement that he prepared literally on the back of an envelope, acknowledge that she owed him $151,000. She refused to provide him with the written acknowledgement. According to Mr. Dagenais, she signed the statement three separate times, but each time crossed out her signature. He produced the document dated January 4, 2010, which had what appeared to be three scratched out signatures at the bottom. Mr. Dagenais, realizing that Ms. Vassel did not plan to pay, brought this action to recover the amounts that he claims that he lent to Ms. Vassel.

ISSUES TO BE DETERMINED

In order to succeed in this action, it was necessary for Mr. Dagenais to establish, on the balance of probabilities, that the funds in question were advanced to Ms. Vassel, by way of loans, and that these amounts are due and outstanding.

Since the transactions were not in writing, and there is no written acknowledgement of the existence of the loan or the amounts owing, it was common ground between the parties that the decision in this case depended, in large measure, on my assessment of the credibility of Mr. Dagenais and Ms. Vassel. In order to assist in this determination, I will now review the evidence advanced on behalf of Mr. Dagenais and Ms. Vassel In more detail.

MR. DAGENAIS' BACKGROUND AND EVIDENCE

Turning first to Mr. Dagenais, his evidence was that he lives alone in Port Colborne in the house in which he grew up. His mother, who is now in a retirement home, previously lived in the house with him. Mr. Dagenais retired in 2004, after working for the St. Lawrence Seaway for many years. He apparently accumulated significant saving during his working life and receives pension payments of approximately $1,800 per month.

In 2007 he suffered a stroke and was in the hospital for six months. The residual effects include weakness in his arm and hand. He has not driven since August of 2008 when he lost his license after an impaired driving conviction. Since his stroke, he has received assistance from his sister, Denise Taylor, who lives close to his house and who gave evidence at trial. She provides transportation for Mr. Dagenais, including for groceries, medical appointments and banking, and also speaks to him by telephone several times a week.

According to the evidence of both Mr. Dagenais and Mrs. Taylor, Mr. Dagenais is a simple man, living a simple life. He watches a lot of television; he is frugal, and generally does not make large purchases, which, according to the evidence of Mrs. Taylor which I accept, was corroborated by the pattern of withdrawals from his bank accounts in the period prior to July 2009. According to Mr. Dagenais' evidence, his principal diversion outside the home consisted of visits to the Sundowner Gentlemen's Club. He said that he would sometimes visit twice in one week, but some weeks did not visit the club. He said that he spent $250 to 300 each time in the private VIP area of the club, spending time with a number of different exotic dancers and paying $20 after each song.
He said that his encounters with the dancers involved mostly talking to them; some "fooling around", in his words; but no lap dancing and no sex. He said that in this context he first met Ms. Vassel, who used the name Linda Lee. She was one of the exotic dancers he had encounters with in the VIP area of the club. In his evidence in chief, he stated that he thought he met her in February 2009, but conceded in cross examination that it could have been much earlier than that. He

claimed that she started coming to his house uninvited, stating in cross examination that she must have obtained his address from the phone book. He stated that she would park on the street near his house, but would not park in his driveway, or directly in front of his house.

According to Mr. Dagenais, she started asking him for money in July 2009, the first request being on July 22nd for $1,200 to travel to Jamaica for her mother's funeral. He said he made it clear to Ms. Vassel that the amount given to her was a loan and that she agreed that she would pay him back. He said that she asked for various sums of money on a numbers of occasions, from July of 2009 to January 2010 for various purposes, including her father's funeral in Jamaica, to repay a loan that her brother owed to bikers, and to allow her to make a movie in Toronto. He said that she was insistent in asking for money, often in tears. He said that in each case he told her that he was loaning the money to her and that she agreed to pay him back.

His evidence was that in order to obtain the cash, she drove him, in his car to a number of different branches of Desjardins and TD Canada Trust, even though his accounts were in Port Colborne and he had not been to the other branches before, and that she always stayed in the car when he went into the branch. He also stated that Ms. Vassel spoke of going to Jamaica together for a vacation, and also mentions moving into his house with him, but neither of these things happened.

Although there were no promissory notes or other written acknowledgement of a debt from Ms. Vassel, Mr. Dagenais relied on certain documentary evidence to support his testimony about the amounts he said that he loaned to Ms. Vassel. Mr. Dagenais produced bank statements for three bank accounts; one at Desjardins and two at TD Canada Trust in Port Colborne, as well as a summary of withdrawals from these accounts, from January 22, 2009 to January 13th, 2010.

According to the evidence of Mr. Dagenais and Mrs. Taylor, that summary was prepared by the two of them from Mr. Dagenais' bank account records shortly after Ms. Vassel refused to sign the written acknowledgement dated January 4, 2010, prepared by Mr. Dagenais. Mr. Dagenais and Mrs. Taylor thought that Ms. Vassel's refusal to sign the acknowledgement occurred on January 4 or 5, 2010, although Mrs. Taylor stated during re-examination that she thought it could have been later in January of 2010. The summary they produce showed a total 46 withdrawals on 32 different dates, totaling $132,845. Of these transactions, there were 31 withdrawals of $1,200 or more, totaling $127,345. Another summary submitted in evidence showed nine different branches of TD Canada Trust where withdrawals occurred during this period.

Mrs. Taylor also produced a summary of telephone calls from Ms. Vassel to Mr. Dagenais during this period, using phone records produced by Ms. Vassel. This summary showed that on a number of occasions Ms. Vassel called Mr. Dagenais on the day prior, or the day of these withdrawals, sometimes a number of times on the day in question.

Ms. Vassel's Background and Evidence

Turning now to Ms. Vassel, her evidence was that she is 41 years old and has worked at the Sundowner as an exotic dancer for six years, making an average of $300 to $500 per night. She said that she had known Mr. Dagenais as a regular customer of the club since shortly after she started working there. He would buy drinks for her and would pay her to dance and he would do the same for others as well. She said that he started asking to see her for dates outside the club and she agreed to do so, on the same basis as she did for other customers, charging $300 to $500 per visit. In the case of Mr. Dagenais, these dates involved going to his house, watching television, talking and driving him in his car to Park, to Tim Horton's and to the bank. She agreed with Mr. Dagenais' evidence that she and Mr. Dagenais did not have sex. She said that when she drove him to the bank branches, it was at his request and that she would stay in the car to respect his privacy.

She also said that on occasion, when returning from the bank, he would boastfully show her a packet of cash he had withdrawn, stating that she could have lots of money if she slept with him. When asked about the phone calls to Mr. Dagenais, she stated that she often spoke on the telephone to good customers, including Mr. Dagenais, and that Mr. Dagenais often left word at the club for her to call him. She also explained that she often lost the signal using her cell phone, which explained multiple calls in a day.

In cross examination, she was asked about her failure to produce bank records which could have shown whether or not there were deposits corresponding to Mr. Dagenais' cash withdrawals. She claimed not to have a bank account during that period, explaining that her business operated in cash. She acknowledged owing over $50,000 to the Canada Revenue Agency for unpaid

GST. She was unable to explain how Mr. Dagenais could have spent $130,000 in less than six months, although she stated he had a couple of other favorite girls at the club, on whom he could have been spending money.

Some aspect of the evidence of both Ms. Vassel and Mr. Dagenais were corroborated by the evidence of Eden Harlow, another exotic dancer at the Sundowner. She stated that Mr. Dagenais had been a customer of the club since she first started working there in 2004 and that he often came twice in a week. Consistent with the evidence of both Ms. Vassel and Mr. Dagenais, she saw him with Ms. Vassel in the VIP area of the club, as well as with other dancers. However, she was not aware of his having given gifts to other girls at the club, as suggested by Ms. Vassel. She stated that he had never offered her money for sex, but had once offered to take her for a vacation in Jamaica, but they had not gone. She also said that in January 2010, she asked him to dance, but that he declined, telling her that he was waiting to dance with [Ms. Vassel] and confided that he was sleeping with her.

ASSESSING THE EVIDENCE OF MR. DAGENAIS AND MS. VASSEL

In assessing the evidence of Mr. Dagenais and that of Ms. Vassel, I am troubled by some aspects of the evidence of both of them. Mr. Dagenais' evidence was sometimes muddled and hard to fallow. As well, his evidence that the visits by Ms. Vassel to his house were entirely unwelcome and unwanted, is not consistent with the evidence of Mrs. Taylor, which I found to be credible. Mrs. Taylor stated that in her frequent conversations with Mr. Dagenais, he sometimes mentioned Ms. Vassel, including discussions they had about taking a vacation together in Jamaica and moving in together, which caused Mrs. Taylor concern. As well, sometime in the latter part of 2009, Mrs. Taylor became aware that Mr. Dagenais had been making significant cash withdrawals from his bank account, but Mr. Dagenais did not tell her he was loaning money to Ms. Vassel until January 2010.

Notwithstanding the misgivings I have referred to about Mr. Dagenais' evidence, I accept as credible the basic thrust of his evidence relating to the significant withdrawals from his bank accounts in the period July of 2009 to January 2010. That is, Ms. Vassel asked him to provide her with significant sums of money for various purposes and that he provided those sums to her by way of loan, with the understanding from Ms. Vassel that he would be repaid.

In giving his evidence, he was understandably emotional about what had happened, and no doubt embarrassed about having to tell his story in court in an attempt to recover his loss, but I commend him for his fortitude in pursuing this remedy, and accept his evidence with respect to the amounts advanced to Ms. Vassel by way of loan. Although there is no written acknowledgement of loans, the documentary evidence that does exist demonstrated that Mr. Dagenais made significant withdrawals from his banks accounts during the period, that were not consistent with his prior spending pattern. During that period, Ms. Vassel was seeing Mr. Dagenais outside the club and taking him to bank branches where he made withdrawals. In my view, whether those visits to Mr. Dagenais outside the club were on an uninvited basis, as contended by Mr. Dagenais, or on a paid basis as alleged by Ms. Vassel, makes no difference for this purpose. As well, in almost every case, Ms Vassel called Mr. Dagenais on the day prior, or the day of the withdrawals, consistent with the conclusion that the withdrawals were made at her request.

Ms. Vassel's counsel argued that it made no sense that Mr. Dagenais would loan such a significant sum of money to someone he did not know very well. However, there is no other explanation on the evidence as to what happened to the funds withdrawn by Mr. Dagenais. In any case, given the discussions Mr. Dagenais and Ms. Vassel about moving in together and vacationing together in Jamaica, which I accept occurred, it is hardly accurate to say that they barely knew each other.

Ms. Vassel's counsel also pointed out the clear, collected and straight forward manner of Ms. Vassel's evidence as compared to Mr. Dagenais, arguing that Ms. Vassel's evidence was more worthy of belief for that reason. While Ms. Vassel's evidence was indeed easier to follow, I did not find it to be more credible than the evidence of Mr. Dagenais, which I prefer and accept on the crucial points as to whether Ms. Vassel received sums of money from Mr. Dagenais and the characterization of these amounts as loans. Among other things, I was skeptical about Ms. Vassel's explanation for failure to produce bank records that may have been helpful in making the determination in this case; nor did I find credible her explanation for the pattern of multiple phone calls to Mr. Dagenais, coincident with bank withdrawals.

Ms. Vassel's counsel also argued that it was inconsistent for Mr. Dagenais to take the position that he had withdraw an additional sum of $2000 on January 13th,

2010 to loan to Ms. Vassel when, according to the evidence, he had concluded as of January 4 or 5 that Ms. Vassel would not be paying him because she declined to sign the written acknowledgement that he prepared. However, I note that Ms. Vassel does not dispute that she refused to provide the written acknowledgement requested by Mr. Dagenais in January 2010, and that her dealings with Mr. Dagenais ended shortly thereafter. Therefore, while I agree there is doubt on the evidence whether the withdrawal on January 13 as advanced by way of loan to Ms. Vassel, (depending on the actual timing of the presentation of the written acknowledgment to Ms. Vassel), I do not agree with the argument of Ms. Vassel's counsel that the alleged inconsistency in Mr. Dagenais' evidence cannot be reconciled with the conclusion that the significant withdrawals made from Mr. Dagenais' account prior to January 2010 were advanced by way of loans to Ms. Vassel.

Accordingly, after weighing all the evidence, I find that Mr. Dagenais has established on a balance or probabilities that Mr. Dagenais withdrew significant sums of money from his bank accounts as outlined further below and advanced them to Ms. Vassel by way of loans and that such amounts are due and outstanding.

In his submissions Mr. Dagenais' counsel suggested that it may be appropriate to exclude from the amount to be recovered the smaller withdrawal amounts included in the summary of withdrawals prepared by Mr. Dagenais and Mrs. Taylor. I agree that such amounts should be excluded since they are equally consistent with the withdrawal of funds for Mr. Dagenais' personal use, rather than being for the purpose of advancing funds to Ms. Vassel.

I am therefore excluding from the amount recovered, all individual withdrawal amounts that are less than $1,200. I chose that amount since Mr. Dagenais was very explicit in his testimony that the first of the withdrawals of July 22nd, 2009 was made in order to loan that amount to Ms. Vassel for a specific purpose, and I find that withdrawals for less than that amount would be consistent with the personal use of those sums by Mr. Dagenais. I am also excluding the $2,000 withdrawal made from TD Canada Trust on January 13th, 2010, given the uncertainty on the evidence as to the timing of Mr. Dagenais' request that Ms. Vassel provide a written acknowledgement of her debt to Mr. Dagenais. Accordingly, there will be judgment for Mr. Dagenais in the amount of $125,245 plus pre-judgment interest from January 31st, 2010 to the date of the Judgment, and post-judgment interest thereafter, in each case at the prescribed rate.

Having completed his comments, Judge Lococo looks up from his text and invites a response from the attorneys. I'm completely stunned and sick to my stomach. It takes everything in me to not jump up and protest that the judge is committing a gross miscarriage of justice.

Either this guy is completely naïve about what goes on between customers and girls in strip clubs, or he doesn't care and he's knowingly shafting me! I can't believe that a judge can be so obviously biased. I've got to appeal this!

Zijad and Clark Peddle leave the room for a few minutes and then return.

Peddle addresses the court: "Your Honour, the parties have agreed that costs will be in the amount of $10,000 inclusive of interest and disbursements." "Thank you," replies the Judge. "Just let me do an endorsement then. Okay, the endorsement reads: For oral reasons given, judgment for the plaintiff. The defendant shall pay the plaintiff:

1. The amount of $125,245.

2. Pre-judgment interest at the prescribed rate from January 31, 2010 to the date of the judgment.

3. Cost fixed at $10,000 inclusive of disbursements and HST.

4. Post –judgment interest at the prescribed rate."

We leave the courthouse, and my lawyer tells me to come see him the next business day. I tell him right away that I felt his closing argument hung me.
He disagrees, but doesn't say much. I ask him for a copy, and he promises to send it to me.

"This is bullshit!" I erupt. "That judge twisted everything to make Dagenais look credible."

Zijad says that we'll talk about it when we get together later, and he heads out quickly. Peddle walks by sporting a disgusting smirk. *God, how I despise that man!*

I return home and prepare to meet a few friends who'd planned to take me out for my birthday. I'm in no mood to eat but I don't want to let them down. I begin getting dressed to go out, but I soon have a change of heart. I decide to call my friends and tell them that I'm just going to stay in. I order pizza and wings, pick up a six-pack of beers and throw my own party – with me as the only guest.

As the beer sedates me, I try to remember the judge's reasons for his judgment, but I can't recall the details. I can't wait for Monday to hear what Zijad has to say.

Saturday I go to the Niagara gorge and hike for about four hours. I manage to banish all thoughts of the trial from my mind as I enjoy some vigorous exercise amid the natural splendors of the Glen Trails. When I get home I take a long hot bath and, for the first time in a long time, I feel safe in my own home. *Now that I've lost in court, why would anyone come after me?* I watch movie after movie on TV and then fall asleep on the couch. I get up around three o'clock and look out the window from time to time. All is quiet. There are no signs of any vehicles on my lane. All the same, I feel uneasy so I get dressed and drive over to a nearby Tim Horton's with my laptop and do some reading over a coffee. I decide to do some internet research on what you can do if you're the victim of an unjust court ruling. I read till about nine in the morning. *Thank God for Google.*

I'm extremely upset that Paul repeatedly lied in court, even though I know that none of his lies should have surprised me. Having decided to fabricate a lawsuit against me, probably at the urging of his siblings, he had no choice but to see it through and lie through his teeth. And yet his performance was so *unconvincing*, at least I thought so. Of course, I *knew* that he was lying, and that *he knew* he was lying. Couldn't a neutral observer see that as well? Wasn't it obvious that he was uncomfortable in his own skin? Or could his confused demeanor and awkward body language be interpreted in another way? *"Poor old guy! What he's been through! To be taken advantage of like that by a heartless, gold-digging stripper. Thank goodness he was able to find the fortitude to fight back!"* Didn't the judge imply that he was thinking along these lines when he referred to Paul's "courage"? And didn't he alibi Paul's more obvious lies – like the whopper about me forcing my attentions on him – by referring to his "understandable embarrassment" in telling "his story"?

Courage??? The very idea that Paul showed courage in going after me is enough to make my blood boil! What was "courageous" about Paul fabricating a story about me borrowing over a hundred grand so he could then sue me and rob me of my only real asset in the world – my home?

A chill runs through me. That's exactly where things stand. If this judge has his way, I *will* lose my home. I'll be forced to sell my property to comply with his court order.

But isn't it obvious that none of this makes any sense? If I had borrowed all that money, why would I be in such dire financial straits? Why is Revenue Canada freezing my bank account so they can grab every penny I deposit? Why am I falling behind in my mortgage payments so often, and forced to make payments through Western Union rather than my bank? Why am I driving on bald, leaking tires and not replacing them with a new set? Why am I scrambling desperately to find work rather than taking the time off, as my doctor advises, to attend to my medical problems? *Why?*

And then I remember exactly "why" none of those questions seemed to have entered the thinking of the esteemed Judge Lococo. Even though I'd repeatedly asked Zijad to provide the court with evidence of my obvious financial distress, not to mention other information that could have refuted Paul's lies, Zijad always insisted, "we have nothing to prove." He was like a broken record, telling me, over and over, that the onus of proof was on the side of the plaintiff, and that Dagenais' case was so flimsy it couldn't possibly meet the minimum standards of proof for a civil suit of this kind.... And yet, at trial, our failure to present certain pieces of information – notably my bank records – *was* used against me by the judge! As a matter of law, maybe the judge *shouldn't* have used that against me. But in light of what actually happened in court, wasn't it now clear that the judge *couldn't* have used that "failure" against us if Zijad had prepared a thorough and thoughtful defense? Had this now-obvious mistake been due to my lawyer's incompetence and inexperience – to a misguided faith in the impartiality of the judicial system? *Or had it been due to some more deliberate, even sinister motivation?*

I recall Zijad asking me to write down the questions I wanted him to ask Paul during cross-examination. But when I did so, he never followed through adequately –

not even when I encouraged him to press Paul to admit that he'd made a habit of asking me to call him and to call him back repeatedly. Those phone records that the judge had made such a big deal of were actually proof of Paul's obsession with me – and of my unwillingness to give him my cell-phone number so he could call me. How could Paul's lawyer have gotten away with presenting them as evidence of my badgering him for loans! The more I think about this and about Zijad's very weak closing argument, the more I'm convinced that Zijad may have deliberately sabotaged my case.

On Monday morning I meet Zijad at his office. After greeting me with a cheery "good morning," he quickly gets down to business. *Blah, blah, blah* – the same old bullshit! The main item on my agenda is the trial transcripts. I want them, and I want them A.S.A.P., because I need to study them carefully to decide how to proceed with the appeal I'm determined to launch. I'm also anxious to expose Paul as a liar and get him charged with perjury. Even my friend Eden had lied in court saying that Paul had never offered her money for sex, when he actually had. I remember she'd said exactly that when Zijad had interviewed her.

As I delve deeper into my case, and the possible connection between it and the intimidating behavior of the stalker vehicle, it occurs to me that during the pre-trial "discovery" session I had experienced a feeling of deep unease with some of the questions that Clark Peddle had asked me about certain notorious bikers. I'd felt really threatened during that interrogation. I need to get a hold of the transcripts from that discovery session along with everything else.

Zijad tells me he doesn't have a copy but that he should be able to get one from the courthouse or from Peddle. He says he'll obtain copies for both of us. But I sense he's stalling me.

Weeks pass and I'm growing more and more frustrated with my inability to obtain the documents I've asked for: the trial book and the transcript of the earlier "discovery" session, as well as other items. The appeals court may not consider it, but I'm determined to prove that Paul lied to the court. I already have recordings of girls telling me about their activities and conversations with Paul, but all of it is "hearsay" and therefore inadmissible in a court of law according to my lawyer. I need stronger evidence - and I need it from the horse's mouth.

I give a lot of thought to how I might be able to draw Paul out and get him on record saying things that contradict his trial testimony. I know he won't talk if he knows it's me, and I need to get him to respond to a whole list of "cues" that I've come up with. Using an old-fashioned public phone, I dial Paul's number and turn on my recorder. When he answers, I pretend to be my friend Eden.

"Eden": Linda Lee is not talking to me anymore.

Paul: Good…

"Eden": Yeah, because I paid for a cab ride a couple of times and she didn't show up at my house.

Paul: Pardon?

"Eden": I paid for a cab ride to come over…

Paul: Yeah?

“Eden”: … and she didn't come over.

Paul: Oh…

“Eden”: Did she ever do that to you?

Paul: Yes, ah.... Leave her alone.

“Eden”: Yeah?

Paul: Yeah.

“Eden”: Did you....

Paul: How you feeling babe?

“Eden”: I'm all right…

Paul: Long time, I never seen ya…

“Eden”: I know..... How did you ... But how did you fall in court? Your sister told me that you planned it.

Paul: No, I didn’t plan nothing.

“Eden”: No?

Paul: You know that…

“Eden”: Oh…

Paul: It was a drop, eh?

“Eden”: It was a what?

Paul: You know, a drop?

“Eden”: Okay…

Paul: You had to step down…

“Eden”: Okay, and you fell. So you didn't plan it?

Paul: Yeah, I forgot about it, and I fell on my leg. Yeah…

“Eden”: Okay…

Paul: And I went down.

“Eden”: Oh..... So, anyways I got your number from... umm... what’s her name? Dakota...! What's her stage name, I can't remember?

Paul: Dakota…

“Eden”: Umm, the white girl you usually get... Ah what's … I know her real name.

Paul: The white girl?

“Eden”: Yeah, really nice…

Paul: Yeah.

“Eden”: Umm, I forget her name... You take her in the back room sometimes.

Paul: Oh yeah, Sexy Stackson still there?

“Eden”: Sexy Stackson, yeah…

Paul: Oh Sexy Stackson!!!

“Eden”: Yeah, she wants to know if you’re ok.

Paul: Oh yeah?

“Eden”: Yeah.

Paul: Someday I'll come around.

“Eden”: Yeah, okay.

“Eden”: Well, we miss your VIP dances…

Paul: Pardon?

“Eden”: We miss your VIP dances!

Paul: I know.

“Eden”: Yeah.

Paul: I miss your’s too…

“Eden”: Aha.

Paul: Yeah, everybody except that Linda Lee. I'm finished with her.

“Eden”: Yeah?

Paul: Don't say nothing to her!

“Eden”: I won't.

Paul: Don't even say that you talk to me!

“Eden”: I won't. You know what else she told me?

Paul: What?

“Eden”: A lot of times when she used to call, umm call you, and uh, you tell her to come over, and you pay for the cab?

Paul: I did even… I didn't pay her for a cab. I have never been in a cab.

“Eden”: You never paid for a cab ride?

Paul: No.

“Eden”: No?

Paul: Never!

“Eden”: Umm, but what about … she, she’s really mad at me.

Paul: So what?

“Eden”: Yeah, she said …

Paul: Mmm … her

“Eden”: I know.

Paul: You've got lots of friends.

“Eden”: True, but you know what she keeps saying? Like she calls you so many times, and a lot of the times she never shows up at your house, and you used to get mad at her.

Paul: So what you want me to do? Don't bring that up any more!

“Eden”: What?

Paul: That stuff.

“Eden”: Umm, but was that true though, cause I kind of like her….

Paul: Well, what you want me to do?

“Eden”: Huh?

(Break it seems he's talking with someone)

Paul: You were the one that was in court, eh?

“Eden”: Yeah, I felt bad for it.

Paul: Who…

“Eden”: I felt bad for it.

Paul: For her?

“Eden”: For showing up, to talk against you... Cause you’re a good customer.

Paul: I know.

“Eden”: Yeah.

Paul: I was mad too.

“Eden”: I know

Paul: You had nothing to say anyways, you didn't know nothing.

“Eden”: Yeah.

Paul: Right…

“Eden”: True.... Yeah... the only thing I have to say is that when you did come to the club you asked me to tell her to call you.

Paul: No, I never…

“Eden”: Huh?

Paul: No.

“Eden”: You never did that?

Paul: No!

“Eden”: Remember, you’re talking to me though…

Paul: Yeah.

“Eden”: Remember, you’re talking to me. You used to tell me to tell her to call you.

Paul: No I didn't!

“Eden”: Hmmm. Anyways, oh well, that's all I could say is … umm, she is really, really mad.

Paul: Oh, I told you, leave her alone.

“Eden”: Yeah, she is really mad, because she says you lied so much on the court.

Paul: I lied?

“Eden”: Yeah…

Paul: Don't even talk about the court. It's over, it's over.

“Eden”: Yeah, but she is so mad!

Paul: I'm going to get in a lot of shit.

"Eden": Yeah?

Paul: I'm going to be in a lot of shit talking to you.

"Eden": Oh yeah?

Paul: Yeah.

"Eden": Okay.

Paul: Court is over with, leave it alone.

"Eden": Okay.

Paul: All right.

"Eden": All right.

Paul: If she don't want to talk to you, forget it.

"Eden": Okay ... Hmm.

Paul: Someday, I'll come over... I'll…

"Eden": But she is so mad.

Paul: All right!

"Eden": Yeah I'd....

Paul: All right, don't worry about her, I told you. I told you, okay? I got to go.

"Eden": Okay ... Bye.

As I hang up the phone, I'm thinking: *Wow. Somebody is watching this guy like a hawk. What a weird conversation! Paul actually sounds worried he's going to get in shit talking about this stuff on the phone.*

Later that day, I visit Zijad to discuss the appeal. We have a very lengthy conversation.

"So, Zijad, I want to hear what you've got to say now."

"What have I got to say…? Two options, appeal it or don't appeal it."

"Okay, I'm appealing it. What's the grounds for getting it dismissed?"

"Well, any time you've got a case that's built solely on credibility, it's very difficult to appeal it. In this case, what the grounds for appeal would have to be is that this is the type of case that credibility alone shouldn't determine it, just because there's absolutely no documents, no documentary evidence at all. That for a case of over a hundred thousand dollars in loans – like I said, this isn't $130, this is $130,000 of debts – it shouldn't be a case that has to be built only on credibility. The judge came to a wrong conclusion, even by listening to the evidence…. So let's talk about credibility. You said, 'I didn't do it', not like you said, not like you stumbled and came across and said 'Yes, I borrowed the money, yes I took the money'. Then he can say, 'well, you know what, I didn't believe that she stumbled. He cross-examined you for ten minutes'."

"The thing that I fail to accept is that we didn't get a chance to even do anything to him, ask him any questions in depth. Nothing like that. Number two is, I called this fucker this morning…." "Which guy?" asks Zijad.

"What's his name, Paul … I call him Skeletor, I didn't even know his last name until court. He was in my phone as Skeletor. I tried to call him this morning, I'm looking for Paul in my phone – there was no Paul, I had to go to Skeletor. Number two is, I called him and I pretended I was Eden, the girl that was on the stand. He was not at all upset with her, okay? I tried to get it out of him, quite a few things, and he goes 'I can't talk about it, let's not talk about it, I can't talk about that – no, no, no'. But I said, you know, we had fun when we go in the VIP, and he's like 'yeah' – he knows about the VIP."

Zijad nods. "It came out, it came out in court and the judge said 'He stumbled here, here…'."

"No, it didn't come out, the VIP. He said that he fooled around on the floor…."

"But here's specifically what the judge said: he stumbled on a lot of his evidence but I believe him on the *thrust* of the evidence, which is the important stuff. I believe him that Paul loaned you the money. And the reason why I believe that Paul loaned the money to you is because you called him so many times in those six months – so the judge came to the conclusion that there is no other explanation given, which was a mistake for the judge to say that we didn't offer another explanation. We don't have to offer another explanation – they're the ones that have to prove the case."

I nod. "Not only that, if we can get papers of other girls that called – phone records – we'd see. I'll tell you this, a friend of mine came down here for my birthday, treated me nicely to a restaurant, me and my boyfriend were on the, you know, whatever…"

Zijad seems disinterested in what I'm saying, his mind seems to be someplace else. Then his voice goes very low.

"I gotta tell you, I gotta tell you some stuff that I can't really tell you – I could lose my job and not be a lawyer anymore if I give you this advice. The only thing they have on you is the house – they can grab your house, they can put a lien on the house.... If you appeal it, that's all put on hold. I can buy you a lot of time on the appeal – to get rid of the house – okay? – and to disappear. They'll never find you, okay? You'll have, like, I can buy you time – like, whether I'm going to be successful on the appeal, I'm behind the 8 ball. I don't think I'm going to be successful on the appeal."
My mind is still focused on constructing a winning appeal and I'm not paying much attention to Zijad's rambling. "No? Even with him stating that he went to the VIP….?"

Zijad and I are on different wavelengths, talking past each other.

"No," he says, "and it will show on the transcript that he's lying about this, lying about that. But the judge said, 'I believe him on the thrust of the evidence'. Which is that, 'I believe him that he took out the money and loaned it to you'."

"But on credibility, this is perjury. If the case is based on credibility and he straight up lied …."

"The grounds of appeal is, you can appeal credibility if the conclusion that the judge came to based on the credibility is manifestly wrong – and that's gonna be our grounds for appeal. But what I'm doing is buying you time, in my opinion, right? Because there's $130,000 on the line. To appeal it will cost about $10,000."

"I have to appeal it, but I do not have the money up front though."

"How long, like, can you do it in – because I have to order transcripts – a lot of this is my costs and court costs."

"Well, I could pay you over time, like every two, three weeks I could give you some money…."

"If over the next three months you could come up with $10,000…." "Oohh," I moan, "I could come up with, maybe over five months, like if I could come every month and give you like a thousand or two. But that's like me going to work… Like, you know I don't have a $132,000 sitting anywhere…."

"Yeah, I can do that … I can do that, because I'll take it out of our account for the time being. Because what I want to do is buy you some time so you can disappear, okay?"

"Why disappear?" Suddenly, it hits me – I've been hearing but not really listening to what this guy's been saying.

"Not disappear, but get rid of the house. That's the only asset you have – they have nothing else on you, okay?

They have the house and they're going to grab onto it as quickly as they can."

"So we need to get on top of this fast…?" I reply, a little perplexed.

"I have to file for appeal within 30 days. And I will file for it within 30 days.
Once one side files for appeal, the decision is stayed, and they can't go after you until the appeal is disposed of."

"What if he starts today?"

"If he starts today, I start my appeal tomorrow, and whatever he's started he can't do anything with it. It's as though it was never started…."

Slowly, I'm beginning to get what he's proposing. *Maybe he's right. If I can't beat them in the courts, then maybe I should follow Zijad's advice and deprive them of a victory this way. At least this way, they'll have won the legal battle but I'll win the war. The idea has its appeal, but I'm not quite sure about it.* Zijad rambles on and on, and I finally tune back in.

"The guys that I work with are as shocked as I am about how the judge came to this decision. They're pretty much saying that what got me was the optics – honestly, no offense, the optics were: 'black girl, older white man'. This is a white town. Black girl who is, in his opinion, a professional sex worker, in the judge's opinion, and which he doesn't know you, he doesn't know you like I know you – that you're smarter than fuckin' any other girl that I know, okay? It's the optics, right? And the judge saying 'I commend, I commend him for taking this civil step' and, you know, getting the courage to sue you – that, in my opinion, is a lot of bias…."

My mind is still wrestling with his idea about disappearing. *Why would he suggest that? He knows I'm being stalked, so why would he say that? Is there a connection here? What does he know that I don't know?* Zijad is talking about Paul.

"He said that 'every single amount that I took out I gave it to her', right?

That was his evidence. And our case was that, that doesn't make any sense. But then…."

"He also put shingles on his house …." I interject.

"The judge makes a mistake by saying that I'm going to exclude any amount under $1,200, and I'm going to exclude the amount that is after January 4. Based on what? His lawyer didn't advance that argument, I didn't advance that argument, so the judge is making his argument for him. He's tailoring it so that it makes sense to the judge to make that decision. But that's not the evidence – the evidence is – and I asked him several times – if you're telling me that every single amount you took out was given to [Ang], 'yes', not a single amount was used for personal use, 'no'. And then the judge goes ahead and says, well, I'm going to exclude this, this and this because it makes more sense that way. He's saying $150,000, and the judge says, well,

I'll say $122,000 – that's not the case, the case is it's either a hundred and fifty or nothing. You can't exclude amounts – there's no evidence to exclude amounts."

"Plus he put new shingles on his house – so how much is shingles, what's that thing that you put on the outside…?"

"Aluminum sidings…."

"So he covered his house with sidings, is that under $1,000?"

"No…."

"You know what I mean? Can they get records of every other person that calls him? No, he's got *my* records…."

"Yeah, exactly…. You're the one he's pointed a finger at…."

We talk for some time about various details of the case and about the judge, and my anger boils up again.

"That judge is totally biased. Would another court rule like that in Toronto?"

"Every judge is different…." Zijad sighs.

"Who judges the judges?" I ask. I'm wondering, *how can a biased and prejudiced judge like Lococo get away with what he's putting me through?*

"The Court of Appeal…."

"Oh really…?" I answer, not quite sure that Zijad is understanding me. I want to have my chance to expose that judge for what he is – *but is that possible at the Court of Appeal?*

"You have a re-course. You don't agree with what this judge says, you take it up, and it's three judges at the Court of Appeal, not just one."

"The way that the appeal works, it's not a new trial, right?"

"Even if he accepts that he gave you the money," Zijad points out, apparently oblivious to my question. "There is no evidence that it was a loan rather than a gift, because there's no paperwork."

"But, I have this question, what about the fact that he's said he never spent no money within that time period, but he probably did the outside of his house. Can you bring that in at the new…?

"It's possible…." Zijad allows.

"… 'cause that's got to be there," I insist. "And I think that perjury's involved…."

Zijad nods. "Well yeah, perjury's a big thing, and if we can find out who did his house, how much he paid him, right, if you have receipts to show that he perjured himself…."

"Don't let this other lawyer know that part…."

"No, no, no," Zijad says excitedly, "this other lawyer knows nothing…." I wonder about that last exchange. *Is Zijad catching on to the fact that I don't trust him and that I'm suspicious of what might be going on between him and the other lawyer?*

"Last but not least," I suggest, "our framework should be, how many other girls did he see in that place? And how many of the phone records did you obtain? Okay? So, you got hers, but he would come in there and talk to her and blah, blah, blah – so why don't you go get these other girls' phone records? And match? But this is what I'm saying. You can't just basically say that because she calls this many times, there's other girls that are gonna call. They could call as many times too. Do you understand what I'm saying?"

I'm trying to hold back, but my impatience with Zijad's handling of the case is hard for me to suppress. *If Peddle is able to get my records to try to crucify me, why didn't my lawyer go after all the girls who associated with Paul and get their phone records? Was it incompetence or what?*

"I understand what you're saying, but again it's you that he pointed a finger at, not those other girls."

"Yeah, but the thing is…."

"They're the ones who call him too, sure, but they're not the ones – maybe they were the ones who drove him to the bank, true, maybe some of them did…."

"Yeah, but the fact is to dilute that interest in my phone records, because they only have mine. It's not saying that I'm saying that that didn't happen.
I'm just saying that it could dilute it because he did see numerous girls. You know what I mean?"

Zijad nods. "And his sister called him too, and his sister drove him to the bank too. So who's to say then that he didn't give it to his sister."

"Did she say that she drove him to the bank?"

"Yeah, of course she did. She admitted she drove him to the bank." *Funny how whenever Zijad makes what sounds like a good point, my frustration with him disappears momentarily. It's like he's reeling me back in.*

Near the end of our conversation, Zijad sums up his view of the judge's decision: "The problem is, and I'm going to say it again, the optics looked bad…You're a hot dancer, he's Skeletor. The judge is gonna say, 'what the hell is she doing at his house?'"

I'm sick to my stomach as I leave his office, and I head right over to see my friend. It's refreshing to have a real conversation about the case and to be able to speak freely. We discuss my whole situation at length.

After listening to me rant on and on, my friend interjects seeking clarification about how the lawsuit came about.

"It sounds like, at some point, Paul's sister and maybe others in his family realized that a great deal of Paul's life savings had gone missing, and they confronted him about it. But instead of owning up to his actions, he pointed the finger at you. You – and only you – is his explanation for why his money is gone."

"Right," I answer.

"So, Paul and his sister brought the suit against you. To prove that the money went to you, they obtained his bank records and your phone records to show that you were calling him frequently and especially on days when he was making big withdrawals from his bank. They match the days of those withdrawals with the days you were calling him. But to make it look like you were

pressuring him into all this, Paul testifies that he didn't want to have anything to do with you – that all the calls were unwelcome."
"Right."

"And then, when you are unable to explain what Paul actually did with all that money, the judge holds that against you."

"Right again."

"But here's an interesting contradiction. After making the first few loans to you, why didn't he demand that you sign an IOU note? And after you were in debt to him for larger and larger amounts, why would he not want to take your calls? I'd most definitely want to take calls from someone who owes me tens of thousands of dollars. Anyone would. What he said makes no sense."

As an outside observer, fresh to the facts of the case, my friend is able to cast new light on just how truly *incredible* Paul's story really is. He agrees that the judge ignored a lot of inconsistencies and implausible aspects of Paul's story, and that his decision was based not on the weight of evidence but on his "subjective perceptions and biases." But he's also disturbed with what I tell him about my lawyer – his whole approach to the case, and especially his "confidential advice" to me to sell my house and run. "So let's get this straight. For months your lawyer was reassuring you that your defense was a slam-dunk – that you could play totally defensive because the other side didn't have any real evidence to support its claims. According to him, you didn't need to present evidence of Paul's involvement with other girls. You didn't need to talk about your financial troubles and how they're inconsistent with the claim that you had bilked Paul for $130,000. You didn't need to do any of those things because 'they had to prove their case,' and supposedly they couldn't. Then, when he loses the case, your lawyer puts it down to the fact that this is 'a white town' and the white judge 'preferred' the white guy's story to that of the black stripper. Unbelievable! So why didn't he anticipate the judge's bias and prepare for it? And if he's so convinced now that the 'optics' were always against you, why didn't he see that before? And, oh my God, why is he now advising you to do something he knows is *illegal* – to defy the court order and 'disappear'? One thing is clear – you need a new lawyer. This guy has been screwing you over, and he'll continue to screw you over."

"I know what you're saying, and I can't disagree," I say with exasperation. "But I have no money for a new lawyer. My gut tells me that he's actually working with the other lawyer to screw me over. It's so frustrating – but I'm stuck with him."

"What makes you think he's colluding with Dagenais' lawyer?"

"Well, at the end of the trial Paul's lawyer asked for his costs to be included in the judgment. Zijad and Peddle left the room for a few minutes. When they returned, Peddle asked for $10,000 in costs. But later Zijad said that he thought Paul is probably paying him about $20,000. Strange, no? Also, my lawyer allowed Peddle to get away with murder when he went after me about the phone records. Those weren't Paul's phone records, as he implied. They were *mine*, requested as part of discovery. Even the judge was confused on that point.

He said in his judgment that *Dagenais'* phone records revealed that I was badgering him, but it was our side that provided the records, *my records*. My lawyer allowed all that confusion to go unanswered. Plus I had recordings of a few girls who saw Paul outside of the club and a Facebook page of a conversation of a girl talking about her date with Paul, but Zijad said it wouldn't hold up in court. And I think it was deliberate. He can't be *that* incompetent."

My friend shakes his head. "You realize it's going to cost you even more lawyers' fees on both sides to take this case to the appeals stage. And the likelihood is you're going to lose. You have an untrustworthy lawyer who's telling you that up front."

"No, I'm going to be hands on, trust me. I'm going to research everything and examine everything my lawyer writes very carefully before he submits it.... I'm going to allow him to start the process, but in the meantime I'm going to try to find a lawyer who'll work for me on a contingency basis."

When I get home, I start thinking about my phone conversation with Paul again. There's a lot of explosive stuff there. He even tells "Eden": "Don't say nothing to her [Linda Lee]... don't even say that you talk to me." It's obvious that he's trying to hide his involvement with other girls. He even promises that he'll be coming in sometime soon. But not now! The question is why? I can't really believe it! He's put a halt to all his usual habits and activities, even going so far as to end a telephone conversation with a Sundowner girl –

something he used to enjoy doing for just as long as the girl would remain on the line.

I'm pleased with what I've obtained on the recording, but I didn't get very far down on my list of things that I wanted to talk to him about. I'm not sure if I have enough on the recording to make a perjury charge stick.

I listen to the tape over and over again, wondering whom he might be afraid of, who might be listening to his conversation? He tells me he's going to "get into a lot of shit" talking on the phone. *Someone's keeping an eye on him, keeping him in line.* His lawyer in his closing argument to the judge had made a big point about how no significant funds had been withdrawn from his accounts since January of 2010. *No shit! His lawyer and his sister have probably made sure of that! They aren't allowing Paul to do anything that could weaken their case against me. Plus if he's not taking cabs who is driving him to The Sundowner, I'm sure it's not me and damn sure it's wasn't his sister.*

Over the next week I spend several days in the library researching what I must do next – and what needs to be submitted to the appeals court. On the advice of my friend, I consider finding a new lawyer who might take my case on a contingency basis. Niagara lawyers are out of the question – too many of them might have ties to Chris, or Zijad, or Peddle. No I'll need to find someone in Toronto. But even that makes me nervous because I remember Zijad telling me that Chris knows lawyers "from here to Ottawa."

I finally get up the nerve to approach one, and we arrange a phone conversation. I feel safe with this guy because he works for a prestigious law firm – and he's black. Knowing Chris as I do, I doubt that he'd have anything to do with a black lawyer, no matter how good he is.

I make an appointment to meet with this big-city lawyer. He tells me he needs a few things from me before we meet: the trial transcript and copies of as much relevant documentation as I can obtain. I call Zijad to inquire yet again about the court papers, and he sets me up with an appointment and tells me he wants to see me too.

When we meet a few days later, I tell Zijad that the stalker car has started coming down my lane again, but he seems uninterested, even though I tell him that I'd seen it parked in my driveway for several minutes with headlights and engine off. I explain that I'd tried to call the police but that I couldn't get a signal from my hiding place on a farm across the road.

I ask him about how the appeals process works. He explains that the court of appeals has a panel of three judges with the authority to overturn a decision if they find fault with the Superior Court judge's judicial reasoning or application of the law. I tell him I'm in the process of compiling new evidence to present to them, but he says they won't consider it. He explains that that this won't be a new trial, and new evidence is inadmissible.

When I protest that I want to prove that Paul lied in court, Zijad replies: "It doesn't matter. They won't look at any new evidence. All they can do is consider our arguments that the trial judge committed errors in arriving at his decision."

I ask him if he can provide me with copies of the trial papers and the transcript. He tells me he's ordered them, and will make copies for me as soon as possible.

I'll be meeting soon with that new lawyer in Toronto and need to give him copies of the trial book and the closing arguments. I'm getting nowhere relying on Zijad to provide me with anything, so I go to the courthouse in Welland to order the transcripts without letting him know what I'm up to.

I'm furious. I call Zijad to confirm my recollection of Peddle's closing argument. Specifically, I bring up his ludicrous point that Paul had stopped making big withdrawals from his bank accounts after he stopped meeting with "Linda Lee." "No wonder," I point out, "somebody's watching him like a hawk." Zijad confirms that Peddle had emphasized this point in his closing. I ask him again about the transcripts for the closing arguments and discovery and he tells me he's still waiting for it.

While all this is going on, I'm afraid to work, not knowing who might be looking for me and where. My fear actually intensifies whenever I see my lawyer because the first thing out of his mouth is always, "where are you working?"

As I bide my time, I begin to notice that one or more vehicles is visiting my lane again in the early morning hours. Not every night, as before, but once or twice a week. My sleep deficit is growing.

On top of all this, my mortgage company is bugging me about payments that are now running months late. I go to a friend and he lends me the money to catch up on my payments and avoid foreclosure. When I'll be able to repay this loan, God only knows. Over the course of the previous year, I've had to take large personal loans from him and other friends to avoid losing my house. For their sakes, as well as my own, I need to hang on. I need to preserve the equity I've built up and prevent my home from being sold on some auction block for a song. But, quite honestly, I'd rather have that happen than see the Dagenais family steal it from me – however "legally"!

For over a year now, I've had to travel far and wide to find work, only to end up making a pittance in dead clubs in small, out-of-the-way towns. I've had to live with my hydro cut off much of the time because I can't afford to pay my bills. Friends have helped me out with that too from time to time. But how often can you ask for a handout or a loan?

I wait and wait for my lawyer to call me and tell me he finally has copies of the various documents he's promised me. I can't believe how long it's taking, but I've already ordered the trial transcript on my own as well. So, I finally venture down to the Welland Court House and inquire about the delay. The clerk tells me that my lawyer has also ordered them and that they should be there in about a week. I ask her to call me when they arrive. A few days later I receive a call from her, and I rush down to claim one of Zijad's copies. *Thank God, because I have no money to pay for it. Even putting gas in my car is becoming a challenge for me.*

I read the trial book carefully and call my lawyer to tell him that it contains enough bald-faced lies from Paul for him to be charged with perjury. We just need to do a little digging. He advises me that he hasn't picked up the trial book yet. But he seems disturbed that I've gone behind his back to get it.

"Zijad, I'm determined to get on with this – I can't let this guy Paul get away with destroying my life! The trial record is very revealing. After they got my phone records, his sister tried to match my phone calls to the dates of his withdrawals."

Zijad reminds me that all of this had indeed come out in court.

"A lot came out in court that neither of us picked up on immediately. For instance, Eden testified about Paul's threats to kill her and some other girls if they talked to me about him. I think maybe Paul realized he'd crossed a line and could end up being charged. Plus he was under pressure from his sister and maybe others in his family to account for all the money he'd blown over a period of six or so months. No wonder he decided to target me at that point, especially after I told him to get lost. What I find incredible is that the judge didn't even mention that aspect of Eden's testimony in his judgment. Yet he gave a great deal of attention to what Mrs. Taylor had done in matching my phone calls with Dagenais' withdrawals. The judge didn't even consider the possibility that the phone records of other girls Paul was seeing may well have matched up with many of his withdrawals as well."

Zijad tells me he'll pick up the other copy for his own use and get back to me.
"There's a lot of stuff that isn't included, including the closing arguments," I mention. "And I really want to see those closing arguments."

He tells me that every item needs to be ordered separately and that he'll get on top of it.

My woes are accumulating rapidly. I'm in a legal morass and my livelihood has been largely destroyed. I remember Chris's notorious rant where he warned all the black girls at the Sundowner what it would mean to them if they lost their ability to work in his club. How right he was! I've been cut off from customers who have been the mainstay of my livelihood for years, and I'm broke. Not surprisingly, I've also been facing an escalation of threats from my mortgage company and they're now going to court to seize my house.

I go out of town to work for a few days at a club up north. I tell every customer who asks me where I'm from, "Toronto." I keep "eyes in the back of my head" and never have a drink while working. It's a bitch, because nothing is harder for me than to dance for customers without a buzz. I plan specific escape routes from each and every club that I work. I keep running shoes with me in my large purse and park my car nearby. I wonder, *am I succumbing to paranoia, a persecution complex?* And then I remind myself of something one of my friends told me: *being paranoid doesn't mean there isn't someone out to get you!* I've been targeted by Dagenais and his gang, I'm being hounded by my mortgage company, and I've been deprived of my livelihood by a pimp who pretends to be a respectable club-owning "businessman." And there's reason to suspect that the lawyer to whom I've confided so much may have sabotaged my legal defense, shared information about me with his pal Chris, and colluded with Dagenais' lawyer for a pound of my flesh. Sometimes "paranoia" has a basis in reality. I have every right to be paranoid!

Business is lousy at this out-of-the-way club. Most of the customers are "regulars" of particular girls and "committed" to them. I make a little money dancing for some out-of-towners, but I quickly become demoralized. After a few days I return home. It's around 5 a.m. I'm tired as hell but I don't dare go inside. I hide in my car and sleep till daybreak. As soon as I go in, I check all the doors and closets and then set my alarm for nine so I can grab a little more sleep before calling Zijad.

When we meet later, Zijad gives me a fist bump instead of his usual hug. He asks me where I've been working, and I answer, "here and there." He asks if I'm able to pay him anything, and I laugh a bitter laugh. I tell him I'm virtually broke and even behind on my mortgage.

"I need to know the name of the biker that Paul's lawyer mentioned during the discovery," I say. "The one he tried to link me to." He tells me he doesn't recall a name being mentioned.

"Come on!" I implore him. "Remember I called you afterwards and asked you how he could get away with threatening to talk about me to bikers?" He answers that he'll try to get the discovery transcript one way or another – either from the court or from Peddle.

“So, how do I go about getting Paul charged with perjury? What steps do we go through for that? Do I go to the police?” He tells me that once we’ve established that he lied about certain things, then we take the transcript and the new evidence that he lied and get the police to look at it. That’s *how* you go about charging him, he says. But it has to be about an issue material to the case. For example, if he said ‘I don’t know what VIP is’ when, six months ago, he admitted to knowing exactly what VIP is – then, that’s not really a material issue.

“Why isn’t it?” I ask.

He explains that the material issue in this case is, did Paul lend you the money?

“Come on, he’s lying about that. If we can show he’s lying about a lot of other things, like his statement that he didn’t give other girls money, wouldn’t that show he’s likely lying about that as well?”

He answers that he needs to look at the transcript. If Paul said he’d only watched shows and bought drinks, and never bought dances, and we can prove that he did, then that *could be* a material issue.

I remind him that in the discovery session – I’m going from memory here – Paul said something about having a girlfriend that he flew out west. Zijad shrugs.

Zijad keeps butting heads with me. No matter what I bring up, he’s always ready with an argument as to why it's not relevant, or why it won't work. *Is Zijad an ass or is it the law? Or is it both?*

I remind him of Paul's trial testimony where he'd said that he didn't have a girlfriend, as well as his sister's evidence that she'd never known him to have a girlfriend. Then I ask him why he didn't bring up the point about the girl who I know went out with Paul on several occasions – the one who mentioned dates with him on Facebook and whose ticket home he paid for.

For the umpteenth time, Zijad makes the obvious point that Paul is pointing his finger *at me* – and asks me how any of this relevant.
"Why isn't it relevant that there were other girls he was seeing, and that he's now denying that? How can you say that's not relevant?"
Zijad replies that all this came out in court.

"How can you say that? You know that a lot of this *didn't* come out in court. And we both know why – because you decided not to introduce it. Even his lie about me agreeing to move in with him – you didn't even push him on that! Plus, in court, Eden said that he'd asked her to go to Jamaica with him.
Why didn't you make more of that? I'm trying so hard to prove my innocence!"

What am I doing? I don't have any money to retain a new lawyer, and I can't be pissing off this guy. I need to backtrack and try to get him to work with me on this at least until I can afford to dump him.

"Sorry, I didn't mean that. But I'm frustrated and I need you to give me some constructive advice rather than just shoot down everything I'm saying."

Zijad seems unfazed, and he proceeds to offer me what might pass for constructive advice. He suggests that, if I can locate a bank account belonging to Paul with $100,000 in it that would certainly help our case. I'm thinking, *is he serious? How would I go about getting information from Paul about a bank account with a $100,000 balance?* I recall once again my repeated suggestions to Zijad that we should have hired a private investigator to look into various aspects of Paul's affairs. That could have been one of them. But how, at this point, could I – on my own – go about investigating what Paul did with all that money? *Some "constructive advice"!*

As we're sitting here talking, I'm thinking that as soon as I leave I'm going to call Paul and get some more of my other questions answered.

Then, rather surprisingly, Zijad starts talking about what a good idea it would be for me to hire an investigator *now. He can't be serious. He knows I have no money for that and it's too late in any case. Why is he talking shit to me?*

I feel like getting into a shit-throwing fight with this guy – just like chimpanzees. I want to see what he'll say next if I counter his crap with some of my own. I say, "Yes, that's a great idea. I want an investigator to go into the Sundowner and get the low-down on everything."

Suddenly, he changes his tune. The Sundowner has nothing to do with my case, he insists. I can't believe my own lawyer can say such a thing. *The Sundowner has everything to do with my case – on so many levels. That's where I met Paul. That's where the witnesses are to Paul's real activities. That's where I made my living – until this case came up and I somehow found myself in trouble with Chris and management. What the fuck is he saying?* Then it occurs to me. Zijad isn't really denying the relevance of the Sundowner to my case – he's protecting *Chris*! He just doesn't want an investigator going into the Downer.

I'm determined to expose more of Paul's lies before the appeals process starts. I have my list of talking points and head toward a friend's house where I'm planning to call Paul. I call my friend and ask her if she'll be at home for a while, explaining I'm just on my way. She invites me over. Over the phone, I tell her about my plans to continue my investigation into Paul's lies and strengthen my argument that he perjured himself. She asks me how I intend to do that, and I tell her that some recorded statements he's made contradict the lies he told in court.

"Not only do I want to destroy his case against me; I want him criminally charged with perjury. And I want to countersue the bastard for all he's worth!"

She thinks it's doubtful I'll be able to get a new trial even if I can prove that Paul perjured himself. I find this upsetting and go off on her.

“This guy has totally disrupted my life with his lies. You think I’m going to sit back and watch him get away with it? You think I’m going to let him destroy me because he got upset that I told him off and because I stopped having anything to do with him for spreading lying rumors about us having sex? Fuck him!”

“I hear you honey, I hear what you’re saying. I get it totally,” she says supportively. “But you need to call your lawyer and see if you can get the case retried now that he’s dead.”

“If I have proof that he lied, of course we can get the case reopened. I can countersue the bastard… Wait a second! What do you mean dead?

Who’s dead?”

“You didn’t know that Paul died?”

“No! What … ? Where did you hear this?

When did this happen?

“A couple of months ago I think.”

“No, this can’t be!”

I pull over and go on line on my phone to see if I can find an obituary, but I soon realize that I’m not remembering the proper spelling of Paul’s last name. So I go to the trunk of my car and retrieve some court papers. There it is – DAGENAIS. I type the name into Google’s search engine and a link to an obituary with Paul’s picture comes up. “He enjoyed taking long drives and playing backyard mechanic. Loving son of Alice Dagenais. Dear brother of Denise, Simon (Rosemary), Suzanne (Gerald), Dianne (Harvey), Raymond, Pauline and Rheo (Lisa).”

It's true – Paul really is dead. I'm not sure what to think or how to react – I just feel numb. *He had all those siblings ... I had no idea. Can it be true that his sister Denise was the only one who cared about all his shit?*

Then it hits me: *Paul must have died shortly after I talked to him on the phone, when I was pretending to be Eden.*

All I know is, I need to talk to Zijad about this, and I head right over to his office.

I wait some time for Zijad, as I don't have an appointment and he's with a client. Half an hour later I get to see him. I tell him Paul is dead. He asks how I know and I say I heard a rumor and did an Internet search. He says no, and I say yes! He gets on the phone to Clark Peddle, and I'm sitting there as he makes the call. The conversation sounds unnatural, even contrived to me. But, of course, Peddle "confirms" to Zijad that Paul is indeed dead.

My lawyer tells me it's too bad he didn't die a month before the trial instead of two months afterward. I tell him I still want him charged with perjury, but Zijad explains that it's impossible now that Paul is dead. Perjury is a criminal charge and only living people can face criminal charges. I feel frustrated as hell. There goes my strategy. But what about getting a new civil trial? Zijad insists that's impossible too. How can the case be re-tried, he asks, if the plaintiff is dead? *Shit! I feel like all the doors are being shut on me! Why did that fucker have to go and die!*

I ask Zijad what I can do, and he replies that all we can do now is proceed with the paper work for the appeal. Then he reminds me that, from his point of view, this is all just a delaying tactic so I can sell my house and split. I tune him out, because I've already decided that I'm not doing that, and I'm more than annoyed that Zijad is giving me this stupid "advice" again. As he drones on about needing money to proceed, I can't help feeling that Paul might be looking down on this scene and laughing.

What impeccable timing for him to die! He doesn't have to face the consequences of his perjury and my lawyer is basically saying that I have no recourse but to commit fraud and run away. What a crock of steaming shit!

I now have Paul pegged for the kind of customer who'd fight for whatever he could get from a woman, and when he's sure he can't get it, he'd go to extraordinary lengths to make her suffer. He was like the guy on an episode of "Boomtown" – a customer who became infatuated with a stripper, began to imagine that he was married to her, and then killed her real husband so he could have her. Paul didn't go quite that far, but he was still a crazy fuck!

Then it hits me like a brick. I yell out, "fuck no, shit!" *Is it possible they'll try to pin Paul's death on me?* I need to find out exactly how he died! I remember that his obituary on the Internet mentioned that he'd died at Welland County General Hospital on November 13, 2011. I call the hospital to see if I can obtain any further information about the circumstances of his death, but they say they can't divulge anything to me because I'm not a family member.

I'm scared, because people might think I had reason to harm him, and I'm not sure I have an alibi for the few days leading up to November 13. As far as I'm concerned, Paul had a lot of life left in him. *Could he have been the victim of foul play? And are the police conducting an investigation? There's nothing in the media to suggest it, but I can't rule out the possibility of an investigation going on behind the scenes.*

Over the next few weeks I feel like a sitting duck, biding my time and waiting to see what might happen. My rule is to never talk to the police, because they will then have your story and their own version of what you've said. So it's always best to talk to an attorney first. I don't know any criminal lawyers, but I get a list of phone numbers off the Internet and keep it freshly written on the palm of my hand for months.

I need to focus – I need to work. With too much on my mind, I head out of town. The last place I want to be is in any strip-club because I now feel particularly vulnerable in those places. But I have no choice. I'm watching every move that everyone makes, and my vigilance is making it hard for me to focus on my work. I always have my escape route planned out, but wherever I go, the money sucks. And the money sucks because I'm preoccupied with watching everything going on around me. I'm unable to give customers the attention they expect. So I get one or two dances but I'm not able to capture the interest of customers the way I used to.

Picture this, I'm sitting with a customer and instead of asking him his name I'm stretching my neck all over the place to see what's going on. If a guy is going to the washroom, I'm on it. So very few customers keep me for more than a song or two. The problem isn't that I lack personality; the problem is I'm not *sharing* my personality. But I can't help it.

This one guy makes a stink saying he isn't going to pay me because my dance was lousy. As he rises to his feet, I push him back into the chair and tell him: "This is a really bad time to fuck with me over twenty dollars. Sorry, I've danced for you and if you want more than a dance I suggest a rub and tug parlor. The law, you peace of shit, is no touching." He hands me the twenty dollars and leaves.

After a few days of work, I'm anxious to get home. I'm so tired that on my way back I have to stop at a gas station. I go inside and explain to the attendant that I'm going to be parked outside taking a nap. He praises me for being smart.

A bit later, the ringing of my phone awakens me. A friend is upset. She can't sleep and needs to talk to me. I don't know why these girls think I have all the answers and smarts.

She tells me that Chris called all the black girls in for another meeting. This time he was even ruder than before.

"I'm totally fed up. We work for ourselves, not for that asshole. We have to pay him to work there and yet he thinks he can order us around and treat us like shit! It's unbelievable."

She's so over-excited that I can't get a word in edgewise.

"Hold on, girl. What exactly happened?"

"You know how on any given nightshift there are anywhere from ten to twenty black girls?"

"Yeah…."

"Chris is saying from now on he's only going to allow two black girls per shift!"

"What???? That's bull. So he'll have sixty to eighty white girls. There's no quota for them, right?"

"Yeah, it's a quota only for us – only two black girls per shift. Isn't this against the law? What can we do about it? Who can I call?"

"The Human Rights Tribunal I guess…."

"So basically the first two black girls who show up for a shift are the only ones who can work. So what the fuck, we're supposed to show up early and get in line, and maybe end up fighting about who was there first? And all the other girls get to prance right by us, no problem. Tomorrow morning, I'm gonna have to get there at 10:00 and sit for two hours until the club opens just to make sure I get my spot."

"Holy!"

"You don't understand how this is going to affect my livelihood, my life! I can't just pick up and move. I've got young kids in school here."

“What about the girls who come in from Toronto? They’re gonna drive for two hours not even knowing about this new rule?” “I guess they’re gonna have to get in the back of the line.”

“If he pulls this off, man he has powers beyond belief,” I say.

“You know he does.”

“No,” I reply with a spirit of defiance, “he’s a racist pig.” I can actually feel the blood rushing through my veins. *How far can he go and how much rope can you give this guy before he hangs himself?*

“So who do I call?”

“Leave it with me for a bit, and I’ll call you back later.”

I get back on the road and head home. I park in my usual hiding spot for a couple of hours before daybreak. As I’m sitting in my car, I recall a conversation with Zijad about Chris.

Zijad: I know Chris is not behind that stuff, but I’m hearing through, here and there, that he is going on saying, I don’t want black girls working at the Sundowner.

Thelma: He doesn’t?

Zijad: Yeah.

Thelma: He wants…

Zijad: He doesn’t, which, he needs a fff…. punch in the mother fucking face.

Thelma: But he's always been racist, that's nothing new.

Zijad: I'm sorta distancing myself from that business.

At daybreak, instead of entering my house and getting some sleep, I head over to Zijad's office even though it won't be open for a few more hours. I see a number of people – lawyers, secretaries – entering a side door and eventually the front door is opened. I go in and ask to see Zijad even though I don't have an appointment. I wait for about an hour before he comes out and greets me.

I thank him for seeing me on such short notice and explain that I have to talk to him about Chris. "You won't believe what he's up to now," I exclaim. He seems eager to hear what I have to say. I tell him about my conversation with my friend and how Chris is establishing a two-black-girl quota for each shift at the Downer. He reacts with shock and I ask him, "can he get away with this?" He responds by saying that this is clearly wrong, and he doesn't understand what Chris is thinking.

I leave Zijad's office with a renewed confidence that we can fight this. I call my friend early in the afternoon and ask her how many black girls had been allowed in to work and she tells me "just two." Several came who were turned away.

"So fuck, this is really happening!"
"Yes," she says.

I get off the phone with her and start doing some Internet research to see who I can contact. A short time later, she calls me back. I'm about to give her the name of someone at the Human Rights Tribunal when she interrupts me and says everything is cool. The quota has been suddenly lifted. I ask her how that came about, but she doesn't know.

But I know how … *confidentiality my ass!*

With my trial book in hand, I head up to Toronto to meet the new lawyer with whom I've had phone conversations and email exchanges. His office is right downtown, smack in the middle of the business district. The building is impressive and the interior beautifully decorated. On the top floor, I encounter an extremely wide hallway with expansive floor-to-ceiling windows. The firm doesn't just have an office – they have an entire floor! The reception area is so impressive that, just from looking at the décor, I know this is way beyond my league financially. Even so the reception staff is kind and warm. After requesting to see the new lawyer, I'm served coffee and settle into a comfortable chair for several minutes. Just as I'm finishing my coffee, almost like clockwork, he appears before me looking like a lion – a lean, tall and attractive black man. *Yeah! There's no way Chris would have any business dealing with this guy. Way too classy and way too black!* I feel a little out of place even though I'm dressed appropriately. At his request, I follow him into a small meeting room near the entrance. He closes the door behind us, pulls out a chair for me to sit on, and then takes a seat directly across from me. Although I'm in a private space, I feel safe. He asks me to explain my situation. I'm not sure how to start. So much has gone on, not only with regard to the trial but in my life! I decide to start with the first time I met Paul. I ramble on and on, because I want this man to know every little detail of what's happened to me. I begin to realize that it might all be too much for him to take in, because I'm even confusing myself. But it's like a dam has broken in my head, and I just have to get my whole story out to someone who might be able to help – and whom I feel I can trust.

He interrupts me and asks to see the trial book. I give him everything I brought with me. Every word he utters is like fresh air to me. I feel hopeful. Even though he's new to my case, this high-powered attorney is grasping the central issues of the case impressively, and it's clear that he's amazed that any judge could have arrived at the decision reached by Judge Lococo. I'm totally comfortable with him doing my appeal. I'm confident he can get this stupid decision overturned.

He mentions his fee, and I almost fall out of my chair. I explain right away I don't have that kind of money, but I do have a house. He asks me to leave the paper work with him so he can look it over. At this stage he's not yet retained. He's going to talk to the other partners in the firm to see if the fee can be reduced. I remember that Zijad is charging me ten thousand for the appeal, with which he is supposedly "buying me time." I'd much rather scrape up that money for this new lawyer. But even that might not be enough to satisfy the partners of this elite law firm.

Our meeting ends and I head back to Niagara. I have a chance here. I want to fire Zijad but I can't until I'm sure I can retain this new guy.

Within a few days, the lawyer calls me back and tells me that all he needs as a retainer is two thousand. I realize that this is an extremely low amount and that I'm being offered a real break. *If I were still dancing at the Sundowner that amount wouldn't be a problem, but the fact of the matter is I'm not, and I just don't have it.* I tell him I'll work on it.

For the next few weeks I try to come up with the money, dancing at shitty bars mainly. But after paying bills and making mortgage payments, I'm left with very little. My timeline is getting shorter, and I need to file with the Ontario Court of Appeals. I come to the dreadful conclusion that I won't be able to come up with the money in time. Holding back my tears, I make one of the hardest calls I've ever made in my life. I *so* want to hire this great lawyer in whom I have so much faith – so much confidence, but instead I must call him and tell him that I can't even pull together a pathetic two thousand dollars. He's very kind and understanding and assures me he'll mail me back all the materials that I'd left with him.

I'm back to square one, and I need to deal with Zijad and get on top of what he's up to. He's already written the factum and other court papers and sent them to me for review, as I'd requested. I know Zijad's plan is to "buy time," and I'm not expecting this factum to be written well. I need to review it, but who am I kidding? I'm not a lawyer and for me it's like reading Chinese.

I remember I have an old friend, Marvin, who knows about the law. I should have thought of him before. I call him immediately. I haven't seen or talked with him in years, but to my surprise he remembers me. I explain my situation, and we set a time to meet. A few days later, I drive an hour and a half to a coffee shop where he's expecting me. I order a coffee and sit waiting for him, with all my paper work spread across a table.

When Marvin enters, we shake hands and remain standing for the first part of our conversation. Then we sit down to review the trial transcript. Now the cat's out of the bag about what I've been doing with my life in recent years. He'd had no idea that I'd become an exotic dancer. I'm expecting the worst kind of reaction from him but all he says is, "when you were in high school, did you think you were going to be doing this"? *Interesting...* I look down, as he continues reading. He doesn't seem to be waiting for an answer, and so I don't give him one.

After a while, Marvin looks up at me and points out that Paul could have bought gold, precious metals or put the money in a family account. "Come to think of it, Paul did come to the club and give a few girls including me a bar of silver," I recall.

He tells me that if I could prove that, it could really help my case. We talk for hours, and the bottom line is, he's going to help me.

I walk away from that meeting feeling better. He'd been very helpful, but even more importantly, I was glad to re-establish my friendship with him. He took my paper work and assured me that he'd start writing my factum and related submissions for the appeals court a.s.a.p.

Marvin has several questions that I can't answer, but he tells me I can get the answers in the documents filed at the appeals court. Later that week a friend drives me up to Osgoode Hall in Toronto, which is where the appeals court conducts its business. I enter this really old building and, after clearing the security check, I locate an office where I'm able to copy all the info Zijad has already submitted. To my surprise, I discover that the application to appeal had been submitted late, after what was supposed to have been the deadline for starting the appeals process. Even so, the application had been accepted and the appeals process was officially underway. I also learn that Clark Peddle hasn't submitted anything as yet.

So Zijad was actually late in filing my application to appeal! Wow! What's going on here? What's he up to? How can he "buy me time" by filing the application late and risking the whole appeals process? Has he caught on to the fact that I'm not selling my house? I don't understand any of this. Is the guy just incompetent or is he trying to screw me over? What if they hadn't accepted the application for appeal on the grounds that it had been filed late? Everything would be over, and Lococo's bullshit order would stand. Peddle would have had his win, period. Is it possible that Zijad is somehow working with Peddle instead of against him?

Later that week Zijad emails me a copy of the factum containing the same information we'd discussed in his office. This is supposedly the factum that he says is destined to be "unsuccessful," but which will also buy me time: the one that he admits I can't and won't win with. Winning, he has said repeatedly, is not the purpose; the purpose is to drag out the process so I can sell my house and disappear!

I tell Zijad not to submit the factum to the appeals court until I've reviewed it. Later that day, he emails me the factum, which I then forward to Marvin. Marvin tells me Zijad's factum needs work and that I should tell him to hold off on submitting it. He tells me he just needs a few more days to complete a factum that will be much better. I agree happily. *This is what I'm talkin' about, being "hands on."*

Zijad isn't happy when I tell him to hold off on submitting his factum because I have another, better version in the works. He says he can't wait.
He's going to Toronto on Monday and he's submitting it, and that's that. Zijad is persistent and isn't taking no for an answer.

I call Marvin and tell him what Zijad has said. Marvin calculates the dates and explains to me that we do have time; it's confusing, but we can submit the factum a few days later than the date Zijad wants to submit it, and we'll still meet the deadline.

I call Zijad and tell him that I want to submit an alternative factum later in the week, but, of course, before the deadline. Monday is not the actual deadline. He responds by saying he's going to be in Toronto, and he's going to submit his own factum, and I shouldn't worry. It's now clear to me that he doesn't want me to submit the alternative factum, and that he's not open to any further discussion about this.

I call Marvin back and report what Zijad said. I'm very apologetic because I realize that Marvin's already done a good deal of work on the factum, and I tell him I'm disappointed, because I'm sure that his factum would be better than Zijad's. Unfortunately, there's nothing I can do. I advise him to stop working on it.

Zijad's shitty paper is going to be submitted, and I need another plan. I call Zijad and ask to meet him. As I sit in front of him, he gives me his lawyer talk, confirming he's submitted the factum on time. Now we're just waiting for the appeal court to give us a date. As soon as he hears from them, he'll call me.

Zijad tells me not to worry. There will be three judges and he'll have about 20 minutes to present our case.

"Three judges, that's good, I can explain everything."

He deflates my hopes immediately. I've got it wrong, he explains. At the Court of Appeal, I can't say a word. I can't explain my side of the story. *Oh my god*! *What the fuck's going on?*

"I can't speak to the judges?" I exclaim.

If I'd known about this I would have insisted upon submitting Marvin's factum and fought hard against Zijad pushing me out of the way and submitting his own work.

Zijad is still at it, goading me to sell and run. But run from what, or whom?

I'm trying to keep myself productive, but I know I've lost the appeal even before we appear in court. It's all going according to Zijad's plan and prediction. I can't work, I can't sleep, I'm just a mess. For days at a time, I lay on my girlfriend's couch sad and hiding out. All I know is, I feel I'm in danger. I don't go home at night to check on my house anymore, and I don't know who to turn to about all the information I've gathered. I can't focus. I feel like I've been set up, but I have no way to prove anything. Every time I explore anything, all I can hear is Zijad saying, *recordings are not permitted; it's too late for this or that. It would have been admissible in the Superior Court, but not in the appeals court.*

What a waste!

I remember talking with Zijad about various precautions that we should have taken in preparing for the Superior Court hearing. "Should have!" But he kept on saying, it's not up to us to prove that the money was not "advanced" to me. I'm thinking, *I've been black for a long time, in fact all my life, and I know I've always had to work harder than my white counterparts in school, at work, and in most everything! Why would a lawsuit be any different?* I call Zijad many times to talk about the case, but he doesn't return my calls or answer my emails. I'm in a state of depression. I keep to myself. My car has become my home. Public parks and parking lots, my "property." … and Tim Horton's is my office.

I get an email from Zijad dated May 3, 2012, at 10:13 a.m. It reads: "The appeal hearing has been set for June 13, 2012. The Court of Appeal has sent a reminder to the other side as they have not yet produced their responding material. I will require payment before proceeding with the Appeal. Let me know when you can arrange for same."

The next day I reply by email:

“Great, nice to hear from you. I've left you a few messages on your voice mail and with your secretary over two months ago and you never returned my calls. I'm very excited that we have a court date. I would still like a copy of the discovery please. I am still waiting for my money from my ex, Aber. He is giving me a hard time... I'm still working on obtaining my money. “I'm still being careful as someone is trying to hurt me and you know how I was let go from the Sundowner over this matter... Since this has begun it's been very taxing on my health and finance matters. Mortgage, bills....

“I'm sure that with this appeal we will win, the law cannot be this big of an ass. I'm sure with our win the other side will pay. I'm sure all provision is taken so I can sue for what I've been through. Even with Paul’s death.

“I'm calling my ex again.
“If the other side don't respond on time what happens? Isn't there a time line of 60 days to respond?
Thanks.”

A short time later, Zijad responds…
“Hi Angela,

“If the other side does not produce material they will not be able to rely on any material or authorities. I hope you are well otherwise. We will be in touch shortly and I will have you come in the next week or two to catch up.
Zijad”

Soon after, I learn from Zijad that Peddle’s file arrived at the appeals court late but it was still allowed …. *Had*

Peddle also been expecting me to sell my house and disappear?

Realizing I have some time on my hands to get out of town and go to work, I go home and pack my bags with several sexy outfits. If I'm lucky, I'll be able to pay some bills.

The management lets me into this new club I've located with no problems. After putting on my makeup and getting dressed, I reach into my bag and realize I've forgotten my shoes. *Fuck!* I can't work in running shoes – that's just not going to cut it with customers. Plus if the manager catches me wearing running shoes I'll be booted out anyway. I have no choice but to leave! As I start up my car I immediately notice that I haven't enough gas to get home. For almost an hour I just sit there contemplating what to do next. My mind is reeling with fatigue and anxiety.

With only a vague plan to head home in my head, I pull out of the parking lot and drive until the needle in the fuel gauge edges past the red zone and finally aligns itself with the black line that indicates I'm running on empty. I have no choice but to call a friend. *Humiliating!* I feel as though I've hit absolute rock bottom.

I pull into a strip mall that, fortunately, has a Western Union service. I can't believe I'm going to have to beg a friend to wire me twenty fucking measly bucks just so I can make it home. Western Union's going to charge about half that amount just for the service.

It would make more sense for me to ask for a hundred dollar loan, but I've exhausted the good will of most of my friends over these tough times.

I explain my situation to my friend and he promptly agrees to send me the twenty… The money arrives thirty minutes later. I'm relieved – but I'm also feeling just two inches tall.

I get home and pack my dancer shoes but then remind myself that I don't have enough gas to return to the club. What's more, it's getting dark. I sit on my couch and gaze out at the shimmering water as night descends over the lake. I move my car down the lane to an abandoned house and park it. Then
I walk back up the lane to my house. I scatter all the newspapers I'd removed from my driveway earlier so that it would look like I'd never came home.

That night and for the next few days I remain at home, sleeping during the day and keeping watch at night. The stalker vehicles are still appearing, but the times have changed and they are less regular. I don't even bother with the cops because I know I'm just going to hear the same song and dance story.

As part of my investigation into the incident with the black SUV at the auto repair shop, I'd asked to see their surveillance video, but the shop manager told me he had no footage because the system wasn't operating.

A few weeks later I notice there's a winery on Lakeshore between the two auto-body shops. I enter and inquire whether they have security cameras recording the exterior of their premises on an on-going basis. The answer is yes, so I call the investigating detective and leave a voice message. My call isn't returned. A week later I return to the winery and ask the manager if the cops had come by to review their surveillance footage. *No!* Now I know for sure that the cops aren't taking me seriously – either that or they just don't care! Whatever these useless cops are thinking, I know damn well that no paper delivery guy is responsible for chasing my car!

My sleep is suffering again. I'm functioning on just a few hours of sleep each day, most of them snatched just after daybreak. I know I'm reaching a breaking point, but I'm driven to get to the bottom of the menacing nighttime visits of the stalker vehicles.

During my stakeouts, I'm trying now to see who's in the car instead of getting the plate numbers. I hide behind trees close to the lane, and the suspicious vehicles often pass so close I could reach out and touch them, and yet I'm never able to see inside.

One night, a little before I'm expecting the stalker to arrive on the scene, I walk down the lane with my flashlight and inspect every private driveway. I see no newspapers. Then I settle in and wait for the car. Three hours pass, nothing yet. I leave my hiding spot and cross the lane to my house. Just as I open the front door, I notice headlights shining from way down the lane. *It's them!* My heart is racing. I slam the door shut and cut across my neighbor's backyard and into my orchard hiding-spot. The car pulls into my driveway, stops briefly and then backs out and heads back down the lane. *That was close*. I'm afraid they might have seen me, but I keep ahead of them, and I haven't crossed the lane directly, so it seems they haven't. It takes several minutes for my shakes to subside.

It's now about four in the morning. It's still dark. I walk down the lane again with my flashlight to see if any papers have been delivered. *No paper, no paper, no paper... None!* Not a single delivered paper along the whole stretch of the lane!

What the fuck! If the cops aren't going to help me, I need a gun.

I walk back to my house in a hurry, with that same thought repeating itself in my head, over and over again. *I need a fucking gun!*

But how and where can I get one?

The only other way to protect myself is to stay out of the bars just in case they start looking for me there, and I'll need to stay away from my home.

I call Zijad and ask again for a copy of the discovery. He tells me to come in so he can update me on everything. I get a ride from a friend and head down to see him that day. As I enter his building he greets me at the front door and we go into his office. I sit but he doesn't. He tells me he can't find the discovery.

"I need it," I insist. "I think it may have some answers in it. This stalking bull started after the discovery."

He tells me he can't find his own copy of the discovery, so what he's going to do is get a copy from the Superior Court or from Peddle. If he can't obtain it that way, he'll order some new copies, at his own expense. Either way, he'll have it in a couple of days.

I'm dolled up, in a tasteful "professional" way, and head to Toronto and Osgoode Hall. Parking is hard to find, so I decide to enter the underground pay lot. As I pull up to the ticket dispenser, I realize it's going to cost me too much to park there, so I decide to back my car out. But, *damn it!* – I'm being blocked by a few vehicles now behind me. I pull off to the side to create a space for them to pass.

I notice a scowling guy in a Mercedes SUV who's obviously annoyed by my actions. As he passes I look closely at him and realize it's that lawyer I met at the club – the basketball guy. I jump out of my car and wave at him, but he drives away quickly into the parkade. I don't think he saw me, but I would love to have talked to him.

I finally find a free parking spot on a side road and rush into the courthouse.
I don't know which room I'm supposed to go to, so I quickly text Zijad and get his answer a few minutes later.

I hurry into the courtroom and spot Zijad waving at me. I sit at the back for a moment but am soon required to stand as the judges enter the room from a side door off to my left. They sit side by side on an elevated platform and look down at us. The room has an impressive, almost other-worldly, appearance, with lots of rich, natural wood that must have been freshly polished because it's shining like glass. It occurs to me that the physical appearance of this courtroom was designed to inspire awe – the idea that visitors are in the presence of a higher power. But I'm under no delusion that this is heaven or that these judges are gods. After everything I've been through, I refuse to be intimidated.

Zijad is invited to begin the proceedings, and, after greeting the judges, he presents a summary of all the issues covered in the factum.

COURT OF APPEAL FOR ONTARIO

BETWEEN:

PAUL DAGENAIS

Plaintiff
(Respondent) and

THELMA ANGELA VASSEL AKA LINDA LEE

Defendant
(Appellant)

APPELLANT'S FACTUM

PART I: NATURE OF THE APPEAL

1. The Appellant, Thelma Angela Vassel a.k.a. Linda Lee ("Ms. Vassel") is the Defendant in an action brought in the Superior Court of Justice for a repayment of a loan. At trial, the Honourable Justice Lococo awarded $125,245.00 to the Plaintiff. The trial Judge also awarded costs of $10,000.00 and pre-judgment interest at the prescribed rate. Ms. Vassel now appeals from this ruling.

PART II: NATURE OF THE CASE AND THE ISSUES ON APPEAL

2. The Plaintiff, Paul Dagenais, brought this action against Ms. Vassel for the repayment of a loan in the amount of $151,000.00. At trial, Mr. Dagenais amended this amount and claimed a total loan of $132,845.00. Mr. Dagenais alleged that from July 2009 to January 2010, he withdrew a total of $132,845.00 in cash from 3 bank accounts and loaned the money to Ms. Vassel.

3. The Appellant states that the learned trial judge erred in:

a. Substituting and relying on his own conclusions rather than the evidence before him.

b. Shifting the burden of proof from the Plaintiff to the Defendant in coming to the conclusion that the money was advanced to the Defendant and that the money was a loan.

c. Neglected to analyze the inconsistencies in the Plaintiff's evidence and failed to provide sufficient reasons as to how the issues of credibility were solved.

PART III: STATEMENT OF FACTS

4. The Plaintiff is a 61 year old retiree and a life long resident of Port Colborne.

Reasons for Judgment of Justice Lococo, dated August 30, 2011, Appeal Book and Compendium, Tab 3, page 69;

5. Ms. Vassel was an exotic dancer, who at all material times worked at the Sundowner Gentleman's Club in Niagara Falls, Ontario. The Plaintiff was a regular customer at the

Sundowner and would go sometimes two or three times per week.

Reasons for Judgment of Justice Lococo, dated August 30, 2011, Appeal Book and Compendium, Tab 3, page 69 and 72;

6. In August 2008, the Plaintiff lost his driver's licence and could no longer drive to the Sundowner.

Reasons for Judgment of Justice Lococo, dated August 30, 2011, Appeal Book and Compendium, Tab 3, page 71;

7. Ms. Vassel stated that the Plaintiff asked her to start going on dates with him outside of the Sundowner. She agreed to do so on the same basis as she did for other customers, charging a fee of $300.00 - $500.00 per visit.

Reasons for Judgment of Justice Lococo, dated August 30, 2011, Appeal Book and Compendium, Tab 3, page 69 and 70;

8. In the case of Mr. Dagenais, these dates involved going to his house, watching television, or driving him around to the park, Tim Horton's and to the bank. It was a common ground that no sex took place between them.

Reasons for Judgment of Justice Lococo, dated August 30, 2011, Appeal Book and Compendium, Tab 3, page 75;

9. It was the Plaintiff's position that after he lost his driver's licence that Ms. Vassel looked up his address in the phone book and started coming to his house without being welcome.

Reasons for Judgment of Justice Lococo, dated August 30, 2011, Appeal Book and Compendium, Tab 3, page 72;

10. According to the Plaintiff, Ms. Vassel started asking him for money in July of 2009 and he began loaning her money from that time period until January 13, 2010.

Reasons for Judgment of Justice Lococo, dated August 30, 2011, Appeal Book and Compendium, Tab 3, page 69 and 72;

11. During the period of July 2009 to January of 2010, the Plaintiff withdrew a total of $132,845 in cash from three bank accounts.

Reasons for Judgment of Justice Lococo, dated August 30, 2011, Appeal Book and Compendium, Tab 3, page 69;

12. There was no Promissory Note or other written acknowledgment of any loans between the parties.

Reasons for Judgment of Justice Lococo, dated August 30, 2011,

Appeal Book and Compendium, Tab 3, page 69;

13. The loans consisted of 46 withdrawals on 32 different dates, with 31 withdrawals being of $1,200.00 or more. The amounts were subsequently all listed on a summary of loans sheet prepared by Mr. Dagenais' sister, Denise Taylor.

Reasons for Judgment of Justice Lococo, dated August 30, 2011,
Appeal Book and Compendium, Tab 3, page 74; Exhibit 1- Summary of Withdrawals, Appeal Book and compendium, Tab 7

14. It is common ground that Ms. Vassel drove the Plaintiff to the bank at his request.

Reasons for Judgment of Justice Lococo, dated August 30, 2011,

Appeal Book and Compendium, Tab 3, page 75;

15. It was the Plaintiff's position that every single withdrawal he made on the list of withdrawals provided at trial were loans made to Ms. Vassel.

Cross-Examination of Paul Dagenais, transcript page 25 and 26;

16. On January 4, 2010, the Plaintiff presented Ms. Vassel with a statement written on the back of an envelope to acknowledge a debt of $151,000.00. Ms. Vassel refused to sign the envelope.

Examination in chief of Thelma Angela Vassel, transcript, page 56;

Exhibit 2 - Envelope, Appeal Book and compendium, Tab 7;

17. Ms. Vassel's position was that she went on several dates with the Plaintiff and he paid her a total of $5,000.00 for the dates.

Reasons for Judgment of Justice Lococo, dated August 30, 2011,

Appeal Book and Compendium, Tab 3, page 69, 74 and 75;

18. In his reasons, the trial Judge held that notwithstanding the misgivings in the Plaintiff's case, he accepted as credible the basic thrust of the Plaintiff's evidence relating to the withdrawals from July 2009 to January 2010, and granted Judgment in the amount of $125,245.00 to the Plaintiff.

Reasons for Judgment of Justice Lococo, dated August 30, 2011, Appeal Book and Compendium, Tab 3, page 77;

19. In arriving at the figure of $125,245.00, the trial Judge excluded all individual withdrawal amount that were less than $1,200.00 and the $2,000.00 withdrawal made on January 13, 2010.

Reasons for Judgment of Justice Lococo, dated August 30, 2011,

Appeal Book and Compendium, Tab 3, page 80;

PART IV: THE ISSUES

20. There are three issues on this Appeal:

a. Did the trial Judge err in substituting and relying on his own conclusions rather than the evidence before him?

c. Did the trial Judge err in shifting the onus of proof from the Plaintiff to the Defendant in arriving at the conclusion that the money was advanced to the Defendant and that the money was a loan?

b. Did the trial Judge neglect to analyze the inconsistencies in the Plaintiff's evidence and failed to provide sufficient reasons as to how the issues of credibility were resolved?

ISSUE 1: Did the trial Judge err in substituting and relying on his own conclusions rather than the evidence before him?

21. The Appellant submits that the trial judge erred in substituting and relying on his own

conclusions rather than the evidence at trial with respect to the alleged loans.

22. An appellate court may substitute its own view of the evidence and draw its own inferences only if the trial judge committed a palpable and overriding error or made findings of fact or drew inferences that are unreasonable or unsupported by the evidence.

H.L. v. Canada (Attorney General), [2005] 1. S.C.R. 401 at para.

23. It was Ms. Vassel's theory at trial that it defied common sense that all 46 withdrawals on 32 different dates, totaling $132,845.00 were all advanced to Ms. Vassel, and that none of the money withdrawn was used for the Plaintiff's benefit including basic living expenses and every day necessities.

24. Specifically, Ms. Vassel's position at trial was that it defied common sense for the Plaintiff to make an additional loan in the amount of $2,000.00 on January 13th, 2010, after she refused to acknowledge any debt, in writing, on January 4, 2010.

25. At trial, the Plaintiff clearly stated that every single amount shown on the summary of loans, including the alleged loan on January 13, 2010, were all loaned to Ms. Vassel.

Q: So it's your evidence that every single one of these cash withdrawals that is shown on the summaries were given - were loaned to Angela?

A: That's right.

Cross-Examination of Paul Dagenais, transcript page 25 and 26;.

26. Notwithstanding the Plaintiff's evidence that every single cash withdrawal shown on the summary of withdrawals was loaned to the Defendant, the trial judge excluded all individual withdrawals amounts from the list that were less than $1,200.00 and also excluded the $2,000.00 withdrawal made on January 13, 2010.

27. Specifically, with the respect to the January 13, 2010 withdrawal, the trial judge stated as follows:

"Therefore, while I agree there is doubt on the evidence whether the withdrawal on January 13, as advanced by way of loan to Ms. Vassel, I do not agree with the argument of Ms. Vassel's counsel that the alleged inconsistency in Mr. Dagenais' evidence cannot be reconciled with the conclusion that the significant withdrawals made from Mr. Dagenais' account prior to January 2010 were advanced by way of loan to Ms. Vassel."

Reasons for Judgment of Justice Lococo, dated August 30, 2011, Appeal Book and Compendium, Tab 3, page 79;

28. The Appellant submits that in light of the evidence of the Plaintiff that every single amount stated in the summary was loaned to Ms. Vassel, it was not open to the trial judge to substitute his own conclusion which could not be justified by the evidence.

29. The Appellant submits that if there is doubt on the evidence whether any single withdrawal was advanced by way of loan to Ms. Vassel, as the trial judge pointed out was the case on the January 13, 2010 withdrawal, then in light of the evidence of the Plaintiff that every single

withdrawal was a loan, there is doubt as to whether any other amount was advanced to Ms. Vassel.

30. The Appellant submits that the trial judge erred by drawing conclusions which were not supported in evidence, to reconcile the inconsistencies in the Plaintiff's evidence.

ISSUE 2: Did the trial Judge err in shifting the onus of proof from the Plaintiff to the Defendant in arriving at the conclusion that the money was advanced to the Defendant and that the money was a loan?

31. The Appellant submits that the trial judge erred in placing the onus of proof onto the Defendant to prove that she did not receive the advances, and relied on her inability to do so in concluding that the money was advanced.

32. In a civil suit, generally, the onus of proof lies on the Plaintiff to prove its case on a balance of probabilities. In *H. (F).v. McDougall*, the Supreme of Court of Canada held that the balance of probabilities standard was the sole standard of proof at common law in all civil proceedings. The party with the onus of proof has the obligation to prove that the existence or non-existence of a fact or issue is more likely than not.

[2008] 3 S.C.R. 41, [2008] S.C.J. No. 54 (S.C.C.)

33. The Appellant submits, that in this case, the onus of proof was on the Plaintiff to prove that money was loaned to the Defendant, on a balance of probabilities.

34. The Appellant submits, that in several areas of the trial judge's decision, it was suggested that

Ms. Vassel's inability to prove where else Mr. Dagenais could have spent that money that he withdrew, supported the conclusion that it must have been loaned to her.

35. The trial judge states that Ms. Vassel was unable to explain how Mr. Dagenais could have spent $130,000 in less than 6 months and in another part of the judgment he stated that there is no other explanation on the evidence as to what happened to the funds withdrawn by Mr. Dagenais. The trial judge also stated the following:

"While Ms. Vassel's evidence was indeed easier to follow, I did not find it to be more credible than the evidence of Mr. Dagenais, which I prefer and accept on the crucial points as to whether Ms. Vassel received sums of money from Mr. Dagenais and the characterizations of these amounts as loans. Among other things, I was skeptical about Ms. Vassel's explanation for failure to produce bank records that may have been helpful in making the determination in this case. "

Reasons for Judgment of Justice Lococo, dated August 30, 2011, Appeal Book and Compendium, Tab 3, page 78 and 79;

36. It follows that the trial judge was looking for evidence by Ms. Vassel to disprove that she had received large sums of money in that period. The trial judge was also looking for evidence from Ms. Vassel to offer an alternate explanation as to what happened to the funds withdrawn by Mr. Dagenais, and because of her inability to do so, the trial judge determined that the funds must have been advanced to Ms. Vassel.

ISSUE 3: Did the trial Judge err in neglecting to analyze the inconsistencies in the Plaintiff's evidence and failing to provide sufficient reasons as to how the issues of credibility were resolved?

37. The Appellant submits that the trial Judge neglected to analyze the inconsistencies in the Plaintiff's evidence and failed to provide sufficient reasons as to how the issues of credibility were resolved.

38. The Appellant submits that there were several inconsistencies in the Plaintiff's testimony. For example, he stated that he met Ms. Vassel in February 2009, then conceded it was much earlier than that in cross examination. Also, he stated that Ms. Vassel's visits to his house were unsolicited and unwelcome, which the totality of the evidence did not support.

39. The trial judge even stated that the Plaintiff's evidence was muddled and hard to follow.

40. The Appellant submits that while the trial judge accepted as credible the basic thrust of the Plaintiff's evidence that he provided significant sums of money to Ms. Vassel, and notwithstanding the inconsistencies, he failed to provide sufficient reasons as to why he preferred the evidence of the Plaintiff.

41. The Appellant submits that the trial judge erred by considering Ms. Vassel's inability to explain where else Mr. Dagenais could have spent the money in issue and her failure to maintain a bank account during these times as issues weighing against her credibility.

Part V: ORDER REQUESTED

42. The Appellant respectfully requests the following Orders:

a. An Order setting aside the judgment of Justice Lococo;

b. Costs of this Appeal and the trial below;

c. Such further relief as Counsel may advise and this Honourable Court deems just.

Zijad concludes his presentation, and it's now time for the judges to pose their questions and make their comments.

The commentary of one judge in particular infuriates me, especially a cynical remark directed at Zijad to the effect that "she should have said it was a gift." It was as though the judge was scolding my lawyer for not persuading me to lie! *Why not make it explicit "your honour"? Why not say: What kind of lawyer are you? Without a signed IOU, Paul Dagenais wouldn't have had a leg to stand on, if only Ms. Vassel had testified that the money had been given to her as a gift! Don't you see: the truth doesn't matter. All that matters is winning the case. The end justifies the means!*

My anger is reaching a boiling point and it takes everything in me to maintain my composure. I want desperately to stand up and denounce the whole sham proceedings. Charles Dickens famously quipped that "the law is an ass." If so, what does that make these judges who are now retiring to a back room to formulate their "learned" ruling?

Zijad walks over to me, leans in close and whispers, "we've lost."

Of course, I know that. Everything has gone according to his prediction. I'm going to lose, so I should just sell and run. But it's a self-fulfilling prophecy.
He barely elaborated on the factum. It was clear to me that he didn't really want to win. His performance was so weak that the other side didn't have to say a word in response to his "argument." Peddle only had to advise the court of Paul's death and identify the executor of his estate. And that was it.

The judges come out of their little rats' nest. I wish they had stayed in it. The predictable BLAH, BLAH, BLAH….

It was over. *I've lost again – how could they not see?* I meet Zijad outside the courtroom and he's chatting with his friends and colleagues.

"That can't be it!" He nods a yes.
"What's next?"
"Next? That's it – there is no next."

He tells me to come meet with him in a few days, and then walks away with his friends. No words of consolation. From the way he's carrying himself, you'd think he'd actually won the appeal.

I'm mad as hell. I walk quickly to my car only to discover a fucking parking ticket on my windshield! I rip it up into tiny little pieces.

I sit in my car and brood. *How can it stop here? How can I let these fuckers win? They've won with lies!* I do a search on my smart-phone and soon discover that my lawyer has lied to me again. I do have *one*, remaining recourse: the Supreme Court of Canada.

I spend several days researching this possibility and decide that this is something I must do. I go to the library in Niagara-on-the-Lake and print a self-help document. It contains forms that I can fill out myself, but I lack some of the required information. I'll have to get this stuff from Zijad.

During one of my sessions at the library, I receive an email from Zijad containing the Court of Appeals decision:

Paul Dagenais Plaintiff

(Respondent) and

Thelma Angela Vassel aka Linda Lee

Defendant (Appellant)

Zijad Saskin, for the defendant (appellant)

Clark Peddle, for the plaintiff (respondent)

On appeal from the judgment of Justice Lococo of the Superior Court of Justice, dated August 30, 2011.

ENDORSEMENT

[1] The trial judge ultimately did not accept the plaintiff's claim that each and every cash withdrawal from his bank accounts during the relevant period went to fund his loan to the defendant. The trial judge was not satisfied that various small withdrawals went for that purpose and he specifically found that a withdrawal made after the date on which the defendant refused to acknowledge that she had borrowed money from the plaintiff was not related to the loan.

[2] A trial judge is not obliged to accept or reject the entirety of the case as presented for the plaintiff. A trial

judge must make findings of fact based on his assessment of the entirety of the evidence. In the course of doing so, he or she may reject some but not necessarily all the evidence given by any witness, including a plaintiff. This trial judge did exactly that. He reviewed the plaintiff's evidence carefully and while he was not prepared to accept the entirety of it, he clearly accepted the thrust of the plaintiff's evidence that he had loaned a great deal of money to the defendant over a six-month period and that he had funded that loan through numerous cash withdrawals from his various bank accounts. The trial judge's finding was not unreasonable and we must defer to it.

[3] The second ground of appeal concerns an alleged reversal of the burden of proof. The trial judge began his analysis by expressly stating that the plaintiff had the onus to prove both that the funds were advanced by way of a loan and that the loan was not repaid.

[4] We see nothing in the reasons which suggests a reversal of the burden of proof. The trial judge in assessing the appellant's credibility properly took into account factors relevant to that assessment, including, for example, the appellant's failure to produce her bank records. In doing so, the trial judge did not place any legal burden of proof on the appellant.

[5] In determining whether the plaintiff had met the burden of proof, the trial judge was obligated to weigh his evidence in the context of the entirety of the evidence, including any alternative explanations advanced by the defendant. The absence of any explanation on certain matters from the appellant and the absence of any evidence to support explanations that were offered were relevant in assessing whether the plaintiff had met his burden of proof. This ground of appeal cannot succeed.

[6] The third ground of appeal is a more general attack on the trial judge's reasons as inadequate. The trial judge analyzed the evidence of both the defendant and plaintiff. His reasons clearly indicate how he came to prefer the evidence of the plaintiff over that of the appellant. In our view, the reasons are both logical and supported by the evidence. They reveal no basis upon which this court can interfere.

[7] The appeal is dismissed. Costs to the respondent are fixed in the amount of $6,000 "all in".

"Doherty J.A." "R.G. "Juriansz J.A." "Ducharme J.A."
I can only shake my head after reading this document. It's time for me to confront Zijad.

I storm over to Zijad's office, composing myself as I enter. I calmly ask for all the paper work I'll need to fill out the forms for the Supreme Court of Canada. Without saying a word, he turns them over to me. It's as though he can't wait to get me out of his office.

I look him straight in the eye and ask him if he thinks the judges were right in their decision. He nods, yes, "probably so."

If looks could kill, Zijad should be dropping to the floor in a bloody mass at this moment. Can he read what's behind the hatred and contempt in my eyes? Does he know what I'm thinking? Does he really think that I missed the meaning of that judge's remark about his bringing the "wrong facts" to the Court of Appeal? Why did Zijad set my appeal up for failure unless he wanted it to fail?

Part of me wishes he can hear my thoughts, but I'm not ready to say them out loud. Not yet.

I retreat to my car and tear through the contents of the box of files he's given me. *Where's the closing argument, and the discovery transcript? Neither is here!*

When I call Zijad and ask him about this, his whispered response is "the name you're looking for is Panetta; that's the name."

By itself this name doesn't ring a bell. I'm expecting to hear a first and a last name. Anyway, I don't trust Zijad; he's always insisted before that he has no recollection of any name being mentioned during discovery. I want proof, not just his say so. When I press him about this, he reassures me he's ordered the discovery.

I return home to examine the contents of the box more carefully. But I can't get the discovery transcript out of my head. That's what I really want to see.

Then it dawns on me that I should just head over to the office where the discovery was conducted to get a copy myself. As I'm pulling out of my lane I pass a Canadian immigration van turning onto it. *That's a first!*

What's up with that?

I head over to the office where the discovery session had been held. When I arrive no one seems to be there, but after a few moments a young man approaches me. I explain to him that my lawyer has ordered a copy of the Discovery Examination. He settles into a chair in front of a computer, asks my name, and does a quick search, but can't find anything associated with my name. Then he tries my lawyer's name, nothing. He asks for a file number and I give him what I think might be the right number, but he's still unable to locate it. He suggests I call my lawyer to get the file number. I explain that Zijad has lost his own copy.

"If copies have already been sent to counsel, then this should be easy." He continues the search on the computer and then in the office's filing cabinets, but concludes that no records of this particular discovery are available.

I call Zijad but his secretary informs me that he isn't in.

An older man at the discovery office intervenes, asking me why I need this document: "Usually it's the lawyers who need these kinds of documents, not clients. You pay your lawyer to take care of your best interests." We exchange some small talk about some black people he knows and he asks me if I'm acquainted with one of them in particular. He's nosy, but in a nice way. But in the end he isn't very helpful.

I leave the office without any documents, but with assurances from the young man that he'll continue the search.

A few days later, he calls me and asks me to return to the office. He's found the file! I'm ecstatic. I ask him to print me a copy and email me the cost. He then advises me that because it's a "first-time copy" it's going to cost me a considerable sum. *A first time copy?*

"It turns out that copies have never been printed either for your lawyer or for the plaintiff's lawyer," he explains. *How very interesting. More proof that Zijad's been lying to me.*

I'm in shock at what I'll have to pay for an original copy, but I agree to make the order. I ask him how long it will take and request that he send me the printed copy with an invoice.

I don't have that kind of money so I have to go call on my friend for help, again. But because he knows the story and the importance of my finding out who is potentially behind the stalking, he agrees to loan me the money.

I sleep in my car, away from my house, and I wait. Finally a few days later I get a call notifying me that the printed copy of the discovery transcript is ready for me to pick up. I rush down to the office immediately.

Once I'm back in my car, I read through the document so quickly that I initially miss the name I'm searching for. I freak out and call Zijad.

"Zijad, the name is missing from the document."

He insists that it must be there. So I re-read it, and yes, sure enough, it's there.

I don't let on to Zijad that I'm catching on to his lies, even though I'd love to present him with the bill for the discovery. I don't bother, because what's really important is that I now have a name.

I go straight to the library and type into the Google search engine: "Timothy Panetta." A few links pop up and I read every single one, with questions:

"Niagara Hells Angel faces charges"

GRANT LAFLECHE AND KARENA WALTER, STANDARD STAFF

“The last original member of the Niagara Hells Angels still standing was charged Wednesday with illegally importing vehicles from the United States. “A five-month investigation by a joint forces police auto theft team led to the seizure of five vehicles and 12 charges against Timothy Panetta of Wainfleet.

“The 39-year-old owns Advantage Auto Sales and Leasing on Allanport Road in Thorold, which was searched by police last month. “A police source from the auto theft team alleged salvage vehicles were purchased in the U. S. and imported into Canada. “ ‘They are being fraudulently registered with their true identities hidden and then sold to the public’, the detective said. “The vehicles included two Chevrolet Suburbans and a Porsche Carrera. One of the five vehicles contained stolen parts, police said. “Police aren't saying where the vehicles originated or their histories. Typically, when a vehicle is fraudulently registered, its flaws are hidden in documentation to increase its sales value. “Two of the vehicles had been sold, while three were for sale, police said. “The auto theft team, spearheaded by the OPP, was assisted by the biker enforcement unit and provincial organized crime enforcement team. “Panetta joined the Hells Angels in 2001, not long after a massive takeover of nearly all of Ontario's biker groups by the gang.

“While gangs around the province abandoned their own colours and adopted the grinning death's head patch of the Hells Angels, Niagara was a special case. “The only biker gang at the time in the region was the St. Catharines chapter of the Hells Angels' longtime nemesis, the Outlaws, who were not about to change colours. If the Hells Angels wanted to put a chapter in the region, they would have to build it from scratch. “In 1998, while the Angels were laying the groundwork for their bloodless takeover of the province, the former national president, Walter Stadnick of Hamilton, met with several local men during a highly publicized Hells Angels ride to Niagara Falls. "This cohort of seven men became Stadnick's handpicked crew to create a Niagara Hells Angels chapter.

Most were known to police, but none had been members of a biker gang before. "The charter members included chapter president Gerald Ward, who is in custody awaiting a court ruling Nov. 21 on whether he directed others to act for a criminal organization. Ward will also be sentenced for trafficking cocaine and possessing more than $300,000 in proceeds of crime. "Other founders included Ward's lieutenant, Kenneth Wagner, who was sentenced Tuesday to 11 years in prison for directing others for a criminal organization, trafficking cocaine and having more than $150,000 in proceeds of crime. "Among the other five was Panetta. In the eight years since the chapter was formed, the Hells Angels in Niagara have been weakened by a series of police crackdowns. Two of the charter members quit the group, and by 2006, only Ward, Wagner and Panetta remained of the founders. "With the arrest of Ward and Wagner in 2006 in the Project Tandem joint forces police investigation, Panetta became the last active original member. "Last week, during judgment on the criminal organization charge against Wagner, a judge ruled the Hells Angels are a criminal organization.

"Police sources say the Niagara chapter is now down to a bare bones six members transferred in from other provincial chapters, such as Kitchener and Hamilton.

"The imported group continues to operate out of the Darby Road clubhouse in Welland, seized during Project Tandem. "A restraint on the building means they can't sell, modify or depreciate the value of the property. “Police sources said the arrests and convictions of the local Angels has disrupted the gang's ability to function in Niagara. “However, as time goes by they expect the replacement members will attempt to fill the void. “Panetta was charged with 12 counts relating to his business, including charges of uttering a forged document, fraud under $5,000, fraudulent concealment, possession of stolen property under $5,000 and common nuisance.

“He was released on bail Wednesday.”

This was on the stcatharinesstandard.ca website.

All of a sudden Zijad is giving me this lead, this “Panetta” name, knowing I'll take it to the cops. But why now? What's his plan? Now he coughs up a name! Very suspicious. There's no way I'm going to the cops with this. I don't trust the cops and I sure as hell don't trust Zijad.

What do I do with this information? Should I disappear as my lawyer has suggested? Maybe Zijad knows more than he's letting on and is trying to protect me in a way. Maybe not. I'm very confused. I pack my trunk with as much clothing and other things as I'll need for a few months, and I leave home.

I spend most days in a library and my nights sleeping in my car. I fill out the various forms that need to be filed with the Supreme Court of Canada, but I realize that I'm no lawyer and that I need my arguments to be presented in a proper way. To get the Court to hear my story, I'm going to have to make a strong argument that my case involves issues of considerable public, and even constitutional, importance. As a nagging toothache returns, I recognize that I'm going to need the help of a friend who I'm pretty sure can do the job....

After three intensive days of work, reviewing and analyzing all the documentation and formulating a series of compelling arguments, the document is finally prepared.

APPLICANT'S MEMORANDUM OF ARGUMENT
PART I – STATEMENT OF FACTS

Issues of Public Importance

1. In the view of the applicant, there are two major issues of public importance posed by the judgment made by Superior Court Justice Lococo on August 30, 2011, and upheld by the Court of Appeal for Ontario on June 13, 2012, in the case of Dagenais v. Vassel (Court File No. C54401).

2. The **first issue** pertains to *inappropriate judicial bias*. It is the claim of the applicant that subjective bias on the part of Justice Lococo against Thelma Vassel, the Defendant, and in favour of Paul Dagenais, the Plaintiff, is the most probable explanation for the specious reasoning, lapses in logic, and errors in law that characterize his "Reasons for Judgment" in favour of the Plaintiff. The applicant submits that this bias must have stemmed, above all, from a prejudicial attitude toward the defendant's occupation as an exotic dancer, compounded by an unfounded suspicion that a frail and aging white male had been taken advantage of by an attractive and much younger black female. Accordingly, in the view of the applicant, and on the balance of probabilities,

judicial bias relating to occupation, age and health status, and possibly to gender and race, played the decisive role in determining Justice Lococo's judgment against Ms. Vassel rather than the meager verifiable evidence available to the court. Furthermore, the brief and thinly motivated decision of June 13, 2012 by the Court of Appeal to uphold the trial judge's original decision as "not unreasonable" and as free of the errors attributed to it in the Appellant's Factum of March 15, 2012 recapitulates the errors and bias of the trial judge. It is the applicant's position that the decisions of the trial judge and the Court of Appeal establish a dangerous precedent allowing a trial judge to attenuate the longstanding principles that the burden of proof rests with the plaintiff rather than the defendant and that the balance of probabilities standard is the sole standard of proof at common law in all civil proceedings.

3. The **second** issue of public importance in the case pertains to *the irresponsible and even life-threatening conduct of Thelma Vassel's defense counsel, Zijad Saskin*, whose inept and possibly unethical handling of her defense appears to have involved, *inter alia*, a breach of solicitor-client privilege and a reckless disregard for Ms. Vassel's livelihood and physical safety. While the details of Mr. Saskin's conduct were not a part of the deliberations of Justice Lococo or the Court of Appeal, the applicant asks the Supreme Court to take into consideration new evidence pertaining to this conduct, which the applicant contends had an important material effect on the outcome of this case.

Nature of the Case, the Issues on Appeal, and the Judgment of the Court of Appeals

4. The appellant, Thelma Angela Vassel (a.k.a. Linda Lee), was the Defendant in an action brought in the Superior Court of Justice for repayment of a loan. Ms. Vassel denied receiving any money from the Plaintiff as a loan. At trial, the Honourable Justice Lococo awarded $125,245.00 to the Plaintiff. He also awarded costs of $10,000.00 and pre-judgment interest at the prescribed rate.

5. The Defendant appealed this judgment to the Court of Appeal of Ontario, citing three major errors on the part of the trial judge:

   a. That he substituted and relied on his own conclusions rather than the evidence before him;

   b. That he shifted the burden of proof from the Plaintiff to the Defendant in coming to the conclusion that the money was in fact advanced to the Defendant and that the money was indeed a loan;

   c. That he neglected to analyze the inconsistencies in the Plaintiff's evidence and failed to provide sufficient reasons as to how the issues of credibility were resolved.

6. The Court of Appeal of Ontario refused to agree that the trial judge had made the errors attributed to him by the Appellant. Asserting that Justice Lococo's judgment was "not unreasonable" and that it "must defer to it," the Court denied the Defendant's appeal and endorsed the judgment of the Superior Court.

Undisputed Facts of the Original Lawsuit

7. The now-deceased Plaintiff was a 61 year-old retiree, a life-long bachelor and a resident of Port Colborne. Either in 2007 or 2008 (there is some controversy about the date), he suffered a stroke and was hospitalized for six months. Following his release, he continued to suffer from physical weakness in his arm and hand. (Mr. Dagenais died in November 2011, little more than two months after judgment was rendered in the case and seven months before the Court of Appeal hearing on Ms. Vassel's appeal.)

8. The now-42-year-old Ms. Vassel was an exotic dancer, who at all material times, worked at the Sundowner Gentleman's Club in Niagara Falls, Ontario under the stage name "Linda Lee." The Plaintiff was a regular customer at the Sundowner, sometimes visiting the club two or three times per week. Except for the period of Mr. Dagenais' hospitalization, these visits occurred frequently between 2005 and 2008, a period during which Ms. Vassel was working regularly at the club. The Plaintiff's visits to the club continued, albeit less frequently, in 2009.

9. At the Sundowner, the Plaintiff was in the habit of spending at least $250 to $300 during each of his visits, occupying his time with a number of different exotic dancers and paying for dances in the private VIP area of the club. Since he admitted to visiting the club two or three times per week over many years, it is reasonable to assume that the Plaintiff may have spent at least $25,000 to $30,000 per year on his activities at the Sundowner prior to his stroke and then again following his hospitalization.

10. No later than August 2008, but possibly much earlier, in 2007 (there is some controversy about the exact date), the Plaintiff lost his driver's license due to an impaired driving conviction and could no longer drive himself to the Sundowner. He became primarily reliant on his sister, Denise Taylor, to transport him for shopping, medical appointments, recreation, family visits and banking. Mrs. Taylor never transported Mr. Dagenais to the Sundowner, as she did not approve of his visits there. Mr. Dagenais stated that he sometimes took taxis to the club, but the evidence was unclear as to how he managed to make his frequent visits there without being driven by Mrs. Taylor.

11. Beginning sometime early in 2009, Ms. Vassel began to spend time with Mr. Dagenais outside of the Sundowner, primarily at his home but also driving him to a nearby park or on errands to shops and banks.

12. Mobile phone records furnished by Ms. Vassel established that on what Justice Lococo described as "a number of occasions" she called Mr. Dagenais at his home, sometimes repeatedly, either the day before or on the same day that he made withdrawals from various bank accounts. Mr. Dagenais' bank records for three separate accounts indicated that he withdrew large sums of money on many of those occasions. A summary of cash withdrawals from these accounts prepared by Mr. Dagenais and Mrs. Taylor indicated that between July 22, 2009 and January 13, 2010 there were a total of 46 withdrawals on 32 different dates (about 7 to 8 per month on average), totaling $132,845. Of these transactions, 31 involved withdrawals of $1,200 or more, totaling $127,345, an average of

$4,108. The average for all 46 withdrawals was about $2,883. The average for the 15 withdrawals under $1,200 was $373.

13. On January 4 (or possibly January 5), 2010, Mr. Dagenais met with Ms. Vassel at the Sundowner club and asked her to sign a statement, dated January 4, 2010 and written on the back of an envelope, acknowledging that she had borrowed $151,000 from him. Ms. Vassal's signature could not be discerned on the document presented as evidence by Mr. Dagenais. However, a few ink markings on the envelope were pointed to by Mr. Dagenais in trial to support his claim that she had signed the statement at three separate and distinct times during their meeting. He claimed that she had promptly scratched out each of the alleged signatures after initially complying with his repeated demands that she acknowledge the debt in writing.

14. Both Mr. Dagenais and Ms. Vassel stated in trial that they had never had sexual relations, either before or after Ms. Vassel began visiting Mr. Dagenais in Port Colborne.

15. In trial, Eden Harlow, another exotic dancer working at the Sundowner, stated that in early January, 2010 she had asked Mr. Dagenais to purchase a dance but that he declined, telling her that he was waiting to get dances from Ms. Vassel, with whom, he claimed, he was sleeping. Ms. Harlow also stated that Mr. Dagenais had threatened to "kill" her if she told anyone about what he had said.

16. Mrs. Taylor stated in trial that Mr. Dagenais began telling her about his encounters with Ms. Vassel sometime in 2009, including discussions they had about taking a vacation together in

Jamaica and also moving in together. She also stated that Mr. Dagenais did not tell her that he was lending money to Ms. Vassel until January 2010, although she was aware by September, 2009 that Mr. Dagenais had recently made some significant cash withdrawals from his bank accounts.

Disputed Facts of the Original Law Suit

17. In trial, Mr. Dagenais claimed that Ms. Vassel started coming to his home uninvited early in 2009 and speculated that she must have obtained his address from the phone book. He further claimed that the visits by Ms. Vassel to his home were entirely unsolicited, unwelcome and unwanted. Ms. Vassel contradicted this account and stated that all her visits to Mr. Dagenais in Port Colborne were prearranged and at Mr. Dagenais' invitation, and that she charged him fees between $300 and $500 per visit, as she did other customers who asked for "dates" outside of the Sundowner.

18. In trial, Mr. Dagenais stated that Ms. Vassel started asking him for money in July 2009, the first request being on July 22 for $1,200 to travel to Jamaica for her mother's funeral. According to Mr. Dagenais, these requests continued until January 13, 2010. He testified that he agreed to all of these requests, under pressure from an often-distraught Ms. Vassel, on condition that all his money transfers to her would be considered loans and that she agreed verbally to repay him. Ms. Vassel denied that she had borrowed money from Mr. Dagenais on any occasion for any purpose and insisted that she had taken money from him only on a "fee for service" basis. She estimated that in the entire

time she had known Mr. Dagenais he may have given her a total of about $10,000, all of which was paid by way of compensation for her time and companionship, both inside and outside the Sundowner. Approximately half of that sum was received for “dates” in Port Colborne in 2009.

19. It was the Plaintiff's position that every single withdrawal indicated on the list of withdrawals produced by Mrs. Taylor and himself and entered as evidence at trial was a loan made to Ms. Vassel. Without admitting to specific knowledge concerning most of them, Ms. Vassel did not dispute that these withdrawals had been made but insisted that she had received no money from Mr. Dagenais as loans and that the approximately $5,000 she did receive from him in 2009 was for services rendered, specifically companionship and time spent driving him to locations of his choosing. The Defendant also claimed that on some occasions when she drove the Plaintiff to a bank he would display large cash withdrawals in a boastful fashion and then offer her large sums to have sex with him.

20. Mr. Dagenais claimed that the January 4, 2010 statement that he drafted on the back of an envelope and that was intended as acknowledgment of Ms. Vassel's $151,000 debt to him was signed by her on that date (or possibly on January 5) on three separate occasions during a single meeting at the Sundowner, but that each time she scratched out her signature during intervals in which he went to the washroom. Ms. Vassel contradicted this testimony by denying unequivocally that she had signed the statement even once, much less three times. She also stated that he had presented this statement to her while in a very

agitated and angry state of mind, shortly after she had told him that she was going to discontinue seeing him. The reason she gave for this decision was that he had been lying to her co-workers about their sleeping together. Although Mr. Dagenais denied telling any of her co-workers that she had slept with him, Ms. Vassel stated that two of her co-workers, one of them being Ms. Harlow and another a dancer named Dakota, had told her that Mr. Dagenais had threatened to "kill" anyone who informed Ms. Vassel about his claims to have slept with her.

21. Mr. Dagenais stated that Ms. Vassel initiated discussions with him about vacationing in Jamaica together and moving into his home. Ms. Vassel denied this unequivocally, insisting that all such discussions had been initiated by Mr. Dagenais. She maintained that she had always rejected these suggestions out of hand, reminding him of the strict fee-for-service boundaries surrounding their relations.

22. The Plaintiff argued that the summary of telephone calls from Ms. Vassel to Mr. Dagenais during the period July, 2009 to January, 2010 when compared to the summary of bank withdrawals made by Mr. Dagenais demonstrated some correspondence between the dates of the calls and the dates of significant withdrawals. Ms. Vassel acknowledged being present at times when Mr. Dagenais made large withdrawals, but denied receiving any loans, or any payments in excess of $500. Concerning the frequency of her calls to Mr. Dagenais, she explained that she often spoke by phone to good customers, including Mr. Dagenais, and that Mr. Dagenais often left word at the Sundowner for

her to call him. She also stated that she often lost the signal while using her cell phone, which explained repeated calls made on the same day, as did his frequent requests that she call him back on the same day.

23. Counsel for the Plaintiff asked Ms. Vassal why she had not produced bank records to show whether or not she had made deposits corresponding to Mr. Dagenais' cash withdrawals, implying that her "failure" to do so proved she was hiding something. Ms. Vassel answered by saying that she didn't have an active bank account during the period in question, explaining that she conducted her business affairs in cash and that the Canada Revenue Agency had effectively frozen her account pending payment by her of over $50,000 in unpaid GST.

24. Mr. Dagenais claimed that the last bank withdrawal he made in order to provide a loan to Ms. Vassel, a sum of $2,000, was on January 13, 2010, more than a week after he failed to obtain Ms. Vassel's signature on the loan statement that he presented to her. Ms. Vassel maintained that she stopped seeing Mr. Dagenais as a customer after he demanded that she sign the loan statement and that the alleged January 13 loan, as with all other alleged loans cited by Mr. Dagenais, was never made to her.

25. It was Ms. Vassel's position that it defied common sense that all of the 46 bank withdrawals listed in the Plaintiff's summary had been loaned or otherwise given to her and that none of this money had been used by Mr. Dagenais for his own benefit, including the purchase of everyday necessities, his spending at

the Sundowner, and his encounters with other exotic dancers outside the Sundowner club. More specifically, Ms. Vassel argued that it made utterly no sense for Mr. Dagenais to withdraw $2,000 on January 13, 2010 and then lend it to her after she had refused to acknowledge any debt, in writing, on January 4, 2010.

Justice Lococo's Judgment

26. Despite some expressed doubts and misgivings about "certain aspects" of Mr. Dagenais' evidence, specifically that it was "sometimes muddled and hard to follow" and "not consistent" with evidence provided by Mrs. Taylor concerning his real attitude toward Ms. Vassel's visits, Justice Lococo nevertheless came to the following conclusion:

"... I accept as credible the basic thrust of [Mr. Dagenais'] evidence relating to the significant withdrawals from his bank account in the period July of 2009 to January 2010. That is, Ms. Vassel asked him to provide her with significant sums of money for various purposes and he provided those sums to her by way of loan, with the understanding from Ms. Vassel that he would be repaid." (RFJ, p. 77)

27. The trial judge stated the following key reason for his acceptance of Mr. Dagenais' evidence with respect to the alleged loans made to Ms. Vassel:

"Although there is no written acknowledgement of the loans, the documentary evidence that does exist demonstrated that Mr. Dagenais made significant withdrawals from his account during the period, [withdrawals] that were not consistent with his prior spending pattern. During that period, Ms. Vassel was seeing Mr. Dagenais outside of the club and taking him to bank branches where he made withdrawals .... As well, in almost every case, Ms. Vassel called Mr. Dagenais on the day prior, or the day of the withdrawals, consistent with the conclusion that the withdrawals were made at her request." (RFJ, p. 77)

28. Regarding Ms. Vassel's evidence, the trial judge commented as follows:

"While Ms. Vassel's evidence was indeed easier to follow, I did not find it to be more credible than the evidence of Mr. Dagenais, which I prefer and accept on the crucial points as to whether Ms. Vassel received sums of money from Mr. Dagenais, and the characterization of these amounts as loans." (RFJ, p. 78)

29. Explaining his attitude toward Ms. Vassel's evidence, the trial judge stated:

"Among other things, I was skeptical about Ms. Vassel's explanation for failure to produce bank records that may have been helpful in making the determination in this case; nor did I find credible her explanation for the pattern of multiple phone calls to Mr. Dagenais, coincident with the bank withdrawals." (RFJ, pp. 78-79)

30. The trial judge entirely rejected defense counsel's argument according to which the "alleged inconsistency in Mr. Dagenais' evidence regarding the alleged January 13 loan to Ms. Vassel] cannot be reconciled with the conclusion that the significant withdrawals made from Mr. Dagenais' account prior to January 2010 were advanced by way of loan to Ms. Vassel." (RFJ, p. 79)

31. The trial judge's principal finding in the case was stated as follows: "Accordingly, after

weighing all the evidence, I find that Mr. Dagenais has established on a balance of probabilities that Mr. Dagenais withdrew significant sums of money from his bank accounts as outlined below and advanced them to Ms. Vassel by way of loan and that such amounts are due and outstanding." (RFJ, pp. 79-80)

32. Notwithstanding the Plaintiff's claim that every single amount shown on the summary withdrawals presented by him in trial was a loan made to Ms. Vassel, including the alleged loan of January 13, 2010, the trial judge excluded all individual withdrawal amounts from the list that were less than $1,200 as well as the $2,000 withdrawal made on January 13, 2010. In making these exclusions, the trial judge affirmed agreement with arguments that smaller withdrawals may have been used by Mr. Dagenais for purposes other than loans to Ms. Vassel and that real doubt surrounded the purpose of his January 13 withdrawal. (See RFJ, p. 80)

PART II - STATEMENT OF THE QUESTIONS IN ISSUE

33. The above statement of facts invites a series of important questions about the judgment rendered by the trial judge as well as the decision of the Court of Appeals to uphold it. These questions pertain to (a) issues already raised in the Appellant's Factum of March 15, 2012 presented to the Court of Appeals (see paragraph 5 above), (b) specious reasoning and logical lapses in the trial judge's findings that were not identified in that Factum, and (c) bias displayed by the trial judge in extending

significant benefit of the doubt to Mr. Dagenais' evidence in unwarranted ways while maintaining a steadfastly skeptical attitude toward all the evidence provided by Ms. Vassel.

34. The **first issue** raised in the Factum presented to the Court of Appeal concerned the question: Did the trial judge err in substituting and relying on his own conclusions rather than the evidence? The Appellant submitted that "if there is doubt on the evidence whether any single withdrawal was advanced by way of loan to Ms. Vassel, as the trial judge pointed out was the case on the January 13, 2010 withdrawal, then in light of the evidence of the Plaintiff that every single withdrawal was a loan, there is doubt as to whether any other amount was advanced to Ms. Vassel." Based on this argument, the Appellant argued that "the trial judge committed a palpable and overriding error by drawing conclusions which were not supported in evidence, to reconcile the inconsistencies in the Plaintiff's evidence."

35. In rejecting this first ground of appeal, the Court of Appeal stated:

"A trial judge is not obliged to accept or reject the entirety of the case as presented for the plaintiff. A trial judge must make findings of fact based on his assessment of the entirety of the evidence. In the course of doing so, he or she may reject some but not necessarily all the evidence given by any witness, including a plaintiff. This trial judge did exactly that. He reviewed the plaintiff's evidence carefully and while he was not prepared to accept the entirety of it, he clearly accepted the thrust of the plaintiff's evidence that he had loaned a great deal of money to the defendant over a six-month period and that he had funded that loan through numerous cash withdrawals from his various bank accounts. The trial judge's finding was not unreasonable and we must defer to it."

36. The applicant submits that the Court of Appeal erred in its assessment that the trial Judge made a "careful" review of the Plaintiff's evidence and that the trial judge's finding was "not unreasonable."

37. The **second issue** raised in the factum presented to the Court of Appeal concerned the question: Did the trial judge err in shifting the onus of proof from the Plaintiff to the Defendant in arriving at the conclusion that the money was advanced to the Defendant and that the money was a loan? The Appellant submitted that the trial judge was looking for evidence from Ms. Vassel to disprove that she had received large sums of money in the period in question. The trial judge also asked Ms. Vassel for an alternative explanation as to what happened to the funds withdrawn to that provided by Mr. Dagenais. Because of her inability to provide a full alternative explanation, the trial judge determined that the funds must have been advanced to Ms. Vassel and by way of loan. The reasoning involved in this determination strongly suggests that the trial judge erred by shifting the onus of proof from the Plaintiff to the Defendant, contrary to the Supreme Court of Canada's ruling in *H. (F). v. McDougall* that the balance of probabilities standard was the sole standard of proof at common law in all civil proceedings. The appellant submitted that, in this case, the onus of proof was on Mr. Dagenais to prove that the money was loaned to Ms. Vassel, on a balance of probabilities.

38. In rejecting this second ground of appeal, the Court of Appeal stated:

"We see nothing in the reasons which suggests a reversal of the burden of proof. The trial judge in assessing the appellant's credibility properly took into account factors relevant to that assessment, including, for example, the appellant's failure to produce her bank records. In doing so, the trial judge did not place any legal burden of proof on the appellant.... The absence of any explanation on certain matters from the appellant and the absence of any evidence to support explanations that were offered were relevant in assessing whether the plaintiff had met his burden of proof. This ground of appeal cannot succeed."

39. The applicant submits that the Court of Appeal erred in its assessment that there was "nothing" in the trial judge's reasons that suggests a reversal of the burden of proof. Furthermore, the court's rejection of this ground of appeal establishes a dangerous precedent by effectively *privileging* a plaintiff's account of particular events in circumstances where a defendant is unable to refute various details of that account or to provide a complete alternative account. In this case, the reasoning of both the trial judge and the Court of Appeal also suggests that Ms. Vassel's "failure" to prove that something did *not* happen (i.e., that she had *not* deposited large sums of money into a bank account) called into question her credibility. Both the Superior Court Justice and the Court of Appeal failed to consider that, even if Ms. Vassel had been able to produce records for an active bank account that showed that no large sums had been deposited during the period in question, this in itself would not have proven that she had not been the recipient of large sums of money from

Mr. Dagenais or that she had not deposited these sums in an undisclosed bank account or otherwise hidden them.

40. The **third issue** raised in the Factum presented to the Court of Appeal concerned the question: Did the trial judge err in neglecting to analyze the inconsistencies in the Plaintiff's evidence and failing to provide sufficient reasons as to how the issues of credibility were resolved? The Appellant submitted that glaring inconsistencies in the evidence of Mr. Dagenais were given insufficient consideration in the trial judge's deliberations and in assessing Mr. Dagenais' credibility. Further, the Appellant submitted that the trial judge erred by considering Ms. Vassel's "inability" to explain how Mr. Dagenais could have spent the large sums of money at issue and her failure to produce records for an active bank account for the period in question as factors that weighed against her credibility.

41. In rejecting this third ground of appeal, the Court of Appeal stated: "The trial judge analyzed the evidence of both the defendant and plaintiff. His reasons clearly indicate how he came to prefer the evidence of the plaintiff over the appellant. In our view, the reasons are both logical and supported by the evidence. They reveal no basis upon which this court can interfere."

42. The applicant submits that the Court of Appeal erred in stating that the trial judge "clearly" indicated how he came to prefer the evidence of Mr. Dagenais over that of Ms. Vassel and that the reasons he gave were "both logical and supported by the evidence." To the contrary, the applicant submits that there are ample grounds

for questioning the quality of that evidence as well as the clarity and the logic displayed by the trial judge.

43. The applicant submits that in addition to the issues explored in the Factum presented to the Court of Appeal there are other serious grounds for questioning the logic, reasoning and attention to detail of the trial judge, as evidenced in his "Reasons for Judgment." Some of these grounds center on the following questions that were left unexplored and unaddressed by the trial judge: (a) Why would Mr. Dagenais lend large amounts of money, not once, but on dozens of separate occasions, to Ms. Vassel without obtaining a signed statement from Ms. Vassel promising to repay him by a definite date? (b) Why would he ask her to swear on a sacred object that she would repay him, suggesting some doubt in his mind about her trustworthiness, but not also ask her to sign a simple IOU statement until dozens of alleged large loans had been made to her? (c) Why would Ms. Vassel have signed an acknowledgement of loan prepared by Mr. Dagenais in early January, 2010 only to then strike out her signature, not once, but three times? (d) Why would Mr. Dagenais have left this statement behind with Ms. Vassel as he went to the washroom on three occasions, giving her the opportunity to scratch out her name, not once but three times, after she allegedly signed the statement for the first time? (e) Why did these last two questions not raise in the mind of the trial judge the possibility that the alleged scratched-out signatures on the January 4 statement of loan were fabricated by Mr. Dagenais to undermine Ms. Vassel's credibility? (f) Why did the trial judge not find it troubling

that Mr. Dagenais demanded that Ms. Vassel sign a loan statement of January 4, 2010 in the amount of $151,000, when, according to the evidence of both Mr. Dagenais and Mrs. Taylor, it was only after January 4 that they compiled a summary of the bank withdrawals in question and decided to sue Ms. Vassel for $132, 845?

44. The trial judge gave no specific reasons for "preferring" Mr. Dagenais' evidence over that of Ms. Vassel beyond his "skepticism" regarding the latter's explanation for "failing" to produce bank records as well as her explanation for the pattern of multiple calls to Mr. Dagenais "coincident with the bank withdrawals." He also gave no reason for accepting Mr. Dagenais' "characterization" of unspecified amounts as "loans." Nor did the trial judge explain the reasoning behind his decision that Mr. Dagenais had "established" that the withdrawals in question were advanced to Ms. Vassel "by way of loan" and that "such amounts are due and outstanding." The decision that these amounts are due and outstanding is particularly curious given the fact that no schedule (or schedules) for repayment of the loans was entered into evidence. How then was the due date (or dates) for the loans established? And how did the trial judge conclude that they are "due" or "outstanding" – and therefore subject to interest?

45. The trial judge's "Reasons for Judgment" contains a contradictory statement regarding the factual basis of the case. Specifically, it is stated on page 73 that the summary of withdrawals prepared by Mr. Dagenais and Mrs. Taylor covered the period from January, 2009 to January, 2010, whereas on page 74 the period

from July 22, 2009 to January, 2010 is identified. This is the most obvious instance of an inattention to detail and carelessness that characterizes the document at many levels. Another concerns the trial judge's arbitrary conclusion that, apart from the alleged loan of January 13, 2010, only withdrawal amounts made by Mr. Dagenais of under $1,200 should be excluded from the monetary judgment made against Ms. Vassel. Yet those amounts totaled only $5,500 over a period of almost six months, about $900 per month on average. This figure is not consistent with undisputed evidence that Mr. Dagenais had been in the habit of spending $2,000 or more at the Sundowner on a monthly basis. Hence, although the trial judge cited Mr. Dagenais' spending habits prior to July, 2009 as a reason to believe his claim that he started making large withdrawals solely for the purpose of making loans to Ms. Vassel, he displayed no interest in considering those habits when deciding what he believed should be excluded from the monetary judgment against Ms. Vassel.

46. The trial judge argued that "in almost every case of withdrawals, Ms. Vassel called Mr. Dagenais on the day prior, or the day of the withdrawals, consistent with the conclusion that the withdrawals were made at her request." But this set of facts can also be viewed as consistent with the conclusion that Mr. Dagenais made the withdrawals in order to pay Ms. Vassel for her time and companionship; that larger sums may have been withdrawn in an attempt to bribe Ms. Vassel to have sex with him; and that major amounts of these withdrawals might have been spent on other activities, including encounters and transactions with other exotic dancers or escorts, deposits in other (undisclosed)

accounts, or even the purchase of precious metals to protect his savings from a global financial crisis. Furthermore, if smaller amounts (under $1,200) were likely used by Mr. Dagenais for purposes other than loans to Ms. Vassel, as admitted by the trial judge, what reasons support the conclusion that the larger amounts could *only* have been used as loans to Ms. Vassel? The trial judge failed to adduce any reasons whatsoever.

47. In making the logical leap just referred to, the trial judge gave undue weight to the evidence that Ms. Vassel sometimes made multiple calls to Mr. Dagenais on the same day, and that there was some correspondence between the dates of those calls and the dates on which he made large bank withdrawals. Ms. Vassel explained that these calls were made entirely at Mr. Dagenais' request, and that they were not always made the day before or on the same day as her visits to him in Port Colborne. If Mr. Dagenais regarded those calls as unwelcome and bothersome, as he claimed he did, why did he continue to receive them? Furthermore, why did he not seek the help of his sister, his other siblings or the authorities in responding to Ms. Vassel's alleged "harassment" much earlier than he did?

48. In drawing the conclusion that the larger amounts could *only* have been used as loans to Ms. Vassel, the trial judge also ignored evidence that Mr. Dagenais habitually spent money on other women besides Ms. Vassel, including other exotic dancers working at the Sundowner. In response to questioning about his activities at the Sundowner, Mr. Dagenais stated that he would "sit and talk" to Ms. Vassel as well as other dancers. When he was asked if he paid Ms.

Vassel for this companionship, he replied: "Always – it seems the way they do it, it's $20 a dance, eh? Not a dance, but $20 after every song. But I never spent too much money with her; I used to go around, eh." When asked if he was saying that he "would go to various different people," he replied "Yeah. Yes." In her evidence at trial, Ms. Harlow confirmed that Mr. Dagenais had been a "good customer" of hers and that, during their times together, he spent $60 to $100 on average for dances in the Sundowner VIP room. She also stated that Mr. Dagenais had offered to take her on vacation to Jamaica, and answered "yes" when asked if she had ever seen him "dance with other girls." This evidence is consistent with Ms. Vassel's claim that Mr. Dagenais was involved with other girls from the Sundowner, both inside and outside the club.

49. The applicant submits that the trial judge's "Reasons for Judgment" displays significant *subjective bias* in favour of Mr. Dagenais and against Ms. Vassel. This bias found expression in the trial judge's pronounced tendency to accord Mr. Dagenais the benefit of the doubt in ways that were completely unwarranted and to maintain a resolute "skepticism" toward the evidence of Ms. Vassel, despite its consistency and straight-forward character. While the trial judge expressed doubts about the credibility of Ms. Vassel's evidence, he was unable to cite even one instance in which she was shown to have lied or dissembled. On the other hand, the totality of evidence reviewed above shows unmistakably that Mr. Dagenais had a marked propensity to obfuscate, contradict himself, and to blatantly lie about many of the facts germane to the case, including his attitude toward Ms.

Vassel's visits to him in Port Colborne, his declared certainty that every single withdrawal he made between July 22 and January 13 was advanced as a loan to her, his denial that he desired and sought sexual relations with her, and his utterly implausible claim that Ms. Vassel scratched out her signature on a statement of loan three times.

50. The subjective bias of the trial judge found clear and damaging expression in his attempts to explain away contradictions in the evidence that undermined Mr. Dagenais' credibility. A case in point is Mr. Dagenais' claim that he loaned $2,000 to Ms. Vassel on January 13, 2010, more than a week after she refused to sign the disputed statement of loan of January 4 and around the time he sent police to the Sundowner to question her. Although the trial judge excluded this amount from his judgment against Ms. Vassel, he nevertheless granted that it was possible, as Mrs. Taylor had suggested, that the January meeting between Mr. Dagenais and Ms. Vassel and their argument over the statement of loan might have occurred after January 13, even though this speculation is highly improbable and no evidence was presented to support it.

51. While serious doubts about the alleged loan of January 13, 2010 do not establish with certainty that Mr. Dagenais lied about that loan, or any loan, his evidence on this matter did suggest a desire on his part to seek maximum damages from Ms. Vassel, as did his claim that every single withdrawal made between July 22 and January 13 were advanced to her as loans. It is not unreasonable to suppose that this desire was motivated by intense animus and even a wish for revenge against Ms. Vassel, and that this

desire, together with the "embarrassment" that the trial judge detected in his demeanor, caused him to lie to the court. The strong likelihood that Mr. Dagenais lied in trial in even small ways should have called into question the credibility of his larger "story." But rather than consider this possibility seriously, the trial judge went out of his way to "commend him for his fortitude in pursuing this remedy." Setting aside his "misgivings" about Mr. Dagenais' extraordinarily confused and muddled evidence, the trial judge expressed sympathy for him by noting that "he was understandably emotional about what had happened, and no doubt embarrassed about having to tell his story in court."

52. In his judgment, the trial judge highlighted the change in the pattern of Mr. Dagenais' spending and withdrawals after he began receiving visits from Ms. Vassel in 2009. He cited this change in behavior as one factor supporting his conclusion that Mr. Dagenais loaned large amounts of money to Ms. Vassel. The reasoning behind this conclusion is by no means clear. However, the apparent sympathy for and favorable bias expressed by the trial judge for Mr. Dagenais may explain why the judge was unwilling to consider the possibility that Mr. Dagenais fabricated his "story" in order to recoup money that he had spent in a variety of ways and to satisfy a grudge against a woman who spurned his sexual advances and whom he came bitterly to resent, particularly after her decision to stop seeing him. Furthermore, the trial judge did not consider that the change in Mr. Dagenais' habits might have been associated with: a) effects of his deteriorating health; b) the disruption of his prior habits resulting from the loss of his

driver's license; c) frustration at his inability to persuade Ms. Vassel to agree to his requests for a more intimate, sexual relationship; and d) his consequent attempts to assuage these frustrations through relationships or sexual encounters with other dancers or escorts. Nor did the judge consider the possibility that, under pressure from his family, in particular Mrs. Taylor, the designated executor of his estate and an individual with experience working in a law firm, Mr. Dagenais decided that the most expedient way to recover the large amounts that he had spent so recklessly over a period of six months was to pursue a legal claim against a single individual, namely Ms. Vassel.

53. While he clearly empathized with the emotionalism and embarrassment shown by Mr. Dagenais, the trial judge displayed no inclination to examine compassionately the facts of the case from the perspective of Ms. Vassel. Not only did he not acknowledge Ms. Vassel's own palpable "embarrassment"; he questioned her credibility and truthfulness in ways that were not clearly supported by the evidence. The size of the claim made against Ms. Vassel, a woman who had been struggling to pay her bills for some time, including a sizeable sum to Canada Revenue Agency, and who would be forced to sell her home in order to comply with a court decision made against her, evidently did not trouble the trial judge, for he made no comment in this regard. Moreover, his very language betrayed the bias against her that informed his "reasoning" and his conclusions in the case. According to the trial judge, Ms. Vassel "failed" to produce her bank account statements in evidence, even though the rules of evidence for a case of this kind did not require that she do

so, and even though bank account statements showing no significant deposits would have proved nothing about whether she had taken the alleged loans or about her credibility. Furthermore, according to the trial judge, Ms. Vassel was "unable to explain" how Mr. Dagenais could have spent so much money in such a short period of time other than by making loans to her. This language of "failure" and "inability to explain" in connection with Ms. Vassel's evidence revealed in subtle but unmistakable ways a willingness on the part of the trial judge to shift the onus of proof from a plaintiff, whose evidence was shot through with inconsistencies, contradictions and implausible claims, to a defendant whose evidence was consistent, plausible and straightforward. Finally, the trial judge's summary of Ms. Harlow's evidence, according to which Mr. Dagenais had "confided" to Ms. Harlow that he was sleeping with Ms. Vassel, provides very strong evidence of a bias favoring Mr. Dagenais. Ms. Harlow's actual words were: "I asked him for a dance and he said he was going to wait for her because he really liked her and he said he was sleeping with her and he told me not to tell no one or he'll kill me." (p.66) Not only did Ms. Harlow not say that Mr. Dagenais had "confided" in her (which implies an intimate, truthful and non-threatening exchange between them), but the alleged threat that Mr. Dagenais made against Ms. Harlow went unmentioned in the trial judge's summary. This begs the question: why would the trial judge summarize Ms. Harlow's very troubling evidence in a way that tended to favor Mr. Dagenais and deflect attention from what could be construed as a criminal threat? The use of the word "confided" by the trial judge in this context might also be read as a subtle attempt on his part to give credence to Mr. Dagenais' claim to Ms. Harlow that he had been sleeping with Ms. Vassel.

54. With respect to **the second issue of public importance** posed by the case of Dagenais v. Vassel, the applicant submits that the trial record, the Factum presented to the Court of Appeal and the gaps in other documentation made to the Court of Appeal attest to the ineptness and incompetence of Ms. Vassel's counsel, Mr. Zijad Saskin. Facts that were not available to either the Superior Court or to the Court of Appeal support the applicant's claim that Mr. Saskin's conduct, involving a breach of solicitor client privilege, was also unethical and that it threatened her livelihood and physical security. Specifically, it is the applicant's claim that Mr. Saskin may have discussed her case with Mr. Chris Rudan, the owner of the Sundowner Gentleman's Club and an individual with whom he had both a personal and professional relationship; that following this breach of solicitor-client privilege, Ms. Vassel's relations with Mr. Rudan and the club management deteriorated markedly; that she was eventually suspended from working at the club, badly compromising her ability to earn money and therefore to fund her legal defense; and that she was thereafter the target of potentially life-threatening intimidation by as-yet-unidentified parties, whom she believes may have been associated with Mr. Rudan and Mr. Saskin. As the above matters had a material effect on the outcome of the case, Ms. Vassel petitions the Supreme Court of Canada to be

allowed to present evidence in support of these allegations.

PART III – STATEMENT OF ARGUMENT

55. (a) It is the position of the applicant that the bias displayed by the trial judge against Ms. Vassel and in favour of Mr. Dagenais, and which was the decisive factor in his decision in the case, stemmed most probably from a prejudicial attitude toward the defendant's occupation as an exotic dancer and sometime paid companion of male "customers," compounded by an unfounded suspicion that an aging white male, who presented himself as a "simple" and rather befuddled pensioner, may have been taken advantage of by an attractive and much-younger black female. The applicant submits that the trial judge had an obligation to resist any influence on his judicial reasoning of prejudicial attitudes and stereotypes that are widespread in the community regarding exotic dancing, an occupation that is legal in Canada and governed by specific provincial and municipal regulations. There is much in his "Reasons for Judgment" to suggest that the trial judge failed in meeting this obligation, not least his failure to acknowledge the existence of prejudicial attitudes towards exotic dancers, and in particular toward black female exotic dancers, as well as his ethical obligation to resist the influence of such attitudes in arriving at a judgment.

55. (b) The trial judge's bias against Ms. Vassel based on her occupation as a black female exotic dancer found expression, *inter alia,* in his differential treatment and comments concerning the evidence of Ms. Eden Harlow and Mrs. Denise Taylor. The trial judge commented that

he found Mrs. Taylor's evidence "credible," while expressing no opinion about the credibility of Ms. Harlow's evidence, which he nevertheless distorted in a way favorable to Mr. Dagenais in his Reasons for Judgment.

56. The evidence that most strongly supports the position of the applicant with regard to the likely *source* of the bias of the trial judge against Ms. Vassel is the comment of the trial judge regarding the demeanor of Mr. Dagenais as he related his "story" in trial. In his Reasons for Judgment, the trial judge wrote: "[Mr. Dagenais] was understandably emotional about what had happened, and no doubt embarrassed about having to tell his story in court." However, the trial judge did not elaborate on this observation, apparently regarding the reasons for Mr. Dagenais' embarrassment and distraught demeanor as self-evident. This posture suggests that he accepted at face value the essential thrust of that "story" – a story in which Mr. Dagenais depicted himself as the victim of a manipulative and dishonest "femme fatale" who set out to force upon him her companionship, to win his confidence and to then pressure him into giving her large sums of money, nominally as "loans," that she had no intention of repaying. To accept this story at face value and to base much of his reasoning on it, the trial judge needed to ignore the fact that key elements of Mr. Dagenais' story were implausible and unsupported by any evidence apart from his own testimony and that other, more well - established evidence clearly contradicted it on key points.

57. The applicant also submits that the trial judge displayed a bias favoring Mr. Dagenais and

unfavorable to Ms. Vassel by not considering other possible explanations for Mr. Dagenais' emotional and embarrassed demeanor while giving his evidence other than the pain of having to recount his alleged folly in making unsecured loans to an exotic dancer. One such explanation was that, as a self-described religious man, he was extremely uncomfortable about lying to the court, particularly after swearing an oath on what he regarded as a sacred object. Another explanation is that he was experiencing great anxiety about keeping his fabricated story straight in his own mind as he told it to the court. Furthermore, it seems likely that, after disclosing to his sister and possibly other siblings that he had squandered large amounts of his life savings over a period of six months, he felt considerable family pressure to rectify the consequences of what he now saw as foolish behavior on his part. Finally, if indeed he fabricated his claim that all the withdrawals in question were made to Ms. Vassel and her alone, then he may well have felt some embarrassment and anxiety in making this claim in her presence. Evidently, none of these possibilities, which are all quite plausible, were given any serious consideration by the trial judge; and the most likely explanation for his failure in this regard was a pronounced bias against Ms. Vassel stemming from a suspicion that, because she was an exotic dancer, she might also be a scam artist. This explanation is likely despite the fact that the trial judge studiously avoided writing or saying anything that could be construed as overtly prejudicial. The only other explanation that can be adduced is sheer incompetence on the part of the trial judge.

58. In light of the above considerations, the applicant submits that *judicial bias relating centrally to occupation/class, age and health status, but perhaps also to gender and race, played the decisive role in determining the trial judge's decision against Ms. Vassel*, rather than the meager verifiable evidence available to the court.

Furthermore, the brief and thinly motivated decision of June 13, 2012 by the Court of Appeal to uphold that decision as "not unreasonable" and as free of the errors attributed to it in the Appellant's Factum of March 15, 2012 recapitulates the errors and bias of the trial judge.

All the Supreme Court forms are now filled out and the main document completed. I'm running out of time, so I decide to drive to Ottawa and submit everything in person. It's a long drive, and once I get there I'm frustrated about getting lost on the damned city's all-too-many one-way streets. It takes me the better part of an hour to find a Staples store. Finally, I locate one, and I rush in and order seven printed copies of my dossier, one of which is sent directly by courier to Clark Peddle. *You'd better believe he's going to sign for it.*

It's now just minutes to five o'clock, and I'm rushing like mad to make it to the main Supreme Court of Canada building to file my submission. I'm very apprehensive about what I'm about to do, but I'm also determined to go through with it.

As I approach the elegant building, I realize that there's no convenient street parking anywhere near the main entrance. My frustration mounts as I drive past several empty lots marked "Reserved Parking."

I drive back toward the downtown area, quickly park my car in a pay lot, and then flag a cab. Thank God this driver knows exactly where I'm going. With just a few minutes to spare, I run up the stairs to a small reception room for the public. Breathlessly, I explain to one of the clerks what I want to do. The staff is helpful but also insistent that I need to present proof that I've sent a copy of the submission to Clark Peddle.

A few days later, I go to Peddle's office, and his secretary confirms they'd received their copy that morning from the courier. I obtain a copy of the receipt from her and immediately fax it to the Supreme Court. My trip back to Niagara had been unnecessary. It's a shame, because I'd given some thought to working in Ottawa for a few weeks.

I have to limit my driving now because I'm still riding on winter tires and they're looking pretty bald. I need to pump air into the front right tire every single day.

A short time later I receive Peddle's formal response to my application to the Supreme Court.

CLARK PEDDLE: responds to the Supreme Court of Canada.

PART 1- STATEMENT OF FACTS

A. overview

1. This is a fact driven case which raises no issues of public or national importance. Thelma Angela Vassel aka Linda Lee (the "Applicant") borrowed substantial

amount of money from Paul Dagenais ("Dagenais") which has never been repaid.

2. Dagenais was a 61-year old retiree and life-long bachelor who resided on Port Colborne, Ontario. After the trial Dagenais passed away and the Court of Appeal added Denise Taylor as estate of Dagenais.

3. The applicant is an exotic dancer who at all material times worked at the Sundowner Gentleman's Club ('Sundowner") in Niagara Falls. Ontario and resided in Niagara-On-The-Lake, Ontario.

4. Dagenais would visit the Sundowner on an average of twice per week where he met and got to know the Applicant.

5. The relationship continued outside the Sundowner premises with the applicant calling Dagenais on numerous occasions, visiting his home in Port Colborne and taking him to various financial institutions in her motor vehicle.

6. The trial evidence demonstrates that Dagenais made substantial loans to the Applicant which have never been repaid.

7. The Respondents ask that this Court dismiss this Application for Leave to Appeal with cost.

B. Facts

8. Dagenais led a frugal lifestyle, would bank his earnings, and would only spend what he needed for his day-today needs.

Transcript of the proceedings at trial before Honorable Justice R. Lococo on August29 and 30, 2011 at Welland, Ontario ("Transcript") page 2, line 13-23, tab 11

9. Prior to meeting the Applicant, Dagenais had suffered a stroke and had been in the hospital for six months.

Transcript, page 3, line 9-13, Tab 12

10. The Applicant began attending at Dagenais' residence in Port Colborne.

Transcript, page 4, line 23-29 Tab 13

11. The Applicant would not park in Dagenais' driveway, and instead park on the street next to the neighbour's house.

Transcript, page 5, line 7-12, Tab 14

12. The Applicant began asking Dagenais to borrow money for her mother's funeral, her father's funeral, to fix her car, to pay her rent, to make a movie, to get a Visa and to settle a debt her father had with bikers.

Transcript, page 5, line 23-32 and page 6, line 3-6, tab 15

13. To obtain the money the Applicant would drive Dagenais to various financial institutions throughout Niagara, most of which he had never been to before.

Transcript, page 6, line 16-31, Tab 16

14. Dagenais would go into the bank and was told not to mention the Applicant's name. He would take out money and give it to her. She would then drive him to another institution because he had reached his daily limit. He would take out $2,000.00 to $3,000 at each of the two or three banks that he visited and loan it to the Applicant.

15. Between July of 2009 and January, 2010 the Applicant drove Dagenais to these financial institutions some 20 times.

Transcript, page 7, line 14-17, Tab 18

16. A summary of the amount loaned from the various bank accounts totaled [SIC] $132,845.00

Transcript, page 8, line 27-32, page 9, line 4-5 Tab 19

17. When Dagenais asked the Applicant if she would repay the loan, she swore on a statue of the Lord that she would. This was important to Dagenais because he is very religious.

Transcript, page 10, line 9-21, Tab 20

18. Dagenais wrote out a note on the back of an envelope stating that the Applicant owed him $151,000.00 and asked her to sign same. She signed on three occasions and then crossed all of them out.

Transcript, page 11, line 7-15, Tab 21

19. Denise Taylor ("Taylor") is the brother of Dagenais and lives about 10 minutes away in Port Colborne, Ontario.

Transcript, page 31, line 3-8, Tab 22

20. Taylor confirms that Dagenais lives a very simple life, his entertainment mainly consists of watching programs on television and he is very frugal with his money.

Transcript, page 32, line 10-14, Tab 23

21. Taylor reviewed Dagenais' bank accounts and noted that there were no large withdrawals prior to July, 2009 and that there were no large withdrawals

after January of 2010. However, there were many large withdrawals between July of 2009 and January of 2010.

Transcript, page 35, line16-25, Tab 24

22. Taylor reviewed Dagenais' telephone records and confirmed that on the some days up to 12 phone calls were made from the Applicant to Dagenais.

Transcript, page 37, line 16-23, Tab 25

23. Taylor cross-referenced the date of the phone calls to the date of the withdrawals and testified that the telephone calls came the day before Dagenais would withdraw funds from the bank accounts.

Transcript, page 37, line 24-32, Tab 26

24. Taylor confirmed that there were no noticeable change in Dagenais' lifestyle from July of 2009 to January of 2010, that he had not purchased any significant assets, and had not transferred monies from his bank accounts to any other locations.

Transcript, page 38, line 4-11, Tab 27C.

Disposition of the Trial Judge:

25. The trial Judge, after weighing all of the evidence found that Dagenais had established on a balance of probabilities that he withdrew significant sums of money from his bank accounts, advanced them to Ms. Vassel by way of loans and that such amounts are due and outstanding.

Reasons for judgment ("reasons"),
Transcripts, Page 79, line 29 to page 80 line 7, tab 28

26. The learned trial Judge devoted 9 paragraphs of his reasons to assessing the evidence and credibility of Dagenais and the Applicant. His conclusions were:

a. "I accept as credible the basic thrust of his (Dagenais') evidence relating to the significant withdrawals from his bank account in the period July, 2009 to July,2010. That is Ms. Vassel asked him to provide her with significant sums of money for various purposes and that he provided those sums to her by way of loans, with the understanding from Ms. Vassel that he would be repaid."

Reasons, Transcripts, Page 77. Line 10-19

b. "although there is no written acknowledgement of the loans, documentary evidence that does exist demonstrated that Mr. Dagenais made significant withdrawals from his bank accounts during the period that were not consistent with his prior spending pattern."

Reasons, Transcripts, Page 77, line 25-29

c. "As well, in almost every case, Ms. Vassel called Mr. Dagenais on the day prior or the day of the withdrawals consistent with the conclusion that the withdrawals were made at her request."

Reasons, Transcripts, Page 78, line 8-10

d. "while Ms. Vassel's evidence was indeed easier to follow, I did not find it to be more credible than the evidence of Mr. Dagenais, which I prefer and accept on the crucial points as to whether Ms. Vassel received sums of money from Mr. Dagenais and the characterization of these amounts as loans."

Reasons, Transcripts, Page 78, line 25-29

e. "Nor do I find credible her explanation for the pattern of multiple calls to Mr. Dagenais coincident with the bank withdrawals."

Reasons, Transcripts, Page 79, line 5-8

f. "However I note that Ms. Vassel does not dispute that she refused to provide the written acknowledgment request by Mr. Dagenais in January, 2010 and that her dealings with Mr. Dagenais ended shortly thereafter."

g. "Accordingly after weighing all the evidence I find that Mr. Dagenais has established on a balance of probabilities that Mr. Dagenais withdrew significant sums of money from his bank account as outlined further below and advanced them to Ms. Vassel by way of loan and that such amounts are due and outstanding."

Reasons, Transcripts, Page 79, line 29-30 page 80, line 4-7

The Court of Appeal stated that:

1) The trial judge ultimately did not accept the plaintiff's claim that each and every cash withdrawal from his bank accounts during the relevant period went to fund his loan to the defendant. The trial judge was not satisfied that various small withdrawals

went for that purpose and he specifically found that a withdrawal made after the date on which the defendant refused to acknowledge that she had borrowed money from the plaintiff was not related to loan.

2) A trial Judge is not obligated to accept or reject the entirety of the case as presented for the plaintiff. A trial judge must make findings of face based on his assessment of the entirety of the evidence. In the course of doing so, he or she may reject some but not necessarily all the evidence given by any witness, including a plaintiff. This trial judgment did exactly that. He reviewed the plaintiff's evidence carefully and while he was not prepared to accept the entirety of it, he clearly accepted the thrust of the plaintiff's evidence that had loaned a great deal of money to the defendant over six-month period and that he had funded that loan through numerous cash withdrawals from his various bank accounts. The trial judge's finding was not unreasonable and we must defer to it.

3) The second ground of appeal concerns an alleged reversal of the burden of proof. The trial judge began his analysis by expressly stating that the plaintiff had the onus to prove both that the funds were advanced by way of loan and that the loan was not repaid.

4) We see nothing in the reasons which suggests a reversal of the burden of proof. The trail judgment in assessing the appellant's credibility properly took into account factors relevant to that assessment, including, for example, the appellant's

failure to produce her bank records. In doing so, the trial judge did not place any legal burden of proof on the appellant.

5) In determining whether the plaintiff had met the burden of proof, the trial judge was obligated to weigh his evidence in the context of the entirety of the evidence, including any alternative explanations advanced by the defendant. The absence of any explanation on certain matters from the appellant and the absence of any evidence to support explanation that were offered were relevant in assessing whether the plaintiff had met his burden of proof. This ground of appeal cannot succeed.

6) The third ground of appeal is a more general attack on the trial judge's reasons as inadequate. The trial judge analyzed the evidence of both the defendant and the plaintiff. His reasons clearly indicate how he came to prefer the evidence of the plaintiff over that of the appellant. In our view, the reasons are both logical and supported by the evidence. They reveal no basis upon which this court can interfere.

PART II-STATEMENT OF THE QUESTIONS IN ISSUE

28. The Applicant says that this case raises the following issues of public or national importance:

1) Subjective bias of the part of Justice Lococo against the Applicant stemming from prejudicial attitude towards the Applicant's occupation as an exotic dancer;

2) The decision of the trial judge and the Court of Appeal establishes a dangerous precedent allowing a trial judge to attenuate the long standing principles that the burden of proof rests with the plaintiff rather than the defendant and that the balance of probabilities standard is the sole standard proof of common law and all civil proceedings;

3) The issues of public importance in the case pertaining to the alleged irresponsible and even life threatening conduct of the Applicant's defense counsel in ineptly and possibly unethically handling of her defense, which is said to have involved a breach of solicitor/client privilege.

29. The Respondents submit that these issues are not raised in this case as:

1) The trial Judge and the Court of Appeal based their findings on the facts after a less lengthy assessment of the credibility of both parties;

2) There was no hint of prejudice on behalf of either the trial judge or the Court of Appeal. There was no bias shown as a result of the Applicant's occupation by either court;

3) The actions of the Applicant's counsel have nothing to do with the merits of this appeal. The alleged conduct was not an issue in either of the courts below and formed no part in their analysis of the case. It should form no part in this Honourable Court's analysis. It simply does not bear upon the merits as between the parties.

PART III- STATEMENT OF ARGUMENT

30. The trial judge reached his conclusion by relying on the evidence before him. In particular, the trial judge carefully reviewed the bank records, telephone records, and banking history of the Respondent Plaintiff both before, during the time in issue and after their relationship ended.

Reasons, Transcripts, Page 77, line 12 through Page 80, line 7.

31. The trial judge did not shift the onus of proof from the plaintiff to the defendant in arriving at his decision. He did note that the Applicant Defendant claimed not to have a bank account during the period, the Applicant Defendant acknowledged owing over $50,000.00 to Canada Revenue Agency for unpaid GST and that the Applicant Defendant was unable to explain how the Respondent plaintiff could have spent $130,000.00 In less than 6 months, all circumstances that bore upon the trial judge in assessing the credibility of the Applicant Defendant. However, these were factors that were weighed by the trial judge in assessing the credibility of the Applicant.

Reasons, Transcripts, Page 75, line 24-29

32. The trial judge considered that the credibility of each party was the main issue in the proceeding, and analyzed it carefully.

33. The trial judge acknowledged and analyzed the inconsistencies in the plaintiff's evidence, but assessed the relative credibility of the parties in a careful manner.

Reasons, Transcripts, Page 77, line 11 through page 80, line 7.

34. In civil case, the treatement [sic] of circumstantial evidence is quite straightforward. It is treated as any other kind of evidence. The weight accorded to it depends on the strength of the inference that can **derived** from it and this is a task for the trier of fact.

Paul's lawyer continued to list The Law of Evidence in Canada, Black's Law Dictionary and a few case studies that had nothing to do with the case.

PART IV- SUBMISSIONS CONCERNING COSTS

If this application for leave to appeal is dismissed, the Respondents request an Order awarding the cost of responding to the Application.

PART V- ORDER SOUGHT

Dismissal of the application for leave to appeal with costs.

[End of Peddle's submission]

All this is basically garbage: just a restatement of the Plaintiff's position and Judge Lococo's judgments, sprinkled with some transparent errors (Denise Taylor was Paul's sister, not his brother) and falsehoods (it was well established by Paul himself that I had never driven him in my car, but only in his), with no attempt to respond to the many strong and substantive arguments I'd presented. None! I'm somewhat baffled by Peddle's failure to re-engage the battle in a serious way, but one thing is certain...this is bullshit! The only thing new from this fucker is his defense of my lawyer, oops ex-lawyer! Peddle cited a few legal precedents, but he didn't address the main points I'd made pertaining to judicial bias and the precedent setting nature of Judge Lococo's judgment.

My friend and I prepare a response....

APPLICANT'S MEMORANDUM OF ARGUMENT RESPONSE

A. Overview

1. The main issue of public and national importance raised by this case concerns the following. The decisions of the trial judge and the Court of Appeal establish a dangerous precedent allowing a trial judge, animated by apparent subjective bias against a defendant, to render a judgment that attenuates the long-standing principles that the burden of proof rests with the plaintiff rather than the defendant and that the balance of probabilities standard is the sole standard of proof in common law and all civil proceedings. The Applicant submits that the attenuation of these principles implicit in the trial judge's decision in this case has wide-ranging and patently unjust implications, opening the way to a proliferation of frivolous and malicious law suits targeting defendants belonging to groups or occupations deemed to be "morally suspect" by segments of the larger community.

2. The Respondents state that this was a "fact driven" case (Memorandum of Argument of the Respondents [MAR] 1). But, as in all civil cases, the facts of this case are very much in dispute. In contrast to the Applicant's Application for Leave to Appeal (ALA), the Respondents' summary of the facts is entirely one sided and sometimes erroneous. Not only have the Respondents failed to provide a balanced and reasonable summary of the often conflicting evidence that the trial judge was obliged to weigh in deciding the

credibility of the litigants; they have also failed to address any of the detailed arguments made by the Applicant showing that subjective bias on the part of the trial judge against the Defendant influenced his decision to "prefer" the often-contradictory, dubious and even demonstrably false evidence of the Plaintiff over the consistent and straightforward evidence of the Defendant, evidence that was never successfully impugned by the Plaintiff.

3. It is the position of the applicant that the bias displayed by the trial judge against Ms. Vassel and in favour of Mr. Dagenais, and which the applicant considers to be the decisive factor in shaping his decision in the case, stemmed *most probably* from a prejudicial attitude toward the defendant's occupation as an exotic dancer and sometime paid companion of male "customers." The applicant submits that the trial judge had an obligation to resist any influence on his judicial reasoning of prejudicial attitudes and stereotypes that are widespread in the community regarding exotic dancing, an occupation that is legal in Canada and governed by specific provincial and municipal regulations. There is in fact a great deal in his "Reasons for Judgment" to suggest that the trial judge failed in this obligation, not least his failure to acknowledge both the existence of prejudicial attitudes toward exotic dancers and his ethical obligation to resist the influence of such attitudes in arriving at a judgment.

4. Against the position of the Applicant, the Respondents assert that: "1) The trial judge and the Court of Appeal based their findings on the facts after a less [sic?] lengthy assessment of the credibility of both parties"; and "2) There was no hint of prejudice on behalf of either the trial judge or the Court of Appeal" (MAR, paragraph 29). However, in supporting these claims, the Respondents entirely ignore the substance of the Applicant's critical analysis of the trial judge's

"Reasons for Judgment" (see Applicant's ALA, paragraphs 33-53) as well as the Applicant's evidence-based arguments (ALA, paragraphs 55-57) that support the conclusion that the trial judge's thinking was "most probably" infected by prejudice, notwithstanding the care he took to avoid making overtly prejudicial references to the defendant's occupation. It should be noted in this connection that the Respondents' assertion that the trial judge and the Court of Appeal "based their findings on the facts after a less [sic?] lengthy assessment of the credibility of both parties" is moot in light of the numerous problems with the "Reasons for Judgment" uncovered by the Applicant and the extremely brief and thinly-motivated nature of the Court of Appeal decision.

5. In light of the above considerations, the Applicant asks that this Court accept the Application for Leave to Appeal and reject the Respondents' request that it be dismissed.

B. The Respondents' Statement of Facts

6. The Applicant stipulates acceptance of the Respondents' statement of facts as contained in paragraphs 2, 3, 4, 20, 22, 23, 25, 26 and 27. Paragraphs 1, 5, 6, 8, 9, 10, 11, 12, 13, 14, 15, 16, 17, 18, 19, 21 and 24 all contain claims that are to varying degrees problematic, either because they are factually incorrect or because they have been formulated in misleading ways. These problematic paragraphs either flatly contradict or are to some extent inconsistent with the statement of facts presented by the Applicant in her ALA and that are never referred to by the Respondents. Furthermore, paragraphs 25, 26 and 27, constituting the subsection entitled "Disposition of the Trial Judge," are simply paraphrases or verbatim quotations from the trial judge's Reasons for Judgment and the ruling of the Court of Appeal. Virtually all of this material was

summarized in the ALA and subjected to a critical analysis by the Applicant – an analysis that has been entirely ignored by the Respondents. Thus, the MAR is characterized by an almost complete lack of engagement with the presentation of facts and arguments contained in the ALA.

7. With respect to the problematic paragraphs in the Respondents' Statement of Facts, the Applicant contests the following paragraphs in particular:

a) "This is a fact driven case which raises no issues of public or national importance. Thelma Angela Vassel aka Linda Lee (the 'Applicant') borrowed substantial amounts of money from Paul Dagenais ('Dagenais') which have never been repaid" (MAR, Paragraph 1). The first sentence of this paragraph makes a claim that has been thoroughly refuted in the ALA. Bias against the Defendant based on a negative perception of her occupation played an important role in skewing the trial judge's objectivity and reasoning in this case. In denying this, the Respondents have an obligation to respond to paragraphs 55-57 in the ALA which adduces clear evidence of such bias. But they have failed to do so. The Respondents therefore have no grounds upon which to assert that this is a "fact driven case" or that it raises "no issues of public or national importance." As for the second sentence quoted above, it asserts as "fact" a claim that has been consistently disputed by the Applicant. The ALA states that "Ms. Vassel denied that she had borrowed money from Mr. Dagenais on any occasion for any purpose and insisted that she had taken money from him only on a 'fee for service' basis" (ALA, Paragraph 18).

b) The Respondents state that "Dagenais led a frugal lifestyle, would bank his earnings, and would only spend what he needed for his day-to-day needs" (MAR, Paragraph 8). Evidence presented in trial by both the Plaintiff and the Defendant flatly contradicts this assertion, as does the Respondents' own Paragraph 4, which states that "Dagenais would visit the Sundowner on an average of twice per week...." The Applicant's ALA elaborates on the financial implications of Dagenais' visits to the Sundowner: "At the Sundowner, the Plaintiff was in the habit of spending at least $250 to $300 during each of his visits.... Since he admitted to visiting the club two or three times per week over many years, it is reasonable to assume that the Plaintiff may have spent at least $25,000 to $30,000 per year on his activities at the Sundowner prior to his stroke and then again following his hospitalization" (ALA, Paragraph 9). It should also be noted that Mr. Dagenais testified that, after losing his driver's license, he often hired taxis to transport him from his home in Port Colborne to the Sundowner club in Niagara Falls. Assuming 100 round trips per year on average, this could easily have cost him an additional $12,000 per year. As Mr. Dagenais was hardly a wealthy man, expenditures of these magnitudes on such recreational activities can hardly be considered indicative of a frugal life-style or consistent with the claim that he spent money only on "day-to-day needs."

c) The Respondents state that the "Applicant would not park in Dagenais' driveway, and instead parked on the street next to the neighbor's house" (MAR, Paragraph 11). The citing of this "fact" is meant to suggest some sinister intent on the part of the Applicant. Yet the reason for the Applicant's behavior in this regard is simple. Contrary to the Respondents' earlier contention that Ms. Vassel would take Mr. Dagenais "to various financial institutions in her motor vehicle," Mr. Dagenais always insisted that she drive *his car* during their excursions. Ms. Vassel parked her car on the street to allow the easy exit of Mr. Dagenais' car from his driveway.

d) The Respondents state that the "Applicant began asking Dagenais to borrow money for her mother's funeral, her father's funeral, to fix her car, to pay her rent, to make a movie, to get a Visa and to settle a debt her father had with the bikers" (MAR, Paragraph 12). No evidence apart from Mr. Dagenais' testimony was presented that Ms. Vassel made any of these requests. Moreover, they are inconsistent with verifiable facts about Ms. Vassel's life. Ms. Vassel's mother died when she was seven years old; her pastor father is still alive and has never had any association with bikers; during the period in question, she had no major automotive repair problems and was not involved in the production of a film. Nor was she paying rent, as she was a homeowner. Furthermore, she denied asking for a loan to pay for a U.S. visa. The ALA states: "[Ms. Vassel] estimated that in the entire time she had known Mr. Dagenais he may have given her a total of about $10,000, all of which was paid by way of compensation for her time and companionship, both inside and outside the Sundowner. Approximately half of that sum was received for 'dates' in Port Colborne in 2009" (ALA, Paragraph 18).

e) The "facts" stated in Paragraphs 13 thru 18 of the MAR are addressed and/or refuted in Paragraphs 19 and 20 of the ALA. In brief, the Applicant denied driving Dagenais to financial institutions in order to borrow money from him. While she acknowledged that he did pay her for services rendered, those sums never exceeded $500 on any individual occasion. Dagenais claimed that a statement acknowledging that Ms. Vassel owed him $151,000 was signed by her on three separate occasions during a single meeting at the Sundowner on January 4, 2010, but that each time she scratched out her signature during intervals in which he went to the washroom. This claim was shown to lack all credibility in the ALA (see Paragraphs 20 and 43 in particular).

f) The purpose of the facts presented in Paragraphs 19 thru 24 of the MAR (which include the problematic paragraphs 19, 21 and 24) is to identify Ms. Vassel as solely responsible for the large bank withdrawals made by Dagenais between July, 2009 and January, 2010 – a pattern of behavior which his sister, Denise Taylor, claimed was inconsistent with his prior habits. The substance of this allegation against the Applicant is answered in Paragraphs 22, 24, 25, 32 and 46 of the ALA. In particular, the Applicant noted the following:

"The trial judge argued that 'in almost every case of withdrawals, Ms. Vassel called Mr. Dagenais on the day prior, or the day of the withdrawals, consistent with the conclusion that the withdrawals were made at her request'. But this set of facts can also be viewed as consistent with the conclusion that Mr. Dagenais made the withdrawals in order to pay Ms. Vassel for her time and companionship; that larger sums may have been withdrawn in an attempt to bribe Ms. Vassel to have sex with him; and that major amounts of these withdrawals might have been spent on other activities, including encounters and transactions with other exotic dancers or escorts, deposits in other (undisclosed) accounts, or even the purchase of precious metals to protect his savings from a global financial crisis. Furthermore, if smaller amounts (under $1,200) were likely used by Mr. Dagenais for purposes other than loans to Ms. Vassel, as admitted by the trial judge, what reasons support the conclusion that the larger amounts could *only* have been used as loans to Ms. Vassel? The trial judge failed to adduce any reasons whatsoever." (ALA, Paragraph

C. Statement of Argument

8. If it can be established that the judgment of the trial judge was likely "driven" in this case not by the strength and credibility of the Plaintiff's evidence but

rather by the trial judge's bias against the Defendant, then the case clearly raises issues of public importance, all the more so if there are indications that it led the trial judge to shift the burden of proof from the Plaintiff to the Defendant and to set aside the "preponderance of evidence" standard that must guide the resolution of civil suits.

9. The Respondents deny that the trial judge displayed any bias and assert that he "did not shift the onus of proof from the plaintiff to the defendant in arriving at his decision." They do not comment on the critical analysis provided by the Applicant of the trial judge's Reasons for Judgment (ALA, Paragraphs 3353) or the Applicant's argument that the source of his subjective bias against the Defendant was a negative perception of her occupation as an exotic dancer and sometime paid companion of male customers (ALA, Paragraphs 5557). Instead, the Respondents construct an argument, replete with standard legal definitions of such concepts as "preponderance of the evidence," that is predicated on the *false premise* that the Applicant's position is that the trial judge ought to have applied the principle of "reasonable doubt" in this case (MAR, Paragraphs 34 thru 41).

10. The Applicant stipulates agreement with the Respondents that: "The Plaintiff has the onus to present relevant evidence to establish a preponderance of probabilities that he is entitled to the damages as alleged. He is not required to prove this case beyond a reasonable doubt" (MAR, Paragraph 35). However the Applicant disagrees with the Respondents that the Plaintiff presented evidence that established a preponderance of probabilities in his favour. In her ALA, the Applicant has provided detailed argumentation showing that the Plaintiff's evidence was not only exceptionally weak but inconsistent, implausible, defiant of common sense, misleading and

false. It offends elementary principles of logic and judicial reason to suggest that this body of evidence establishes a balance of probabilities favoring the Plaintiff. For this reason, the Applicant argued that "the Court of Appeal erred in stating that the trial judge 'clearly' indicated how he came to prefer the evidence of Mr. Dagenais over that of Ms. Vassel and that the reasons he gave were 'both logical and supported by the evidence'. To the contrary, the applicant submits that there are ample grounds for questioning the quality of that evidence as well as the clarity and the logic displayed by the trial judge." (ALA, Paragraph 42). This position was elaborated and supported in detail in the ALA.

11. That bias against Ms. Vassel and in favour of Dagenais influenced the trial judge's thinking, and caused him to shift the onus of proof from the Plaintiff to the Defendant in this case, has been thoroughly documented in the ALA. That one source of this bias may have been a prejudicial attitude toward Ms. Vassel's occupation is supported by the argumentation in Paragraphs 55 thru 57 of the ALA. Among other things, this argumentation cites the perversely selective treatment by the trial judge of the important evidence of Eden Harlow, a coworker of Ms. Vassel at the Sundowner club, and the judge's willingness to accept the "thrust" of Dagenais' story at face value (despite its inconsistencies and implausible aspects) according to which he had been victimized by a devious *femme fatale.*

12. The Applicant reiterates her request to present to this court new pieces of evidence that undermine the case brought against her by the Plaintiff and that point to ethical infractions on the part of her former counsel that have compromised her physical security as well as her ability to fund her legal defense. (ALA, Paragraph 54)

………………………………

I'm very satisfied with the response to Peddle. It blows his weak reply out of the water. But the whole exchange causes me to recall many of the things this lawyer had said during the trial.

I can't help wondering why Peddle made some references to Paul's sister as a "he" or as a "brother." *Could Dagenais' brothers have been more involved in the case – behind the scenes – than appearances suggested? Why have they been so invisible in a case that really should be of no less interest to them than their sister? And yet Peddle keeps referring to them indirectly, seemingly inadvertently.*

Could one or all of Paul's brothers have been involved? Could they be the ones stalking me? I can only wonder.

All I can really do now is wait for the Supreme Court to respond to my application. Will they hear the appeal? It's probably a long shot, but I know that issues of national and constitutional importance are posed by this case.
If they fail to recognize that and deny me a hearing, then I'll have no other option than to publicly denounce them along with the whole damn "justice system." Correction: the *injustice* system! I've already decided that, at the very least, I'm going to haul Zijad's ass before the Law Society of Upper Canada, the professional governing body for lawyers in Ontario. I'm hopeful that they will take an interest in his crooked actions. Maybe that would even lay the basis for a successful civil lawsuit against him.

All I want to do is sleep, but my mind is constantly pushing against my body's desire to surrender to a long and deep slumber. It knows my bill collectors are hard at work, and they never sleep.

In the midst of my running around, I can't believe how often the police are stopping me for this or that, but mostly for no good reason. I wonder if I've been put on some special list for harassment.

I head back to Niagara Falls to stay with a friend. But on my way I decide to stop off at the courthouse in Welland. I stand in line and then fill out forms to obtain copies of the closing arguments in my case. My main interest is Peddle's argument, especially the part about Paul's more responsible banking habits. But I'm also increasingly interested in examining Zijad's statements. In light of everything that's happened and my growing suspicions about him, I'm going to look very carefully at what he said … and didn't say.
Weeks go by and I make repeated phone calls to the court about the status of my order of the transcripts. I have this feeling that they really don't want to give me this information. But I fight on and eventually I get it.

Finally, I sit in my car in front of the courthouse and read the closing arguments.

Superior Court of Justice

Proceedings at trial (**closing addresses**)

Submission – Mr. Peddle

<u>SUBMISSION BY MR. PEDDLE:</u>

Thank you Your Honour. Your Honour, I will be very brief because this trial was a very quick trial and it's not complicated, I don't believe. The plaintiff has proved on a balance of probabilities that it's more probable that my client loaned Mrs. Vassel $130,000 as opposed to her blanket denial that she didn't borrow any money from my client. It is credible that over a six month period, Paul spent an additional $132.000 more than he would have normally spent at the same time - the same times as he met defendant and she spent time with him? She admits calling him numerous occasions, [SIC] sometimes up to 12 times per day.

The calls all pre-date visits and corresponding withdrawals from banks accounts. She admits visiting him, but would not park in his driveway, despite her assertation [sic] that she set up dates with him and spent time in public with him. She avoided meeting his sister ...

THE COURT: Could you slow down please.

MR. PEDDLE: Oh sorry.

THE COURT: Hold on for a second. Okay, sorry, just go ahead.

MR. PEDDLE: I was just saying she avoided meeting his sister, the question is why somebody who has nothing to hide would not want to be seen in public, or even in family, with my client. What are the odds you drive someone to the bank 24 times, by her own admission, and yet you never go into the bank once; not even if there is a lineup, it sort of defies common sense. How do you judge someone credible, such as the defendant, who admits she didn't operate a bank account for the vast majority of the time these loans were being made. She get's re-assessed by Revenue Canada, some $60,000 and my client didn't even learn her real name until told so by the police. The evidence of the exotic dancer, my client and his sister are fairly consistent in the fact that he did visit the Sundowner, and he sometimes went twice a week, and sometimes spent $200 to $300 on each visit.

THE COURT: Just a second.

MR. PEDDLE: There was no evidence, however, that he spent money on any of the girls in terms of buying them gifts, taking them on trips, any type of thing that he would need to do to spend $132,000 in a six month period. I would suggest to Your Honour it's more probable that he was taken advantage of by the defendant. I would understand if Your Honour would take the position that some of the smaller withdrawals, the two to three hundred dollar ones may not meet the standard, but when Your Honour sees consistently six to seven thousand dollar withdrawals in the space of days, from a man who has no extraordinary lifestyle, no mortgage payments, lives in an old home, lives simple, that money has to be going somewhere, and it's all withdrawn for a very specific purpose. In conclusion Your Honour, I want to say, it's more probable, in our position, that the money that was withdrawn ended up with the defendant, because there was no indication, through any of the bank records, that it went anywhere else. My client has not pointed the finger at anybody else. There is absolutely no evidence that it went anywhere else than to this defendant. Those are my submissions Your Honour.

THE COURT: Mr. Saskin.

<u>SUBMISSION BY MR. SASKIN:</u>

Thanks you Your Honour. Your Honour, we have a case here where a significant amount of money was allegedly lent to my client, $132,845, to be exact. As my friend rightfully pointed out, the issue raised her [SIC] is quite simple, did the plaintiff loan to the defendant the sum of $132,000 or any other sum to my client? And Your Honour has to be satisfied on a balance of probabilities that Mr. Dagenais indeed lent $132,000 to Ms. Vassel. In this case, we heard from four witnesses and two of which, in my submission, are central to the issues. The credibility of the witnesses is going to be very, very important in deciding this case and I would submit your Honour that the evidence of Ms. Vassel was straightforward, logical and believable, whereas the evidence of Mr. Dagenais was murky and unclear at best. Before we look at the credibility, it is important to note that we do not have any documentary evidence to support that a single loan was made, let alone s series of 32 loans totaling in excess of $132,000. Your Honour, we are not talking about $130 that a friend gives to another, we are talking about $132,000, life savings of an individual. Yet, there is not a single shred of documentary evidence in support of the plaintiff's contention that he advanced any money to the defendant. There is the envelope at Exhibit Number 2. It simply states, "I owe Paul Dagenais the sum of $151,000." It is not signed by anyone but there are three scribbles underneath.

My client's evidence is that she refused to sign this because simply she did not owe Paul any money. Paul's evidence is that she refused to sign it and that he knew at that time that there was going to be a problem. Paul's evidence was that it was on or about January 4th. His sister evidence was that it was January 4th, 5th, could have been later. However Your Honour, Some nine days later, it is Paul evidence that he loaned Angela another $2,000. Your Honour, it defies common sense that the plaintiff would lend an additional $2,000 to Ms. Vassel just after she refused to sign the envelope. It defies common sense that a frugal man would take out any large sum of money and simply lend it to a stranger whom he says he knew nothing about. And even besides this, there are several glaring problems with the plaintiff's case.

The plaintiff's memory, I would submit, is failing him. He stated that he started going to the Sundowner in or about February 2009. He was very clear about that date. On cross examination, he stated that he drove his car to the Sundowner several times, yet he lost his drivers licence [SIC] in August of 2008 and never got it back. He stated that Angela would come to his house that she was not invited, that she learned from the phone book where he lived, yet he would tell his sister about Angela, about how they would be going on a trip to Jamaica. Again, this doesn't sound like an unwanted stranger, but someone he would tell his sister about.

But what he didn't tell his sister is that he was loaning money to Angela. Why? Because it never happened. The plaintiff's sister can only testify that Paul is a frugal man and that it is unlike Paul – it is unlike for him to do this. Your Honour, I would submit that she is correct, Paul is frugal, he would not do this and he did not do this. The evidence of Mrs. Taylor only reiterated what Paul has told to the court. She has no independent knowledge about the facts, only what Paul told her. Now, on the other hand, let's look at how Ms. Vassel handles her testimony. Your Honour, I submit that she was clear, collected, and told her story in a straight forward fashion. She has known Paul for a while, she got to know him, was comfortable with him. Paul lost his driver's licence and wanted to spend time with Angela. She told him the terms and he accepted. It was the same terms that she told to her other clients. That's how she made her money. She stated that she saw Paul on a number of occasions and that he paid her three to five hundred dollars for her time. She was clear and straight forward that she was paid approximately $5,000 to spend time with Paul and this was not a loan. In summary Your Honour, I submit that the plaintiff cannot prove his claims in this action. These alleged loans are not documented at all and it is common grounds that the defendant refuses the plaintiff's demands that she acknowledges the loans in writing.

The plaintiff did not keep a total of running total of the large sums of cash he claims to have lent to the defendant. It was made after the fact by sitting down with his sister and tell her in his own words what had happened. Instead, the plaintiff relies on his bank statements as proof of these loans and he claims to have lent the defendant every large sum withdrawn from his bank accounts over a six month period. You Honour, this argument, in my submission, is so flawed that it could not possibly be accepted by a court.

The fact is, the withdrawals show that the money was taken out, but that's all it shows. The fact is that these cash withdrawals could have been used for any number of purposes, including just sitting in his house. The defendant submits that the plaintiff's claim is without merit and that it should be dismissed with costs. Barring any further questions from Your Honour, those are my submissions.

THE COURT: No that's fine, thank you.

MR. SASKIN: Thank you Your Honour, and I thank my friend.

THE COURT: Anything in reply?

MR. PEDDLE: I think Your Honour's heard enough, thank you.

Oh, my God, some of the information is missing! But there's no way that the court can tamper with official transcripts. No way! Or is there? What if someone viewed Peddle's statement about Paul's changed banking habits – after his falling out with me – as a potential problem? Maybe Peddle himself? Could he have requested that part of his closing statement be removed? Could a cooperative court clerk or even a judge facilitate such a request?

Casting a very interesting light on the significance of Peddle's "brilliant observation" is what Paul Dagenais himself said on the phone to me just before he died. Believing he was talking to Eden, he'd indicated that he'd soon be returning to his old ways and visiting the club again, while intimating that he could get himself into trouble for even talking about any of this!

In Peddle's closing argument, I distinctly remember him saying that since Paul stopped talking to me, he'd made no significant withdrawals from his account. Of course, it could just as easily have been said that, since Paul's family and Peddle had become involved in suing Thelma Vassel, Paul had been on his "best behavior" – perhaps because he had been placed on a short leash. (Zijad could easily have made this point, but of course he didn't!) But now, in the official transcript of the closing arguments, Peddle's statement has mysteriously disappeared. How very convenient! It's gone, and unfortunately the only person who can verify that something is amiss here is my former lawyer.

I have a distinct recollection of talking to Zijad about that part of Peddle's closing argument – the very point about Dagenais' supposed reformed ways and good behavior after he escaped the grip of Thelma. But there's no way my ex-lawyer will be willing to help or even talk to me now. After all, by now he must know that I called attention to his unprofessional and unethical behavior in my application to the Supreme Court of Canada.

I talk all this over with my friend, and we agree that my first step should be to call the Superior Court where the case was originally heard.

I place the call and ask a court clerk if they keep tape recordings of the trial proceedings. She tells me they do have audio recordings but they're not available to me.

After ruling out the idea that Zijad will ever talk to me, my friend asks me what I'm going to do. I need proof. I sit quietly and think. *How to handle this?*

I seem to have no alternative but to call Zijad. There's nothing else for me to do even though the prospect of hearing his voice sickens me….

Fuck it…

The phone rings…

I can feel my blood racing through my veins, I'm sweating and itchy. My heart is beating so fast I have to control my breathing.

Secretary: Broderick and Partners….

Thelma: Good day, may I speak with Zijad please?

Secretary: I'll try his office, who is calling please?

Thelma: Angela.

Secretary: Thank you.

Zijad: Hello.

Thelma: Hi Zijad…

Zijad: Hi Angela.

Thelma: How are you?

Zijad: I’m good, how are you?

Thelma: I’m miserable as hell – to tell you the truth.

Zijad: Oh, where are you, are you local …?

Thelma: If I’m local? No, not right now, but I was thinking of coming to the Falls in a week or two.

Zijad: Oh, okay, okay.

Thelma: Yeah, umm, the reason for my call right now, I was just wondering how much I owe you.

Zijad: Ahmm, I don’t know, I think it’s like five thousand for everything.

Thelma: Yeah.

Zijad: Yeah.

Thelma: I’m still upset, ahmm …well anyways…

Zijad: A…

Thelma: Go ahead...

Zijad: No, no, I know, like I told you before, I’m not going to, umm, chase you for it or…

Thelma: Yeah, ahmm…

Zijad: Yeah and that’s it, and I think I’ve wrote off, like between the trial and the appeal, it’s like fifteen, but I’ve wrote off most of it.

Thelma: Ok, well I'm going to head back out to Vancouver, ahmm…

Zijad: Okay.

Thelma: And ah, work my ass off. So anyways I was reading over the transcript the other day and ah…

Zijad: Yeah…?

Thelma: I was just pissed off; I just think that what really, okay, okay, I was upset about a lot of things…

Zijad: Yeah!

Thelma: But I think what really nailed it for me is when Peddle was in court, ahmm, and he said that to the Judge that, ah, uhm, between January and June, whatever the timeframe was…,

Zijad: Yeah?

Thelma: That Paul never returned back to the club. I think that what, that's what really nailed it for me in the coffin.

Zijad: Okay.

Thelma: Don't you think?

Zijad: Yeah, there were a lot of things in there that the judge believed that he shouldn't have believed. Thelma: Yeah but…

Zijad: Not just that…

Thelma: But his closing argument.

Zijad: Yeah, a lot of things...

Thelma: But his closing argument, I think that's what really nailed it, when he came at the end there and said Your Honour, like between June to January, January to June since then…

Zijad: January to June after, after the last, ah, money was alleged given to you…

Thelma: Yeah, that Paul never returned back to the club right?

Zijad: Yeah, yeah, yeah…

Thelma: Not that he didn't return to the club, but that, how did it go …?

Zijad: But that's what he said.

Thelma: That no activity came out of his account, or something, I can't remember exactly, but along that line…

Zijad: That after that January there was no big withdrawal any more…?

Thelma: Yeah something like that…

Zijad: All the big withdrawals stopped after January …

Thelma: Yeah, in his closing there, I think that really nailed it for me, because then he's thinking, well since that date, um, then if no money came out of his account, then that means it must have went to her because he stops seeing her, the phone calls stop, and no more money came out of his account, so it must have been her, and I think that really killed me…

Zijad: Yeah, that's possible…

Thelma: And that was in the closing argument right? So…

Zijad: Yes, yes.

Thelma: How else can you do this, well, um, what I'm going to do is give you a call in about two, three weeks when I'm out there and let you know how things are coming, and try to see what I can do to get some money to you.

Zijad: No problem Angela, I really appreciate it. Like I said, take your time and, and whenever you can, if you can, great.

Thelma: Okay awesome, thank you very much.

Zijad: Okay and have a safe trip.

Thelma: Thank you.

Zijad: Bye.

Thelma: Bye.

I feel totally vindicated after this conversation. Zijad has confirmed my recollection about Peddle's closing argument. *He's confirmed Peddle said those things, and those things – those damning things! – have been removed from the official court transcript of his closing argument. Something is very, very wrong here.*

At the same time, I'm absolutely amazed at Zijad's manner after everything that's happened, especially the statements I made about him in my Supreme Court application. He must know about that by now! What kind of game is he playing with me? Still pretending to be a kind and caring friend. Then it occurs to me: he wants me to let my guard down, and let him know where I am.

Is the shadowed force still looking for me? Who is it and what do they want? Do they want a kill?

I've exhausted my legal options for appeal. I'm wiped out financially, and I actually fear for my physical safety, even my life. After taking stock of my situation, I have an epiphany. The issues posed in my case *are* truly important. They affect not only me, but potentially thousands of other women across the country. I can't let this rest. I'm determined to start a campaign, a campaign to expose the corruption and injustice that I've experienced at every level of the judicial system. I'm convinced that bringing this into the public eye may also be the *only* way to protect myself.

My story *will* be told, and justice will be pursued.

With all judicial avenues for appealing the Dagenais lawsuit exhausted, I need to regroup and figure out a way forward. After consulting with friends, I formulate a two-pronged plan. On the one hand, I need to go after Zijad Saskin: his mishandling of my case cries out for a civil lawsuit against him and his firm. On the other hand, I need to bring the issues in my case to the wider public: a book needs to be written that exposes the main issues posed by my legal struggle and the ways in which the judicial system betrayed my constitutional and fundamental human rights – and in so doing failed the democratic rights of all Canadians. *An injury to one is an injury to all!*

The first step in going after Saskin is to submit a formal complaint to The Law Society of Upper Canada. If this regulatory body for the legal profession in Ontario validates the legitimacy of my grievances against him, this will provide a solid basis for pursuing a civil lawsuit.

In the winter of 2013, I make initial contact with The Law Society, speaking on the phone with an Intake Counselor named Taryn. I explain the main elements of my complaint against Zijad Saskin, highlighting in particular his breach of client-attorney confidentiality, his failure and deception with regard to the Discovery Examination transcript, and his advice to me that I should sell my house and run away to avoid obeying Judge Lococo's court order. Shortly thereafter she emails me and asks me to send her copies of a number of documents, including: "Proof of retainer such as Statement of Account, Retainer Agreement, cheque(s) payable to Mr. Saskin (front and back), or cash receipt(s), Final order made at trial in your case, Any notices, decisions, and orders made by the Court of Appeal in your case, Emails from you to Mr. Saskin that he did not respond to, Approximate dates of telephone calls from you to Mr. Saskin that he did not respond to, Any evidence that Mr. Saskin told you to sell your house and disappear." I'm being asked to produce this material by February 28. I promptly provide everything asked for, and more.

Months later, I receive a letter dated June 6 advising me that the Complaints Resolution Department had received my complaint materials and files from the Intake Department and that the matter had been assigned to Danielle Wilson, Complaints Resolution Counsel. At this time, I'm also invited to send copies of any additional material and information I want considered to Ms. Wilson. Which I do … I immediately send in the transcript of the discovery examination, the transcript of the closing arguments for the Superior Court trial, the Appeals Court closing arguments, the Application to Appeal to the Supreme Court of Canada, and other documents. While I'm waiting for a response from Ms. Wilson, I attempt to rectify a curious mistake that has crept into my correspondence with The Law Society. They are addressing me as "Selma" Vassel rather than as Thelma. I can't help wondering about this. Thelma is a far more common name than Selma. But Selma is the name of a city in Alabama that was a flashpoint for the civil-rights struggles of the 1960s: for the voting rights movement of 1965 and for the famous Selma to Montgomery marches led by Martin Luther King. *Do they know I'm black? If so, how? If not, why this apparent subliminal association between me and Selma, Alabama? Very curious indeed....*

A few weeks later, I receive a letter dated June 18 from Danielle Wilson explaining that she had sent my complaint materials to Saskin and had asked him to respond by July 9. Specifically, she asked him to address three issues: "1. That he may have failed to serve you; 2. That he may have failed to follow your instructions; and 3. That he may have failed to respond to your communications." At first I assume that these three broad issues cover *all* of my specific complaints against Saskin. However, she goes on in the letter to explain that The Law Society is investigating the "professional conduct issues" raised in my complaints and that the Society doesn't have jurisdiction to investigate "negligence issues" that may have caused "financial loss or other damage." I can't be sure, but I immediately sense that Ms. Wilson may be laying the basis for refusing to investigate my claims that Saskin advised me to sell my house and disappear, and that he had breached his ethical obligation to keep my case confidential, above all in relation to my Sundowner employer.

I get on the phone to her and press her on these issues, demanding to know if she's going to require Saskin to respond to those complaints. Her response is a little evasive at first, but she then asks me if I have any proof that he gave me such advice or that he breached confidentiality. I confirm that I do, and that I'm able to provide her with recordings of conversations with him that support what I'm saying. She seems to take a genuine interest, but tells me to hold off on submitting the recordings until a later date. I feel reassured that she's taking my complaints seriously. Once Saskin responds, she explains, I'll be invited to review what he's said and provide my own counter-response. I ask Ms. Wilson specifically to send all future correspondence to me by email, and she agrees.

My conversation with Ms. Wilson reverberates in my mind for days afterward. *She seems to have taken a real interest in the fact that I have recordings that support my complaints on the "confidentiality" and "criminal advice" issues. Yet she's told me to hold off on sending her the audio files. Is she going to demand a response from Saskin on these issues or not? Saskin has been given till July 9 to respond. Why is Ms. Wilson not confronting him with the fact that there is evidence supporting the most serious of my complaints?* I grow increasingly anxious as I ponder these questions -- and as more and more time passes.

I originally expected to hear from The Law Society again sometime in July – since Saskin's response is due by July 9. But I don't hear anything from them for months. In October, I contact Ms. Wilson, inquiring as to why everything is taking so long. She tells me she'd sent a copy of Saskin's response to my complaint along with a cover letter dated August 29 to my home in Niagara-on-the-Lake. I explain that I haven't been home on a regular basis and hadn't received the package. I again ask her to send the materials to me by email. She agrees, adding that she will extend the deadline for my written response to Saskin from September 12 to October 15. When I receive her email, I'm unable to open the attachments, so I arrange to pick the documents up at the front desk of The Law Society in Toronto. I have only a few days to compose a response, put together a package of supporting documents, as well as the crucially important audio files (the recordings of my conversations with Saskin), and physically deliver everything back to The Law Society.

I settle down with Saskin's eight-page letter to Ms. Wilson. On my first reading, I'm immediately struck that he hasn't addressed any of my most serious complaints. *Apparently Ms. Wilson didn't ask him to address those issues. Even in the section of his letter where he responds to my complaints about his handling of the appeals process, he makes no mention of my claim*

that he was pursuing the appeal only to "buy me time" so that I could sell my house and disappear without paying off the Dagenais estate. But he did say something interesting. Casting himself as someone sympathetic to my interests and who believed in my innocence, he wrote that he believed Lococo's judgment "would ruin her life." This from the man who had advised me to "sell and disappear"! If I had taken that criminal advice, you bastard, I could have been sent to jail for years! Saskin wasn't trying to save me from ruin; he was actively involved in ruining me!
As for my claim that he breached attorney-client confidentiality by approaching me at the Sundowner in the presence of Chris Rudan, this also is not addressed. Surely, if Ms. Wilson had inquired about that matter, he would have felt compelled to respond. It's pretty clear that The Law Society, against my expressed wishes and despite Ms. Wilson's professed interest in those issues, decided to sweep them under the rug.

Overall, I'm confident that once The Law Society is able to review my response and the supporting recordings, they'll be able to immediately see that Saskin's letter is chocked full of self-serving lies. For example, regarding the discovery transcript, Saskin claimed that I had instructed him to minimize costs pertaining to documents, and that this was why he had never ordered the transcript. But one of my recordings establishes beyond any doubt that he had told me the transcript had been ordered and made available to the Superior Court and Clark Peddle, and that he'd be able to obtain a copy from the court for my review. My recording *proves* that he directly lied to The Law Society about this important issue.

Upon delivering my response and supporting audio files to The Law Society, I'm advised that it will take 60 to 90 days for the investigation to be completed. I'm on pins and needles. *I can't wait to receive the results of the Society's investigation so that I can really nail this bastard, and get him where it real hurts!*

It's now Friday, January 31, ninety days on, and I'm waiting for my phone to ring.

No rings, no emails. It's now mid-day. I decide to call Ms. Wilson before she leaves the office for the weekend.

There's no answer, so I fire off an email. Shortly thereafter, I receive an email reply from her stating that she's going to need an additional 60 to 90 days to wrap up the investigation. I'm pissed. *You're telling me I need to remain in hiding for another 60 to 90 days? I need to move forward! The time-line for a civil law-suit is already dicey after all the delays and "mistakes" on the part of The Law Society. Now she wants another 2 to 3 months! Shit no, this is unacceptable! But what can I do?*

On Monday, I receive a follow-up email from Ms. Wilson, and much to my surprise, she informs me that she has now completed her investigation into Zijad Saskin and that she'll be sending me "the outcome within the next week."

I'm perplexed by this turn of events, but happy that things won't be dragged out further.

About a week later, I receive an email containing Danielle Wilson's report. Just as I'd feared, the report is largely a white-wash of Saskin's conduct, addressing *none* of the most important complaints I'd made against him. To conceal what seems to be a cover-up, however, Ms. Wilson gave my former lawyer a slight slap on the wrist: "Based on my review, I have concluded that, in the circumstances of this matter, the appropriate regulatory response by the Law Society to address the professional conduct concerns under the Law Society's *Rules of Professional Conduct* as raised by the evidence would be to give the Lawyer Best Practices Information on following client instructions. Best Practices Information is a remedial written communication with the Lawyer. Best Practices Information is a form of regulatory response by the Law Society and is remedial guidance as to how the situation could have been avoided. Best Practices Information represents significant professional governance action and is part of the Lawyer's Law Society record. Therefore, I have given the Lawyer Best Practices Information and closed the file."

There was more, of course, but it was all about secondary issues, alongside pedantic explanation about the Law Society's mandate to evaluate "professional conduct" issues only, as opposed to professional "negligence" issues. *As if Saskin's breach of attorney-client confidentiality, his advice to me to sell and run, and his repeated lying to me should not be of any concern to this august "regulatory body" of the legal profession in Ontario!*

My course is now clear. There is only one way forward. *Public exposure of all this bullshit!*

"To shun one's cross is to make it heavier," Henri Frederic Amiel once said… And now I say, *the time has come for me to pick up my cross!*

Read updates and post your thoughts at
www.tokillanakedbird.com

Manufactured by Amazon.ca
Bolton, ON

14152461R00219